WITHDRAWN

GENERATION ME

Why Today's Young Americans
Are More Confident, Assertive, Entitled—
and More Miserable Than Ever Before

Jean M. Twenge, Ph.D.

Free Press

New York London Toronto Sydney

*f*P
FREE PRESS
A Division of Simon & Schuster, Inc.
1230 Avenue of the Americas
New York, NY 10020

Copyright © 2006 by Jean M. Twenge, Ph.D.

FREE PRESS and colophon are trademarks of Simon & Schuster, Inc.

For information about special discounts for bulk purchases,
please contact Simon & Schuster Special Sales at
1-800-456-6798 or business@simonandschuster.com

Book design by Ellen R. Sasahara

Manufactured in the United States of America

3   5   7   9   10   8   6   4

Library of Congress Cataloging-in-Publication Data

Twenge, Jean M., 1971–
Generation me : why today's young Americans are more confident, assertive,
entitled—and more miserable—than ever before / Jean M. Twenge.
p.   cm.
Includes index.
1. Young adults—United States. 2. Youth—United States. I. Title.
HQ799.7.T94 2006
305.2420973'090511—dc22   2005058514

ISBN-13: 978-0-7432-7697-9
ISBN-10: 0-7432-7697-3

The author gratefully acknowledges permission from the following source to reprint mate-
rial in its control: Universal Syndicate for Calvin and Hobbes © 1992 by Bill Watterson.
Dist. by Universal Press Syndicate. Reprinted with permission. All rights reserved: 57, 151;
Doonesbury © 1993 G. B. Trudeau. Reprinted with permission of
Universal Press Syndicate. All rights reserved: 62–63.

To Craig,
for proving that some dreams really do come true

Contents

Introduction   1

1 You Don't Need Their Approval: The Decline
   of Social Rules   17

2 An Army of One: *Me*   44

3 You Can Be Anything You Want to Be   72

4 The Age of Anxiety (and Depression, and
   Loneliness): Generation Stressed   104

5 Yeah, Right: The Belief That There's No Point
   in Trying   137

6 Sex: Generation Prude Meets Generation Crude   159

7 The Equality Revolution: Minorities, Women,
   and Gays and Lesbians   180

8 Applying Our Knowledge: The Future of
   Business and the Future of the Young   212

   Appendix   243
   Notes   248
   Acknowledgments   275
   Index   279

GENERATION ME

Introduction

Linda was born in 1952 in a small town in the Midwest. After she graduated from high school in 1970, she moved to the city and enrolled in secretarial school. It was a great time to be young: Free Love was in, and everybody smoked, drank, and had a good time. Linda and her friends joined a feminist consciousness-raising group, danced at the discos, and explored their inner lives at est seminars and through meditation. The new pursuit of self-fulfillment led Tom Wolfe to label the 1970s the "Me Decade," and by extension the young people of the time the "Me Generation."

Compared to today's young people, they were posers.

Linda's Baby Boomer generation grew up in the 1950s and early 1960s, taught by stern, gray-suit-wearing teachers and raised by parents who didn't take any lip and thought that *Father Knows Best*. Most of the Boomers were well into adolescence or adulthood by the time the focus on the self became trendy in the 1970s. And when Linda and her friends sought self-knowledge, they took the ironic step of doing so en masse— for all their railing against conformity, Boomers did just about everything in groups, from protests to seminars to yoga. Their youthful exploration also covered a very brief period: the average first-time bride in the early 1970s had not yet celebrated her 21st birthday.

Today's under-35 young people are the real Me Generation, or, as I call them, Generation Me. Born after self-focus entered the cultural mainstream, this generation has never known a world that put duty before self. Linda's youngest child, Jessica, was born in 1985. When Jessica was a toddler, Whitney Houston's No. 1 hit song declared that "The Greatest Love of All" was loving yourself. Jessica's elementary school teachers believed that their most important job was helping Jessica feel good about herself. Jessica scribbled in a coloring book called *We Are All Special*, got a sticker on her worksheet just for filling it out, and did a sixth-grade project called "All About Me." When she wondered how to act on her first date, her mother told her, "Just be yourself." Eventually, Jessica got her lower lip pierced and obtained a large tattoo on her lower back because, she said, she wanted to express herself. She dreams of being a model or a singer. She does not expect to marry until she is in her late twenties, and neither she nor her older sisters have any children yet. "You have to love yourself before you can love someone else," she says. This is a generation unapologetically focused on the individual, a true Generation Me.

If you're wondering what all of this means for the future, you are not alone. Reflecting on her role as a parent of this new generation, *San Francisco Chronicle* columnist Joan Ryan wrote: "We're told we will produce a generation of coddled, center-of-the-universe adults who will expect the world to be as delighted with them as we are. And even as we laugh at the knock-knock jokes and exclaim over the refrigerator drawings, we secretly fear the same thing."

Everyone belongs to a generation. Some people embrace it like a warm, familiar blanket, while others prefer not to be lumped in with their age mates. Yet like it or not, when you were born dictates the culture you will experience. This includes the highs and lows of pop culture, as well as world events, social trends, economic realities, behavioral norms, and ways of seeing the world. The society that molds you when you are young stays with you the rest of your life.

Today's young people are experiencing that society right now, and they speak the language of the self as their native tongue. The individual has always come first, and feeling good about yourself has always been a primary virtue. Generation Me's expectations are highly optimistic: they expect to go to college, to make lots of money, and perhaps even to be famous. Yet this generation enters a world in which college admissions are increasingly competitive, good jobs are hard to find and harder to keep, and basic necessities like housing and health care have skyrocketed in price. This is a time of soaring expectations and crushing realities. Joan Chiaramonte, head of the Roper Youth Report, says that for young people "the gap between what they have and what they want has never been greater." If you would like to start an argument, claim that young people

today have it (a) easy, or (b) tough. Be forewarned: you might need ref-
erees before it's all over.

I have researched generational differences for thirteen years, since I
was a twenty-one-year-old undergraduate working on my B.A. thesis.
When I began, most of what had been written about generations was
based on an amalgam of personal experience and educated guesses: it spec-
ulated about possible differences, but had little proof they actually existed.
I read book after book that said things such as young people now are more
likely to come from divorced homes, so they are more anxious and cynical (but were they really?). And, people born after 1982 entered a more
child-centered society, so they would be more group-oriented (but was
that really true?). It was all very interesting, but all very vague and non-
scientific. I kept thinking, "Where's your proof? Has anyone ever found
the real differences among the generations, instead of just guessing?"

The next year, I entered a Ph.D. program in personality psychology at
the University of Michigan. I soon learned that academic psychologists
measure personality traits and attitudes with carefully designed and vali-
dated questionnaires. Best of all, many of those questionnaires had been
used thousands of times since they were first written in the 1950s, 1960s,
and 1970s, and most people who filled them out were college students and
schoolchildren. That meant I could compare scores on these measures and
see exactly how young people's personalities and attitudes had changed
over the generations. To my surprise, no one had ever done this before.

This book presents, for the first time, the results of twelve studies on
generational differences, based on data from 1.3 million young Americans. Many of the studies find that *when* you were born has more influence on your personality than the family who raised you. Or, in the words
of a prescient Arab proverb, "Men resemble the times more than they
resemble their fathers." When you finish this book, you'll be ready for an
argument about which generation has it easy or tough and why—you
might even want to start it. At the very least, if you're part of Generation
Me, you can use this book to bean that annoying guy who says that people your age are lazy and shiftless. Who says books can't be useful?

This book focuses on the current generation of young people, born in
the 1970s, 1980s, and 1990s, whom I call Generation Me. Right now in
the 2000s, this group ranges from elementary school kids to thirtysomething adults. Although thirty years is a longer-than-average span for

a generation, it nicely captures the group of people who grew up in an era when focusing on yourself was not just tolerated but actively encouraged. A member of this generation myself, I was born in 1971. Like most of us who came along after the Baby Boom, I'm too young to remember Vietnam, Woodstock, or Watergate. During the summer of 1980, when every tree held a yellow ribbon for the Iran hostages, my main activity was running when I heard the chimes of the ice cream truck. Since I'm at the leading edge of this group, however, I'm also too old to have pierced anything except my ears or to have ever owned a Justin Timberlake poster. But when I talk about Generation Me, I'm also talking about myself.

Why the label Generation Me? Since GenMe'ers were born, we've been taught to put ourselves first. Unlike the Baby Boomers, GenMe didn't have to march in a protest or attend a group session to realize that our own needs and desires were paramount. Reliable birth control, legalized abortion, and a cultural shift toward parenthood as a choice made us the most *wanted* generation of children in American history. Television, movies, and school programs have told us we were special from toddlerhood to high school, and we believe it with a self-confidence that approaches boredom: why talk about it? It's just the way things are. This blasé attitude is very different from the Boomer focus on introspection and self-absorption: GenMe is not self-absorbed; we're self-important. We take it for granted that we're independent, special individuals, so we don't really need to think about it.

This is not the same as saying that young people are spoiled. That would imply that we always got what we wanted. Although some parents are indeed too indulgent, young people today must overcome many difficult challenges that their elders never had to face. While families could once achieve middle-class status on the earnings of one high school–educated person, it now takes two college-educated earners to achieve the same standard of living. Many teens feel that the world demands perfection in everything, and some are cracking under the pressure. Many people reaching their twenties find that their jobs do not provide the fulfillment and excitement they had anticipated, and that their salary isn't enough to afford even a small house. There's an acronym that describes how this growing self-reliance can be stressful: YO-YO (You're On Your Own).

I am also not saying that this generation is selfish. For one thing, youth volunteering has risen in the last decade. As long as time spent volunteering does not conflict with other goals, GenMe finds fulfillment in helping others. We want to make a difference. But we want to do it in our own way. GenMe also believes that people should follow their dreams and not be held back by societal expectations. Taking a job in a new city far from one's family, for example, isn't selfish, but it does put the individual first. The same is true for a girl who wants to join a boys' sports team or a college student who wants to become an actor when his parents want him to be a doctor. Not only are these actions and desires not considered selfish today (although they may have been in past generations), but they're playing as inspirational movies at the local theater. These aspirations are also being touted by politicians, even conservative ones—such opportunities are what George W. Bush is talking about when he says that "the fire of freedom" should be spread around the world.

This is the good part of the trend—we enjoy unprecedented freedom to pursue what makes us happy. But our high expectations, combined with an increasingly competitive world, have led to a darker flip side, where we blame other people for our problems and sink into anxiety and depression. Perhaps because of the focus on the self, sexual behavior has also changed radically: these days, parents worry not just about high school sex but about junior high school sex.

All of this, and we don't even have a name. People born in the late 1960s to the 1970s are often labeled "Generation X," but they have not been reexamined since being named in the early 1990s, long before their primary identity veered from slackers to Internet millionaires. It's just not clear that the GenX label fits now that flannel shirts are out. One advertising executive called the early 1990s depiction of this generation as bored cynics "the most expensive marketing mistake in history." Some descriptions (and birth years) of GenX overlap with what I call Generation Me, but it's clear that the GenX description is incomplete and often misguided. And the generation born in the 1980s and 1990s—today's children, teenagers, and people in their early twenties—has no name at all. Some marketers have used "GenY," which simply parrots the GenX label and thus probably won't last long: who wants to be named after the people older than you? Some have called young people the "Net Generation," as this is the first generation to grow up with the Internet, but this label has not caught on (and being the first to experience something doesn't mean much; the Boomers were the first "TV Generation," but later generations have clearly trumped them in their attachment to the boob tube). "Millennials," a somewhat better name, has also yet to stick, and of course that whole millennium thing is so 1999. But combine this label with the Net Generation idea, and you can name this generation after a version of Windows: the Millennium Edition. The convenient abbreviation? ME.

A neat twist on the Generation Me label—and in the same computer-oriented vein—is iGeneration. The first letter is nicely packed with meaning: it could stand for Internet (as it does in iMac and iPod) or for the first person singular that stands for the individual. Its pronunciation also appropriately suggests vision, either the things inside young people's heads that are usually glued to the computer or the TV, or the vision of young people in shaping a new world. It's an appropriate name for a generation raised with on-demand "iMedia" like TiVo, the Internet, and the ever-present iPod.

I don't really expect the Generation Me label to replace the GenX, GenY, and Millennial labels, though I'd welcome it if it did (iGeneration or iGen might have a better shot). The GenX label has been with us since the early 1990s and is fairly well established, so those of us born between the mid-1960s and the late 1970s are probably stuck with it—though we'd love to shake that slacker stereotype. Those born after 1980 do not yet have a coherent generational identity or name, but this should arrive sometime in the next ten years. What it will be is anybody's guess. Generation Me is a description as well as a label, a way of capturing our most distinctive trait—the freedom and individualism we take for granted. After the relatively unified mass of the Baby Boomers, the rest of us can only hope to be understood; we might not be precisely defined.

My perspective on today's young generation differs from that of Neil Howe and William Strauss, who argue in their 2000 book, *Millennials Rising*, that those born since 1982 will usher in a return to duty, civic responsibility, and teamwork. Their book is subtitled *The Next Great Generation* and contends that today's young people will resemble the generation who won World War II. I agree that in an all-encompassing crisis today's young people would likely rise to the occasion—people usually do what needs to be done. But I see no evidence that today's young people feel much attachment to duty or to group cohesion. Instead, as you'll see in the following pages, young people have been consistently taught to put their own needs first and to focus on feeling good about themselves. This is not an attitude conducive to following social rules or favoring the group's needs over the individual's. When the United States entered the war in Iraq, new enlistments in the military went down, not up; this generation is no more inclined than Boomers were to get killed in a foreign war. Even the subtitle *The Next Great Generation* displays the hubris fed to the young by their adoring elders. When the World War II generation was growing up during the 1920s, no one was calling them the Greatest Generation and telling them they were the best kids ever. That label was not even applied to them until 2001, more than fifty years after their accomplishments during the 1940s.

Strauss and Howe also argue that today's young people are optimistic. This is true for children and adolescents, who have absorbed the cheerful aphorisms so common today (Chapter 3 of this book, for example, is titled "You Can Be Anything You Want to Be"). Yet this optimism often fades—or even smashes to pieces—once Generation Me hits the reality of adulthood. If you are a Baby Boomer or older, you might remember the 1970 book *Future Shock*, which argued that the accelerating pace of cultural change left many people feeling overwhelmed. Today's young people, born after this book was published, take these changes for granted and thus do not face this problem. Instead, we face a different kind of collision: Adulthood Shock. Our childhoods of constant praise, self-esteem boosting, and unrealistic expectations did not prepare us for an increasingly competitive workplace and the economic squeeze created by sky-high housing prices and rapidly accelerating health care costs. After a childhood of buoyancy, GenMe is working harder to get less.

This book focuses on changes among young Americans—and on trends that have arrived at different times, or not at all, in many other cultures. However, many of the changes here can be generalized to other nations, particularly other Western nations such as Canada, Great Britain, Australia, and Germany. These cultures have also experienced the movement toward focusing on the needs of the self, as well as the dark flip side of increased depression and anxiety. Developing countries might well be next. Like McDonald's and Coca-Cola, American individualism is spreading to all corners of the globe. If current trends continue in developing countries, Generation Me boomlets might soon be arriving around the world. The more exposure kids get to American culture, the more they will rebel against the family-first, group-oriented ethos of many cultures around the world.

This generation is not only the future: we are now. The accelerated pace of recent technological and cultural change makes it more important than ever to keep up with generational trends. A profound shift in generational dynamics is occurring right now in the 2000s. Baby Boomers, usually defined as people born between 1946 and 1964, have dominated our culture since they were born, because of their large numbers. But this won't last forever: the first Boomers turned 60 in January 2006. Though they are loath to admit it, Boomers have already lost their grip on the marketers and advertisers of the world. As early as June 2000, *Time* magazine announced the "Twilight of the Boomers." Business and marketing have already moved on to GenMe, which, as of 2005, completely dominated the lucrative 18-to-35 age group as well as the teen and tween age brackets. These are the consumers everyone wants to reach, and it's time to understand them.

And I do mean understand, not change. In the final chapter, I provide some advice on how to combat the more negative aspects of current generational trends, but I am not suggesting that we return to the supposedly ideal days of the 1950s (which, of course, were ideal only for some people). Nor am I suggesting that these trends are this generation's "fault." Instead, young people today should be seen as products of their culture—a culture that teaches them the primacy of the individual at virtually every step, and a culture that was firmly in place before they were born. Asking young people today to adopt the personality and attitudes of a previous time is like asking an adult American to instantly become Chinese. Morris Massey, for years a popular speaker on generations, put it this way: "The gut-level value systems are, in fact, dramatically different between the generations. . . . The focus should not be so much on how to change other people to conform to our standards, our values. Rather, we must learn how to accept and understand other people in their own right, acknowledging the validity of their values, their behavior." As Massey points out and research supports, our value systems are set in childhood and don't change much thereafter. Massey's favorite question is "Where were you when you were ten?" Put another way, you can't teach an old dog new tricks.

I'm not trying to stereotype the generations. The studies I discuss here show what people from certain generations are like on average. Many of these studies show very strong, consistent change, but of course there will always be exceptions to the rule. Some members of the World War II generation lost their virginity at 15, and some members of GenMe waited until they were 30 to have sex. Yet at the same time, there is no denying that sexual activity now begins, on average, sooner than it did fifty years ago (particularly among young women). The same is true for psychological states: some older people are depressed just as some younger people are, but there is some very convincing evidence that depression and anxiety are markedly more prevalent among younger generations. These shifts in averages are important. Marketing studies, for example, find that generational styles influence purchasing decisions as much or more than sex, income, and education.

My empirical research on change over time in personality and attitudes provides the backbone to this book: it shapes the chapter topics and provides the basis for how GenMe really differs from previous generations. This makes the book unique among those that discuss generations, because it summarizes psychological data—and a very large amount—collected at various times. I haven't surveyed the generations as they are now, with Boomers middle-aged and GenMe in youth and rising adulthood. Instead, I've found data on what Boomers were like when they were young in the 1960s and 1970s and compared it to data on young people from the 1980s, 1990s, and 2000s. This is an enormous benefit, as I can be confident that the changes aren't due to age or to people misremembering what they were like when they were young (how many parents have fudged a detail or two about their own teenage years?). I've provided more details about this method in the next section and in the Appendix.

I have also gathered a large amount of supplemental data from various sources. For example, the Higher Education Research Institute has conducted a nationwide survey of over 300,000 American college freshmen every year since the late 1960s. The *Statistical Abstract of the United States* is a gold mine of statistics going back decades (I often joke that it is my favorite book: what it lacks in plot it more than makes up for in information). Many other surveys, polls, research studies, and books reveal the true feelings of today's young people. I have tried to bring to life a wide range of research on generational differences in personality, attitudes, and behavior—my own research and others', and from both academic and popular sources.

I have supplemented this numerical data with more qualitative opinions from a number of sources. Over two hundred of my students at San Diego State University shared their stories through written essays. This was a very diverse group, including students of every ethnicity and background, ranging from first-generation college students to upper-middle-class kids. Another fifty young people from around the country contributed stories and thoughts through my website, www.generationme.org. I have also drawn on my own stories and those of my friends and family, most from Texas and the Midwest, where I lived before moving to California in 2001. In all cases, I have changed names and, in some instances, identifying details, and stated ages reflect the person's age at the time of the quote.

I also include ample references to popular culture, including television, movies, music, and magazines, without which a book on young people today would not be complete. This is where the culture lives and breathes, especially for a generation that has always enjoyed cable TV with one hundred channels. And our pop culture refers constantly to the self and individuality. My husband got used to my folding down pages in magazines and seeing me suddenly rush for a pen while watching TV. I was astounded at how often I heard the word "self" from so many different sources. I had never really noticed it before, as most of us haven't: like fish swimming in the ocean, we don't notice the water because it is all around us and has always been there.

Even the most innocuous TV comments now catch my attention. During a recent episode of her eponymous talk show, Ellen Degeneres said that the most important thing is "how you feel and being happy." It's a statement most young people take for granted. Dan Atkins, 17, says in *Growing Up Digital*, "my basic philosophy toward life is: do whatever makes you happy." But when I asked my mother (born in 1943) about this, she said, "In the early 1960s, most people would have said the most important things were being honest, hardworking, industrious, loyal, and caring about others. I can't even remember thinking about whether I was 'happy.' That's not to say we weren't happy—we just didn't focus on it." We do now. Here's Mario, a recent college graduate quoted in the book

Quarterlife Crisis: "I just try to do whatever will make me happier, and think of myself first." Welcome to Generation Me.

HOW IT ALL STARTED

The idea for this book began when I was a 21-year-old college student at the University of Chicago in 1992, working on my B.A. thesis. Unfortunately, and unknown to me at the time, my thesis was a rather undistinguished project that would ultimately be rejected by four journals and never published. However, an intriguing tangent of this work led to the thirteen years of research and twelve publications in prestigious scientific journals that form the basis of this book.

One of the questionnaires I used in my ill-fated B.A. project was the Bem Sex-Role Inventory, which measures personality traits associated with one sex or the other. For example, "assertive" and "acts like a leader" are items on the "masculine" scale, and "compassionate" and "yielding" are items on the "feminine" scale. I had always been fascinated by how gender shapes our personalities, and still had a copy of the scale I'd received nine years before at a Texas Tech University program designed to show middle school students what college was like (the program bore the clumsy name "Shake Hands with Your Future," and, now that I've been to college, I think it would have been more accurate if it had included beer).

For my B.A. thesis, I gave this questionnaire and one about appearance choices to 150 college students, mostly by hijacking people everywhere I went. People filled out questionnaires at loud parties, during particularly boring classes, and between bites of barely tolerable food in the dining hall. Several questionnaires bore water stains from being penciled in at a swim meet. Most people were willing to help, although as word got around, the occasional potential victim would duck around a corner if I appeared carrying pencils.

I went about analyzing the data on my ultimately doomed project, looking for correlations between all kinds of things like hair length, earrings, and—yes—that test of gender-related personality traits. That's when I noticed something interesting: about 50% of the women in my sample scored as "masculine" on the test, meaning that they had endorsed significantly more of the stereotypically masculine traits (like "assertive") than the feminine items. When the test was written in 1973, only about 20% of women scored that way. This was completely tangential to the main question of my amateurish thesis, but interesting nevertheless.

I immediately thought that this might be a difference between generations—being a woman in 1973 was surely quite different from being one in 1992. On the other hand, my sample was far from random and consisted of students at the University of Chicago, a group not known for its normalcy: the school is intensely intellectual and proud of its asocial nerdiness. In his popular syndicated column, "The Straight Dope," Cecil Adams once wrote that U of C undergraduates, like insects that eat book paste, developed their "intellectual predilections as the consequence of an unhappy sex life." So what if he was a biased Northwestern grad—he was basically right. So I didn't think much of it. Besides, I had a B.A. thesis to write, and it was going to change the world! (Insert ironic eye-rolling here.)

By the next fall, I was a graduate student at the University of Michigan, collecting more data on my gender role project. This time, participants from an undergraduate class filled out questionnaires in a large classroom over a few evenings. The generational difference popped out again: more than half of the women in the sample had high scores on the scale of stereotypically masculine personality traits. I couldn't write it off to campus this time—the Michigan undergraduates were distressingly *normal*—and these differences were even more interesting than the main results of my thesis (did you know that college women, on average, own fifteen pairs of shoes, compared to five for men?).

But what did I have? Two recent samples to compare to the original one in 1973. What had happened in between those years? Were my samples just a fluke? Fortunately, this scale had been used by a large number of people over twenty years, so the data had to be out there. One spring day in 1994, I decided I just had to find out if women really did embrace more stereotypically masculine traits now, and I developed the method I ultimately used for all of the studies in this book. (As for the results of the "masculine" traits study, you'll find them in Chapter 7.)

The method is really pretty simple, though it's a tremendous amount of work. I begin by searching computer databases for journal articles, master's theses, and dissertations that used a particular scale. I keep only those that used a normal population of a specific age—usually college students or children. Then I search to find them at the library or in full text databases online, since only the entire article or thesis will have what I'm looking for: the average score of the sample on the questionnaire. Once I find all of the data, I can then graph those scores by the year the data were collected, showing me how scores changed over a range of years—not just from one year to another, but across the entire time period. Because the samples are roughly the same age (say, college students), this shows how young people differ from one generation to the next. No one had ever done this type of analysis before, so I started from scratch developing a way to find and analyze the data.

I did most of these searches in the labyrinthine stacks of the graduate library at the University of Michigan, a building so vast and confusing that red and yellow lines are painted on the stone floor to help people find the exits. The university had added on to the library in 1970, smushing two buildings of different styles and floor heights together with limited access between the two. The older building ended up with floors like "4A" (reminiscent of the magical seventh-and-a-half floor in *Being John Malkovich*) connected by narrow, apparently randomly placed staircases. The tall shelves filled with books created a nerdy form of a Halloween cornfield maze. I would often sit looking through journals only to see some poor soul walk past me, double back again, and then stand under the dim lights with a look of utter confusion on his or her face. During those years, I probably helped more people escape from the Michigan library than anyone else. I imagined these rescued students stumbling gratefully into the thin winter sunlight, relieved that they weren't going to wander around the library for hours until someone finally found them, weak and dehydrated, on floor 1A between HM and HQ.

During these projects, I probably pulled half a million journals off the shelves. ("I hope you're not allergic to dust," my dissertation adviser quipped.) When I left one section of the library to move to another, I would leave behind several teetering stacks of colorfully bound journals, each about four feet tall. I felt sorry for the work-study students who had to reshelve my looming piles of discarded books, many of which were twenty or thirty years old. They must have thought someone left them as a joke, or that a book monster was loose in the library, pulling down old journals from the rusty shelves to create random stacks in scattered carrels. But there were perks as well. One of my favorite finds was an advertisement in a 1920s journal that announced a contest with a $20,000 prize, an enormous sum in those days. The money would go to anyone who proved he or she could perform telekinesis (moving an object with only the force of your mind). I was amused to see that one of the judges for the contest was Harry Houdini. A few issues later came the unsurprising conclusion: no one won the prize.

I also used the Interlibrary Loan Department to obtain endless dissertations and master's theses, another great source of data. I requested so many that the staff began to grimace when I walked up to the desk. I couldn't get every thesis that way, but I soon found out that the Library of Congress in Washington, D.C., has a copy of every American doctoral dissertation on microfiche. I made many trips there, usually staying with friends in Baltimore, where I slept under a comforter that, despite my friends' best efforts, was their cat's favorite alternative litterbox. Fortunately, the data I got during the day and the great conversations with my friends in the evenings more than made up for it—what's a little cat piss when you're finding out how generations really differ?

The dissertations were a study of change in themselves. The earliest, from the 1940s and 1950s, were on transparently thin, onion-skin paper, with blurred typewriter print—there were no photocopiers, so documents had to be typed on carbon paper, with the copies made as the typing was done. Apparently, the library copy was never the original, and the type blurred as the typewriter keys struck through several layers of paper and carbon. Who knew? Certainly not a child of the computer age like me.

A little later, after copiers became more common, dissertations were still typewritten but clearer. In the 1950s and 1960s, almost every male student thanked his wife for typing his dissertation. I could just see those poor women, tired from a day in the secretarial pool, coming home to struggle through their husbands' scribbled sentences. By the late 1970s and 1980s, dissertations almost always appeared in the then-ubiquitous, straight-serif font of the IBM electric typewriter. Slowly, computer fonts began to appear; someone had bought one of the first Apple Macintoshes, and would get overly creative using more than one font in a document. By the 1990s, almost every dissertation was in Times New Roman. No one thanked his wife for typing his dissertation anymore, and many of the dissertations were written by the wives themselves, who were now getting their own Ph.D.'s. The modern age had arrived.

After years of doing library searches, I overloaded on the tedium. Fortunately, by then I had wonderful and enthusiastic graduate students to help. But I still feel a misty wave of nostalgia when I remember the library stacks I frequented in just about every place I lived and visited, including Iowa, Michigan, Texas, Ohio, Pennsylvania, Wisconsin, Washington, D.C., and California. Every time I went to the library, it felt like a treasure hunt: somewhere amid those dusty books was the answer, and all I had to do was find it. I imagined the numbers I sought flying off the candlelight-yellow pages, swirling into the air between the metal shelves of the stacks, drawing a picture of change across the generations. (What can I say? I was an overeager graduate student.) Even as the years passed and I started new projects, I knew that those dusty books I mined contained a rich vein of information from which to reassemble the remarkable story of past and future generations. This book tells that story.

1

You Don't Need Their Approval: The Decline of Social Rules

Getting dressed in the morning is a fundamentally different experience today than it was forty years ago. For all of Generation Me's lifetime, clothes have been a medium of self-expression, an individual choice in a range of alternatives and comfort. Contrast this to past decades, when men wore ties most of the time and women did not leave the house without crisp white gloves and a tight girdle. Pictures of crowds in the early 1960s show quaint sights like men wearing three-piece suits at baseball games and ladies lined up in identical-length skirts. To GenMe, these images look like people on an alien planet—who wears a suit to a baseball game?

Even our shoes are different. Today's casual footwear is called tennis shoes because people once wore them only to play tennis or basketball. Not even kids wore these types of shoes on the street—their shoes were made of stiff leather, just like adults'.

Now that's all but forgotten. Except in the most formal of workplaces, few men wear suits to work anymore, and virtually no one wears them to baseball games. Women have (thankfully) abandoned wearing tight girdles and white gloves everywhere they go (and many young women don't even know what a girdle *is*). The trend toward more informal dress has accelerated in the past ten years, with many companies opting for "business casual" and others going for just plain casual. The trend reached all the way to the top in July 2005, when about half the members of the Northwestern University women's

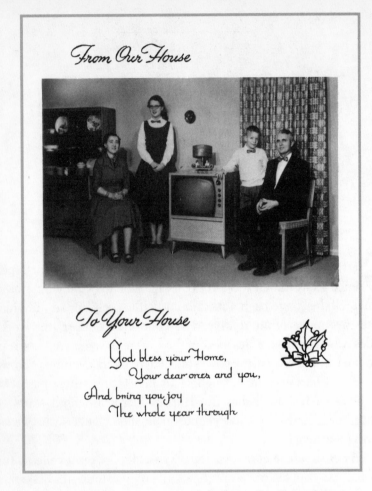

Holiday card, Minnesota, 1955. Not only are the clothes formal, but so is the posing and demeanor. The perfect family was proper and composed.

lacrosse team wore flip-flops during their White House visit, resulting in a picture of the president of the United States standing next to several young women wearing shoes that were once reserved for walking on sand or showering in skuzzy gymnasiums. Although most people still want to look good, we are a much more informal and accepting society than we once were. This is a perfect illustration of generational trends in attitudes, as the entire point in dressing up is to make a good impression on others and elicit their approval. You don't dress

Lots of Love
from Our
Family
🌸

Best Wishes for a
happy and healthy
2005!

Holiday card, Massachusetts, 2004. Formal clothing is no longer
necessary to make a good impression. It is now more important
to be relaxed, natural, and happy.

formally for yourself or for your comfort; if you really wanted to do
things "your way" and just for yourself, you'd wear jeans to work. And,
of course, many of us already do.

The strict rules of previous decades went far beyond appearance.
Beneath the wool suits and tailored hats, yesterday's men and women
were bound by another type of conformity. Male or female, you were considered strange if you did not marry by age 25 and even stranger if you
married outside your race or religion. It was expected that you would
have children—it was not considered a choice. Your race and sex dictated your fate and behavior. When war came, you went to fight if you
were male and able. Overall, duty and responsibility were held more
important than individual needs and wants. There were certain things
you did, certain things you said, and certain things you didn't talk about.
End of story.

Today, few of these rules apply. We are driven instead by our individual needs and desires. We are told to follow our dreams, to pursue happiness above all else. It's OK to be different, and you should do what's right
for you. Compared to Boomers in 1973, GenMe is twice as likely to agree
with the statement "There is no single right way to live." Young people
say that the most important quality a child can learn is "to think for himself or herself," and only half as many young people as old say that obedience is a good lesson for children.

The choices of the individual are now held so paramount that the most common advice given to teenagers is "Just be yourself." (Not that long ago, it was more likely to be "Be polite.") Filmmaker Kevin Smith (*Clerks*) says, "My generation believes we can do almost anything. My characters are free: no social mores keep them in check." Or take Melissa, 20, who says, "I couldn't care less how I am viewed by society. I live my life according to the morals, views, and standards that I create."

This is the social trend—so strong it's really a revolution—that ties all of the generational changes together in a neat, tight bundle: do what makes you happy, and don't worry about what other people think. It is enormously different from the cultural ethos of previous decades, and it is a philosophy that GenMe takes entirely for granted. "As long as I believe in myself, I really do not care what others think," says Rachel, 21.

GENERATIONS AT THE CINEMA

This ethos appears frequently in popular movies; my favorite examples involve what I call "the apparent time traveler." The main character in these films is supposed to be a real person in the 1950s, but he or she actually represents the enlightened voice of the twenty-first century, which makes him (or her) the hero of the film. In 2003's *Mona Lisa Smile*, Julia Roberts plays a professor at Wellesley College in 1953. Soon after arriving, she rallies her students against the restrictions of early marriage and training for motherhood. When she critiques sexist advertising during a class, we in the audience all know exactly what she is doing, but few people in the 1950s would have seen it before—or even thought to do it. Roberts's character has clearly taken the time traveler shuttle to the future and absconded with a copy of the 1987 feminist antiadvertising film *Still Killing Us Softly*.

The Majestic, released in 2001, is an even worse movie. Jim Carrey's character, a Hollywood screenwriter, gets blacklisted and takes refuge in a small town. After he is asked to testify, he manages to convince the entire town that McCarthyism is bad and that free speech is our most treasured right. When I watched this movie (I was on a plane; it was not a matter of free will), my mouth dropped almost to the floor as the whole town united behind the accused writer and the main female character said, "It doesn't really matter if you are a Communist or not—this is

America and you can be one if you want to. It's nobody's business." Uh, not really. Had this actually been the 1950s, an accused Communist would have been everybody's business.

Movies that admit to time travel are somewhat more enjoyable. In *Pleasantville*, two teenagers from 1998 help a 1950s town find passion and the freedom of ideas. Every character who discovers an individualistic freedom like sex or intellectual questioning instantly turns from black and white into color. The film sinks into predictability once discrimination against the "colored" people begins. (Get it?) *Back to the Future*, probably the only good movie among these four, also promotes the individualistic ethos but has a better story. When Marty McFly travels from 1985 back to 1955, he finds that his father George lacks assertiveness and mumbles a lot. Marty teaches George to stand up for himself, and, in a fit of sudden self-confidence, George punches the local bully and gets the girl who will become Marty's mother. When Marty returns to 1985, his parents are now successful, rich, and still in love with each other. George has even become a published novelist. ("If you put your mind to it, you can accomplish anything," he says, repeating Marty's radical-for-1955 advice.) Believing in yourself has clearly paid off.

Other movies travel across cultures rather than time, but they promote the same message. In 2002's *Bend It Like Beckham*, an Asian-Indian girl living in London wants to play soccer. Her parents, already taken aback that their older daughter did not have an arranged marriage, want the younger Jess to learn to cook and be a proper young lady. The plot comes to a head when Jess must shuttle back and forth between a game and her sister's wedding. By the end of the movie, Jess wants to join a professional women's soccer team and move to America. Her parents, finally convinced that it's right for Jess to follow her dreams, reluctantly agree. The overall message of all of these movies—whether they travel in time or cultures—is to rebel against restrictive social mores. Don't follow the rules; do whatever makes you happy.

And sometimes you don't even need to travel. The biggest box-office draw in late 2004 and early 2005 was *Meet the Fockers*, the sequel to the highly successful comedy *Meet the Parents*. The movie revolves around the culture clash between the conservative Byrnes family and the hippie Focker family. The Fockers provide most of the comedy in the film, with their sex therapy business, their leather sandals, and their display of their son's ninth-place ribbons (because, they say, "It's not about winning—it's about what's in your heart"). But by the end of the movie, the Fockers are not the ones who have been convinced to change—it's the straight-laced Byrnes family who learns from *them*. Mr. Byrnes, played to crusty perfection by Robert De Niro, learns to loosen up and show emotion toward his daughter. He also decides that it might be good for him and his wife to enjoy more physical affection in their marriage, and puts some of Mrs. Focker's sex tips to good use. Hippies may be laughable, but they teach us how to live. No need to walk around all uptight like that—which, of course, you must be if you're not a hippie. I'm exaggerating a bit, but the movie does make it very clear which message is paramount, and it's definitely Let It All Hang Out.

These movies dramatize two interlocking changes: the fall of social rules and the rise of the individual. As the individualistic viewpoint became prominent, concern with the opinions of others plummeted. This chapter discusses the decline in the need for social approval, and the following two chapters document the ascendance of the individual self. Over the last few decades, the entire nation has experienced the transfor-mation parodied in an episode of *The Simpsons*, when Springfield's usual "Do What We Say Festival" (started, they say, in 1946 by German set-tlers) is replaced with the new "Do What You Feel Festival."

DANCE PARTY REVOLUTION
(AGAINST CONFORMITY)

In a famous piece of art, Andy Warhol copied the instruction cards from the 1950s Arthur Murray dance school. Each black and white card showed shoe prints where the student was to stand on each step. Warhol meant the piece to capture the conformity of the times, when learning to dance involved precise rules designed to present a graceful picture to those watching.

For all of GenMe's lifetime, however, dancing has been an individual, free-form event. For the 90% of songs that are fast dances, you don't even need a partner, and you move to the music any way you want. The few slow dances involve a little more closeness but no real skill: the girl's arms go around the guy's neck, his arms go around her waist, and you both shuffle around in an endless circle until the song is over. (I can hear the strains of Chicago's "You're the Inspiration" and feel the sweaty pain of a junior high school dance even now.)

Even in this modern slow dance, it's not necessary to learn any rules or to move harmoniously with a partner. I've seen this generational divide play out at wedding receptions over and over, including at my own. For the father-of-the-bride dance, my dad automatically assumed the dance position of his generation, with one hand up to hold mine and the other at my waist. He then began to move in some kind of cadenced waltz step. I'd never danced this way before. It was all I could do not to fall down.

I'm not sure what wedding receptions will look like in the future; I can't imagine a father of the bride doing the junior-high-slow-dance circle shuffle with his daughter. But the GenMe father of the bride of the future might not know how to couple-dance any other way.

DO YOUR OWN THING

Consider this scenario: You are seated at a table with six other people. Four lines are drawn on a chalkboard at the front of the room: a medium-length target line, along with line A, medium, line B, short, and line C, long. You're to say which of the lines is the same length as the target. You're all ready with the obvious answer of A, but the six others go first and say line C. What do you do?

When Solomon Asch first performed this experiment in 1951, 74% of people gave the group's incorrect answer on at least one trial, and 28% did on the majority of trials. People felt the need to conform to the group and not to stand out. The study became one of the most famous in social psychology, taught in every class as an example of the social nature of human beings. Yet some have pointed out that this was the essence of getting along in 1950s society, when no one wanted to be thought of as different. But when researchers tried to replicate the study in 1980, they got completely different results: few people conformed to the group anymore. Apparently, it was no longer fashionable to go along with the group even when they were wrong. The authors of the study concluded that the Asch study was "a child of its time."

Throughout the 1970s, self-help books and therapists actively encouraged people to flout social rules, telling readers they should stop caring about what others think. A central chapter in the 1976 megabest-seller *Your Erroneous Zones* by Wayne Dyer is called "You Don't Need Their Approval." The author argues that people can do anything they put their minds to, and that others' opinions only get in the way. (It's probably no coincidence that both the cover and back of the book feature oversize pictures of the author, complete with a 1970s powder blue V-neck shirt and the resulting display of male chest hair.) Dyer rants on and on about how courteous acts like giving a wedding gift or attending a funeral are "musterbation," his double-entendre term for unnecessary social rules. Dyer argues that seeking approval from parents, teachers, and bosses undermines self-reliance and truth. "Needing approval is tan-tamount to saying 'Your view of me is more important than my own opin-ion of myself,'" he writes. Another self-help book carries on the tradition with the title *What You Think of Me Is None of My Business*. Unlike the Baby Boomers who learned these new standards as adults, GenMe takes these attitudes for granted and always has.

"Do your own thing" is the central ethos of modern parenting. In 1924, a group of sociologists did an extensive study of the citizens of a place they called Middletown (later revealed as Muncie, Indiana). When mothers were asked which traits they wanted their children to have, they named strict obedience, loyalty to church, and good manners. In 1988, few mothers named these traits; instead, they chose independence and tolerance. Modern mothers might be gratified to learn that these values now appear frequently. In *Growing Up Digital*, an 11-year-old girl says, "I think the individual determines what is cool, and it is his or her opinion. What is cool to one person might not be to another. The days of con-formity are over." Danielle, 29, agrees. "I refuse to do something because it's what everyone else is doing, or because it's the socially acceptable thing to do at the time," she says. When I asked my undergraduate stu-dents to name the characteristics that best described their generation, the two most popular answers were "independent" and "open-minded."

GenMe has been taught these values almost since birth. *Free to Be You and Me*, one of the most popular children's films during the 1970s and 1980s, trumpets individuality in forty-five minutes of catchy songs and stories. Many people I know have it practically memorized; my third-grade class in Irving, Texas, watched it almost every Friday in the early 1980s. One song says, "When I grow up I'm going to be happy and do what I like to do." Another skit gives examples of animals dressed by their owners ("Don't dress your horse in a nightgown just cuz he can't stay awake") and concludes, "A person should wear what he wants to, and not just what other folks say."

A 1977 manual for teachers stated as its central philosophy, "I am a self and you are a self and I don't want to be made to feel guilty if I am not like you nor should you be made to feel guilty if you are unlike me." Amanda, 22, says that one of the main lessons in her Girl Scout troop was "being different is good." It's a mantra GenMe has heard over and over. We absorbed the lesson of tolerance with our baby food—not just for race and religion, but for sexual orientation, beliefs, feelings, and all kinds of other intangibles. Just about the only difference that wasn't good? Someone who was prejudiced.

"For my grandparents, questioning their religion, their country's system of government, or what they ate was not acceptable. The fear of standing out or being judged by others for their beliefs was strong," says John, 25. "My generation is much more independent. I pride myself on being a free and independent thinker. My wish is to break down the walls that humans have socially constructed." A book on generations in the workplace notes that today's young people were instructed to "Never just do what an adult asks. Always ask, 'Why?'"

This means that GenMe often takes for granted the nullity of others' opinions. Cynthia, 26, wrote about the breakup of her marriage: "When I decided to get divorced, at no moment did I ever care about what others would say about my decision." In an earlier time, of course, the social ramifications of a divorce would have been a major concern. Now little social stigma is attached to divorce, and most people consider it completely acceptable to divorce if you are unhappy—or to leave the mother of your children. A prime example from the lower end of popular culture is Britney Spears's husband Kevin Federline, who left girlfriend Shar Jackson when she was seven months pregnant with their second child. Some people saw this behavior as not just acceptable but laudatory. "I was excited to see Britney, her fiancé, and future stepdaughter, on the cover," Kristy Nichols of Cleveland wrote to *People* magazine. "It's refreshing to see that her fiancé chooses to be with her because of love and not with Shar Jackson just because they have children together." *Just* because.

WHO CARES WHAT YOU THINK?

Not caring what others think may also explain the decline in manners and politeness. Because we no longer believe that there is one right way of doing things, most of us were never taught the rules of etiquette. Although it's fine to wear white shoes after Labor Day and use whatever fork you want, most etiquette was developed to provide something often lacking in modern life: respect for other people's comfort. "Society has gotten increasingly callous and me-centered, and we're fed up with [the results]," says Corinne Gregory, founder of a class called the PoliteChild. Diane Diehl, who runs a similar class, agrees. "Kids are being encouraged by pop culture to be disrespectful and self-destructive, and their parents are frightened and looking for help." A high school teacher told me that she noticed her students don't "clean up nice"—they find it difficult to not swear and to speak more formally when necessary. They talk to older people and authority figures the same way they talk to their friends. A business book relates the story of a company founder who visited one of his shops and asked a young employee how she was doing. "Well, a little hungover this morning, but okay," she replied.

Basic consideration for others seems to be on the wane as well. I am continually amazed at how many people drive down the street blasting music from their car stereos, often with their windows rolled all the way down. Some drivers soup up their car engines so they will make even more noise. Others will carry on loud conversations in hotel hallways at all hours of the day and night, or will allow the room door to swing open and then slam shut so loudly that the walls shake. In both of these situations, the perpetrators seem not to realize—or care—that their actions are disturbing dozens—and sometimes hundreds—of other people.

It goes beyond manners—people today are less likely to follow all kinds of social rules. Business professor John Trinkaus finds that fewer people now slow down in a school zone, and fewer observe the item limit in a supermarket express lane. More people cut across parking lots to bypass stoplights. In 1979, 29% of people failed to stop at a particular stop sign in a New York suburb, but by 1996 a stunning 97% of drivers did not stop at all. In Trinkaus's most ironic finding, the number of people who paid the suggested fee for lighting a candle at a Catholic church decreased from 92% to 28% between the late 1990s and the early 2000s.

In other words, 72% of people cheated the church out of money in the most recent observation.

Cheating in school has also increased. In 2002, 74% of high school students admitted to cheating, up from 61% in 1992. In 1969, only 34% of high school students admitted to cheating, less than half of the 2002 number. This continues into college; a 2002 survey found that 80% of students at Texas A&M University admitted to cheating. Technology has facilitated this dishonesty, with students passing answers through camera cell phones and downloading papers on the Internet. Other times all it takes is good old-fashioned money: one of the heirs to the Wal-Mart fortune allegedly paid her college roommate more than $20,000 to write papers for her.

Not only are teens more likely to cheat, but they are resigned to cheating among their peers. In a 1997 survey, 88% of high school students said that cheating was common at their school. Three times as many high school students in 1969 compared to 1989 said they would report someone they saw cheating. Also in 1989, an incredible 97% of high school students said they had let someone else copy their work. The disregard for rules continues outside the classroom: in 2000, 26% of high school boys admitted they had shoplifted from a store at least once.

This breakdown in consideration and loyalty, and the increase in cheating, reaches all the way to the top. Business scandals like those at WorldCom and Enron demonstrate that many people have little problem with breaking rules and telling lies in an attempt to make more money. Even honest businesses disregard other time-tested social rules, such as loyalty to employees. Companies are now more likely to raid pension funds and engage in mass layoffs to prop up a sinking stock price. Others ship jobs overseas if it will save money. "Downsizing" and "outsourcing" are the modern corporate equivalents of rudeness—and a lot more devastating. Because GenMe grew up with this kind of ruthlessness, it should not surprise us that they think little of some occasional homework copying. It also suggests that the corporations of the future are going to need much stricter oversight to make sure that cheating and scams are kept to a minimum. Cheating on tests easily translates to cheating on the balance sheet. Expect to see more laws, like Sarbanes-Oxley, that ask corporations to prove that they are not cheating their stockholders. Even with these laws, more stock reports, research, and articles will have to be taken with a grain of salt—in an increasingly competitive world, the temptation to cheat will be ever stronger for GenMe.

CALL ME BETH

Boomers laid claim to the phrase "question authority" during the 1960s. But GenMe doesn't just question authority—we disrespect it entirely. "Older generations trusted God, the church, government, and elders," says Kevin, 22. "I have questioned things and people that earlier generations never would have thought to." This is the eventual outcome of increased informality and the loosening of social rules, and many people would rightly argue that questioning things is good. Sometimes "traditions" are outmoded and need challenging.

But sometimes GenMe takes the questioning of authority a little too far. Education professor Maureen Stout tells the story of a young man in her class who did not turn in his research paper. "After a lot of excuses and arguments he finally came out with it," Stout writes. "He believed he was entitled to do just as he pleased and refused to recognize my authority, as the instructor, to determine what the assignments in the class should be. It was as simple as that." In *Generation X Goes to College*, Peter Sacks relates his frustration with the community college students he taught after spending ten years as a journalist. Students seemed uncomfortable with the idea that he knew more than they did, and even with "the idea that my knowledge and skills were important or even relevant." Student after student balked when he corrected their essays, several complaining that his comments were "just your opinion."

I recognized this phrase immediately, as I'd heard it over and over from my own students. I heard this complaint even when I corrected obvious errors like run-on sentences and incorrect punctuation, things that were clearly not a matter of opinion. Even multiple-choice tests weren't free from this kind of challenge. In one class, I decided it might be a good idea to review the correct answers to exam questions—it would be a way to correct misconceptions and help the students learn, I thought. Almost immediately, several students began to argue with me about the questions, claiming that the answer they had chosen was right. Since there wasn't a grading mistake, I was forced to explain again why the answers were correct, but they continued to argue. It was the worst class I'd ever had. After it was over, an older student—who had not been one of the arguers—came up to me and said with disbelief, "Twenty years ago when I got my first degree, we never questioned teachers like that."

Sacks interviewed a veteran teacher who described a "real qualitative shift" in college students during the late 1980s (not coincidentally, exactly when the first GenMe'ers arrived). He said they had "a sense of entitlement" and were "not very deferential. Some are outright hustlers and try to browbeat professors into giving good grades." Another fellow professor advised Sacks to adopt the more informal approach that she used. In her first class, she always announced: "I have some expertise and you have some expertise. My job is to facilitate this process. And please call me Beth."

The message: We are all equals here. I might have a Ph.D. and years of experience, but that doesn't mean I know any more than you. This is, of course, a lot of the reason for the crumbling of authority and the new acceptance of questioning those in charge. This new democracy in education and the workplace has been energized by the new informality in dress and names. While the boss was once "Mr. Smith" or "Mrs. Jones," now bosses are instead "Mike" or "Linda." "Mr." and "Mrs." sound too stiff and formal—and old-fashioned. When we're all on a first-name basis, the specter of authority takes yet another step back into the shadows of a previous era.

Classrooms are increasingly structured for teachers to be "facilitators" rather than authority figures. Lecturing is frowned upon; "collaborative learning" is in. Class presentations and group projects are common. Sometimes the teacher hardly says anything. In *Growing Up Digital*, Don Tapscott describes a Web-page class where "students learn to cooperate, work in teams, solve problems, and take responsibility for their own learning—by doing." If they don't understand something, they are supposed to ask each other, not the teacher. "And who's the last person you ask for help?" says the teacher. "You are," the students reply. The teacher goes on to say: "I don't teach. If I teach, who knows what they will learn. Teaching's out. . . . If they stop and think about it, they are the authority! They are in charge of their own learning."

The curriculum reflects this lack of a central authority as well. It is no longer enough to teach only the "classics"; these are now known as DWMs (Dead White Males). Few academics still agree that there is a "canon" of Western literature that all students should learn. Instead, students must take classes teaching a variety of perspectives, in which the works of women and minorities are also covered. Whether you agree or disagree with this "multicultural" approach to education, it's clear that we no longer answer to one definite authority. There are many opinions, and each is considered valuable. Though this has many advantages, it does mean that people will be much less likely to conform to societal rules—after all, which rules would they follow? Which culture or society is "right"? We are taught that none of them is, or all of them are.

Unless it's the Internet. Like most people old enough to remember a pre-Internet world, I marvel that we ever got along without it. (How *did* we find movie showtimes in the early 1990s? Oh, yeah, that weird recording where a teenager with acting aspirations would read off the movies and times.) As fantastic as the Internet is for doing research, it also democratizes the source of information. Suddenly, you don't have to write a textbook or have a column in a major newspaper for thousands of people to read your words—just put up a Web page or a blog, and eventually someone, and maybe even lots of people, will stumble across it. In this environment, there is no authority: information is free, diffuse, and comes from everyone. (Whether it is correct is another matter.) Tapscott argues that the current generation of young people is very contrarian. Unlike the passivity of TV, the Web is often interactive. Message boards and chat rooms promote two-way dialogue—of information, opinion, and sometimes insult (called "flaming"). "Because they have the tools to question, challenge, and disagree, these kids are becoming a generation of critical thinkers," writes Tapscott. It's yet another force toward chucking those pesky rules. And in many Internet situations, you can abandon social roles entirely. Want to be a different age or sex? Go ahead. As a famous *New Yorker* cartoon showing two dogs in conversation puts it, "On the Internet, nobody knows you're a dog."

Parental authority also isn't what it used to be. "Parents are no longer eager to be 'parents.' They want to love and guide their children as a trusted friend," says family studies professor Robert Billingham in a recent *Chicago Sun-Times* article. Chicago-area parent Richard Shields says that his 17-year-old son is his best friend. He prefers them to have fun together rather than impose strict rules or discipline. "It's better for them to see our values and decide to gain them for themselves," he says.

This also means that children play a much larger role in family decisions. The kids who chose their own outfits as preschoolers have grown into teenagers who help their parents choose which car to buy or even where to live. The *Sun-Times* article interviewed a large group of teens and their families, finding one where a teenage daughter helped her father decide on a new job, and another where the two teenage kids make all of the home-decorating and electronics-purchasing decisions. Forty percent of teens see their opinions as "very important" in making family decisions. In an earlier era of greater parental authority, that percentage would have been close to zero. One family's two daughters convinced their parents to buy a second car. "I always stress to my girls to be opinionated," said Christine Zapata, the girls' mother. "I guess that sort of backfires on me sometimes."

I wonder what will happen when this generation has their own children. Will they continue the move toward lesser parental authority, or insist that they retain the authority they have grown accustomed to? If GenMe teaches our own children to be individualistic as well, we may have a full-scale battle of the wills once our kids become teenagers themselves.

BEING DIFFERENT IS GOOD, EVEN WHEN YOU'RE GETTING MARRIED

As one of society's most long-lived traditions, marriage and weddings illustrate the move away from social rules better than anything. In 1957, 80% of people said that those who didn't marry were "sick, neurotic, or immoral." Now, of course, when and whether you marry is considered a personal choice. Whom you marry is also fast falling into that category. My parents, a Catholic and a Lutheran (though both white and alike in every other way), were considered a "mixed marriage" at their wedding in 1967. People in my mother's Minnesota hometown whispered about it behind cupped hands for weeks. In contrast, no one blinked an eye when my brother married my sister-in-law in 2003, even though she is Jewish and this is a much larger religious difference. My Catholic relatives danced the hora at their wedding and had a great time, and my parents and I attended my niece's naming ceremony with tremendous pride.

Interracial marriage has also become much more common, doubling since 1980 and now accounting for 1 in 17 marriages. Yet until the Supreme Court struck down miscegenation laws in 1967, whites and blacks could not legally marry each other in sixteen states. In fact, the last antimiscegenation law was not officially repealed until November 2000, in Alabama. Now these unions are everywhere, and between almost all ethnicities and races. My next-door neighbors for three years were a Mexican-American man and his half-Jewish, half-Italian wife, and I've lost count of the number of Asian-white marriages among people I know. Almost half of Asian women will marry a white man. In a 1997 survey of college freshmen, a whopping 95% agreed that "in dating, the important thing is how two people get along, not what race or religion they may be." In 2000, 41% of high school seniors said they had dated someone of another race.

Many young people I've talked to mention interracial dating as the biggest difference between them and their parents: many of their peers date across racial lines, but their parents don't agree with this. Several young women from Texas and North Carolina told me that if they dated a black man their fathers would meet the poor guy at the door with a shotgun. Yet most of GenMe finds this perplexing: who cares what race someone is? In one survey, only 10% of white young people said that marrying someone from their own ethnic group was important; however, 45% said it was important to their parents. Of young Asian-Americans, 32% said same-ethnic-group marriage was important to them, but 68% said it was important to their parents. Interracial marriage is likely to become even more common in the future as more and more young people meet and date people from different backgrounds.

When we marry to our other-race, other-religion, and possibly same-sex partners, we don't follow all of the wedding rules of previous generations. In the mid-1960s, *Brides* magazine insisted that "the only correct colors" for wedding invitations "are white, ivory, or cream, with absolutely no decorations such as borders, flower sprays, and so on." In other words, your invitation had to look just like everyone else's. Now, of course, people use wedding invitations in every possible theme and color—and wording. My parents, who live near Dallas, received a wedding invitation a few years ago with a picture of a cowboy and cowgirl inviting guests to "c'mon over for a big weddin' to-do." The reply card

Weddings, once governed by strict conventions for dress
and behavior, now have few rules. It's your wedding,
so you can wear shorts or a bikini if you want to.

choices were "Yes, we'll be there with our boots on" and "Shucks, we can't make it."

People are bending tradition in other ways. Some brides with male friends have a man of honor, and some grooms have best women. When former *Beverly Hills, 90210* star Tori Spelling married Charlie Shanian in 2004, she had five bridesmaids and two bridesmen, and he had five groomsmen and three groomswomen. Another trend encourages brides to let each bridesmaid choose the style of her gown—it's no longer required that they all wear the same dress, a rule now seen as overly conformist. Many couples write their own vows, wanting a ceremony personalized to speak for their own individual love. I once saw a ceremony that was written specifically for recovering addicts—not exactly the Book of Common Prayer. And the new trend in wedding photography is toward "journalistic" style; the photographers capture moments as they happen, putting less emphasis on formal posing. Wedding aren't about rules any-more, but about individual expression. Wedding gown designer Reem Acra says a bride should choose the look that encapsulates her personal-ity. She says, "I always ask my brides, 'Who are you and what do you want to tell everybody?'"

THE CHURCH AND COMMUNITY
OF THE INDIVIDUAL

GenMe is also less willing to follow the rules of organized religion. Church attendance across all faiths has declined 30% since the 1950s, and about half of that decline occurred since the 1980s. Unlike the Boomers, who seek spirituality as a chosen quest, GenMe is not very reli-gious. Only 18% of 18-to-29-year-olds attend religious services every week. Among high school seniors, most of whom still live with their par-ents, the figure is still only 26%. Even in the South, fewer than 1 out of 3 high school seniors attends religious services weekly. The number of college freshmen who named no religious preference doubled between 1985 and 2003, and the number of students who said they prayed weekly decreased from 1996 to 2003. It will be interesting to see if this genera-tion returns to churchgoing and religion once more have children them-selves.

In *Emerging Adulthood*, Jeffrey Arnett describes the belief systems of young people as "highly individualized," which he calls "make-your-own-religions." He found that only 23% of young people are "conservative believers"; the remaining 77% were agnostic/atheist, deist, or liberal believers (who believe in a religion but question some aspects of it). Many don't adhere to a specific belief system because, as Melissa says, "I believe that whatever you feel, it's personal. . . . Everybody has their own idea of God and what God is. . . . You have your own personal beliefs of how you feel about it and what's acceptable for you and what's right for you personally." In an April 2005 poll, 3 out of 4 American Catholics said they were more likely to "follow my own conscience" on difficult moral questions rather than follow "the teachings of Pope Benedict."

Many young people abandon organized religion because of, you guessed it, the restrictive rules it often imposes. Interviewed in *Emerging Adulthood*, Dana said she attended Jewish services growing up, but stopped going when she got older because "there was this pressure from the people at the synagogue to be, like, kosher, and I just didn't like having anyone telling me what my lifestyle should be." Beth was raised Catholic but by adulthood came to believe that humans all have natural, animalistic urges; she stopped believing because feeling guilty "made me unhappy." Charles grew up Episcopalian but stopped attending because "I realized I was not being encouraged to think for myself. . . . It is, literally, 'This is black. This is white. Do this. Don't do that.' And I can't hang with that."

Many of the churches that have grown in membership in the past few decades are the fundamentalist Christian denominations that do require more strict adherence. However, these churches promote a very personalized form of religion. Many fundamentalist Christian faiths ask one to believe that "Jesus Christ is your personal savior" and that "He has a plan for your life." I heard these phrases from my high school classmates in suburban Dallas very often; many spoke with pride about having "a personal relationship with God." Rick Warren, author of the popular Christian book *The Purpose-Driven Life*, writes, "Accept yourself. Don't chase after other people's approval. . . . God accepts us unconditionally, and in His view we are all precious and priceless." These denominations teach that one's personal faith guarantees acceptance into heaven, not the good works you perform and the way you treat others (which traditionally defined a proper spiritual outlook and its rewards). Even if you are a murderer, you will be saved if you accept Jesus as your personal savior. Of course, most adherents strive to live good lives, but personal beliefs are considered more important.

Churches are not the only group hurting for members. As Robert Putnam documents in *Bowling Alone*, memberships in community groups have declined by more than one-fourth since the 1970s. Groups like the Elks, the Jaycees, and PTA groups have all seen memberships fall. Putnam labels the trend "civic disengagement" and concludes that it is linked to generational shifts. The title of his book comes from the observation that people used to bowl in organized leagues but now bowl alone or in informal groups. Young people would rather do their own thing than join a group.

We're also less likely to trust our neighbors, and less likely to believe that the world is a welcoming place. In 1976, 46% of high school students said that "most people can be trusted" (versus "you can't be too careful in dealing with people"). By 1997, teens' trust in others had slid to 26%. In 2000, 64% of 18-to-24-year-olds said that most people are "just looking out for themselves" rather than "try[ing] to be helpful," and 53% said that most people "would try to take advantage of you if they got a chance." Among 45-to-54-year-olds, however, the majority said that most people would be helpful and fair. GenMe trusts no one, suggesting a culture growing ever more toward disconnection and away from close communities. Trusting no one and relying on yourself is a self-fulfilling prophecy in an individualistic world where the prevailing sentiment is "Do unto others before they do it to you."

THE WORLDWIDE CONFESSIONAL

Maria, 20, says her mother's motto is "Other people don't have to know about the bad things that happen in the family." It's a belief that few in GenMe share. We think that confession is good for the soul, and this no longer means whispering to a priest in a dark booth. It means telling everyone about your experiences and feelings, no matter how distasteful. Shannon, 25, grew up in an abusive household and overdosed on crystal meth when she was 18. In therapy, she learned not to be ashamed of what happened. "You can't build a wall around it—it is better to talk about it and get it out in the open," she says. "I go around to people I just met and tell them my story, hoping they will learn something from my experience."

When I recently asked my students to relate true stories for an extra-credit assignment, I assured them they could tell their own story in the third person if they didn't want me to know it was actually about them. Not one took me up on the offer; instead, I got myriad first-person stories, with names attached, about teenage sex, drug abuse, psychological disorders, ugly divorces, and family disagreements. One student wrote about losing her virginity at age 14 to a man who had only eight toes. So many students wrote candid essays about sex that I finally took it off the list of topics because I had more than enough stories. None of the students cared if I knew details of their personal lives that other generations would have kept as carefully guarded secrets.

This applies in spoken conversation as well. Jenny, 22, is an undergraduate at a small college in the South. When we met at a psychology conference, I asked her about her career plans. Within two minutes, she was telling me about her broken engagement and how her former fiancé had been depressed. This was all done without pretense or embarrassment. In a recent survey of men, 62% of those 18 to 24 said they are comfortable discussing their personal problems with others, compared to only 37% of those age 65 and older. Many older people are amazed that young people will readily share their salary numbers with others, the disclosure of which once carried a strong taboo.

GenMe is also much more open about emotions. "In my generation, as opposed to my parents' or my grandparents', we are told to express our feelings and anger and sadness about our surroundings and not to hold them in," says Ashley, 24. She's not sure this is a good thing, however. "We are an emotionally spoiled generation," she says. "It can lead to more dramatic emotions when you are always discussing, sharing, analyzing them as our generation is led to feel they should do."

But that's not the message young people receive from most of the culture. Even sharing feelings that might muddle a situation is encouraged. In a 2001 episode of the teen show *Dawson's Creek*, one character does not want to confess her romantic feelings to her former boyfriend, who is now dating someone else. "If it broke my heart, I have no right to say so," she says. Her roommate can't believe what she's hearing. Clearly meant to be the show's Voice of Reason, she announces, "You have the right to say anything you want when it comes to how you feel."

TMI COMING UP!

Health issues are also the subject of much more honest and open discussion. Not that long ago, it was not acceptable to talk about health problems, particularly women's health problems. I once asked my grandfather why they had only one child. "Too expensive," he said, though I knew he had made a good living. When I told my mother about this, she said my grandmother hadn't been able to have any more children. I asked why. "All he ever said was that she had 'female problems,'" my mother said. It was a term I'd heard before—for a certain generation, "female problems" was the closest anyone would ever come to uttering words like breast cancer, hysterectomy, endometriosis, uterus, infertility, or even menstrual period.

These days, of course, few people have qualms about using any of these terms, especially when talking with family or close friends—or, as it turns out, even with total strangers. I often read the message boards on ConstantChatter.com. In the "All Things Family" section, there are boards dedicated to pregnancy, childbirth, and trying to conceive. Women on these boards discuss everything, and I mean everything: not just morning sickness, but miscarriages, PMS, the precise appearance of cervical fluid, and the color of menstrual blood (brown or red today?), DTD (doing the deed), and BD (baby dancing) with their husbands. How often, and in what position, is also openly discussed, including any problems that might have arisen—or, sometimes, have not arisen (wink). Common phrases on these boards include "TMI coming up!" or "Sorry if TMI!" TMI, for those of you who are not GenMe, means "Too Much Information" (also called an "overshare"). I'm convinced the phrase was coined because there is so little that is now TMI, but we need a way to warn people before things become really gross. Of course, after warning about the TMI, everyone goes ahead and posts the details anyway.

There are also several support boards for women who have miscarried or lost a baby. Many tell their stories online. In one post, I read a woman's heartbreaking story of giving birth to a deformed child who died just a few hours after delivery. Her signature, which appears under every post she makes even to an open message board, includes the burial picture of her dead son.

These boards are extremely helpful, as they provide an enormous amount of information and support to women going through difficult life experiences. They're wonderful things—but an earlier generation of women would never have dreamed of discussing these topics in a public forum, and maybe not even with their closest friends. We live in a much more open age. In a 1990s study, 33% of women in their forties said that tampon commercials should not be aired on TV, whereas only 5% of women under 30 felt this way. Younger women said their main problem with feminine hygiene ads was that they insulted their intelligence with "outdated notions of modesty." Maybe it all started when we read those Judy Blume books that talked about Margaret getting her period and Tony having wet dreams. We've been able to talk about periods and wet dreams even before we had them, so it's no wonder we're so frank about everything. Now there are not only tampon commercials, but ads for condoms, "personal lubricants" like K-Y jelly, and erection drugs (my favorite: the one where the guy throws the football through the hole in the tire swing. So subtle).

GENERATION DIRECT

This openness extends to all kinds of communications at work and at home. Some older business managers complain that young people today are too blunt. These managers say that young employees ask for instant feedback that's straightforward and uncomplicated, and give it in return. Some managers are surprised at young people's willingness to critique the performance of older people—it's a combination of the eroding respect for authority and the compulsive honesty of the younger generation. "I feel like the X'ers are so 'in your face,'" said one manager.

Young people see their directness as an asset. In one episode of the teen soap *The O.C.*, 16-year-old Seth makes a sarcastic comment, after which his father tells him, "Watch your mouth—I was trying to be polite. You might want to give it a try." Seth replies, "No, thanks, I'd rather be honest." So, to some GenMe'ers, if you're not true to yourself, and you conform to someone else's rules, you might be seen as dishonest or a victim of peer pressure—and avoiding that is more important than being polite. In his book *What Really Happened to the Class of '93*, Chris Colin describes Becky, a classmate who is unfailingly proper and polite; as a result, he complains that he can't "catch an unfettered glimpse of Becky's *core self*." Previous generations were unconcerned about seeing someone else's "core self," but for GenMe "not being yourself" equates to being somehow unwhole and false. Kim, 21, says her mother worries too much about other people's opinions; her mother says Kim should be ashamed when she doesn't take care with her appearance. Kim disagrees. "She should be ashamed of herself for being fake," she declares.

One student of mine took this principle a little too far. Aaron, 22, was the kind of student a teacher dreads—well intentioned and even sweet, but unable to keep his unorthodox opinions to himself. By the end of the term, the other students were openly hostile toward him because he interrupted the class so many times. He didn't see things this way, however. "You might view me as a 'rebel without a cause,'" he wrote. "But I do have a cause. It is being true to me. When I am true to myself I feel confident and content. When I am untrue to myself I feel uneasy and fake. I have to be honest with myself as well as others." In other words, it's more important to be true to yourself than to be liked.

Overall, GenMe appreciates directness. "The older generations are so cautious and political in the way they phrase everything that half the time I don't know what they mean," said one young employee. Lynne Lancaster, one of the authors of the business book *When Generations Collide*, gives a nonbusiness example that perfectly captures this trend. Trying to teach her young stepsons better table manners, she said, "You see, when you're part of a family system, in which all of the parties have mutual respect and caring, it's important to recognize the cultural norms and behave appropriately." When the kids stared back with blank looks, their father—who knew how to relate to this generation—barked out, "Dammit! You both need to use a fork!" It worked.

#$@%&*%$!

These days, saying anything you want often includes words you might not want to say in front of your grandmother. Whether you're for or against this trend, it's clear that swearing is just not the shocker it used to be. The relaxation of the rules against swearing mirrors the same social trend as all of the others here—we swear because we don't care as much about what other people think.

Sixties radicals threw around words like "motherfucker" because they knew it would shock the older generation. It was their way of declaring their independence and showing that they didn't care if people disapproved of them. The shock value still exists to an extent, but many young people swear now just because that's the way they talk. The 1994 movie *Clerks* is a pretty accurate illustration of how young people talk, with about two swear words in every line. It proves the adage that "fuck" is the most versatile word in the English language, since it can be a noun, a verb, or an adjective. (Or even an adverb, as in Mr. Big's famous line in *Sex in the City*: "Absofuckinglutely.")

This comfort with profanity is especially common in college—even, as I found out, in official contexts. My first day of undergraduate orientation at the University of Chicago began with a meeting in a large Gothic hall. After being welcomed by two administrators, a third came to the podium and asked us to note a change in the test schedule: the swimming test would be held tomorrow instead of today. A guy wearing swim trunks and a Big Bird intertube then walked down the center aisle, threw his hands up in frustration, and said, "Aw, fuck!"

As it turns out, the whole thing was staged—with administrative approval—by the campus comedy troupe, Off-Off-Campus. I remember being both stunned and pleased—people can swear in official meetings in college! This was not high school anymore! This was like summer camp with fewer rules! Sure enough, we had a discussion about "shitwork" in one of my sociology classes, and nobody even blinked. Everybody in my dorm swore like sailors. It was a huge adjustment to go home for Thanksgiving break and not tell my mother that the turkey was "really fuckin' good." (My advice to college students everywhere: *Don't* do this.) When I did let such words slip out, my mom's eyes would widen and she would put her hand over her mouth. Few of us in GenMe, of course, cover our mouths after someone swears. We may have when we were about 10 . . . but not if we got HBO.

There has been much public hand-wringing over the number of four-letter words now heard regularly in movies and on television—or, actually, five- and three-letter words. Network TV began allowing "bitch" in the 1980s, and the 1990s brought the best gift late-night comedians ever got: the ability to say "ass" on TV. David Letterman liked this so much he started a segment called "big-ass ham" just so he could say it over and over. And of course, characters on HBO and in R-rated movies utter four-letter words as if they were being paid for each usage. People against this trend often use an argument that should now sound familiar. American culture has become crude, rude, and socially unacceptable. Whatever happened to politeness and manners? Nobody cares what anyone thinks anymore. (I say @$#% them. Just kidding.)

WHAT THE DATA SAY ABOUT CONFORMITY AND THE NEED FOR SOCIAL APPROVAL

Do you like to gossip sometimes? Have you ever pretended to be sick to get out of doing something? Have you ever insisted on having your own way? Before you vote, do you carefully check the qualification of each candidate? Are you always polite? Are you always willing to admit it when you've made a mistake?

If you answered no to the first three questions and yes to the next three, you have a high need for social approval. You want other people to see you as a good person, and you place high value on conventional behavior. What other people think matters a lot to you.

You are also probably not a member of Generation Me. These questions are from a measure called the Marlowe-Crowne Social Desirability Scale. The scale measures a person's "need for social approval," and people who score high on it, according to the scale authors, display "polite, acceptable behavior" and follow "conventional, even stereotyped, cultural norms." My student Charles Im and I analyzed 241 studies that gave this questionnaire to college students and children, 40,745 individuals in all.

Not surprisingly, scores on the need for social approval have slid downward since the 1950s. The average college student in 2001 scored lower than 62% of college students in 1958. Put another way, the 2001 student scored at the 38th percentile compared to his or her 1958 peers. These percentiles work just like those on standardized tests—imagine your child taking a test and scoring at the 50th percentile one time and the 38th percentile another time. You would consider her average the first time, but be fairly concerned about her slipping performance the next.

I also wondered if children would show the same results—was it only college students who changed, or were kids also seeking social approval less? Sure enough, the results were similar. Children ages 9 to 12 showed rapidly decreasing needs for social approval. For example, the average 1999 GenMe fifth- or sixth-grader scored at the 24th percentile, or lower than 72% of kids in the 1960s. This is an even larger change than for the college students—you would be pretty upset if your child came home with a standardized test score in the 24th percentile. These results told me that the decline in social approval was pervasive: even children as young as 9 showed the generational trend, with kids from GenMe scoring lower than kids from earlier generations.

The Baby Boomers, of course, began this trend. In fact, the data show that the need for social approval reached an all-time low in the late 1970s to the early 1980s. This is not that surprising—the Boomers practically invented youth rebellion in the 1960s. By the 1970s, the rebellion was mainstream, and the defiance of authority an accepted social value. Take the line Yippie radical Jerry Rubin used in the late 1970s—if someone called him on the phone when he was otherwise occupied, he would say honestly, "Can't talk to you now—I'm masturbating."

The 1980s, on the other hand, returned society to a somewhat more conventional existence. Slowly, men cut their hair (except for Ponch and Jon on CHiPs), pant legs went from flagrantly bell-bottom to normal (at least until their resurgence around 1996), and pot smoking declined. It was not quite as necessary to rebel to fit in—which was always a rather ironic notion anyway. GenMe turned this trend around to an extent, no longer thinking of social approval as something to be completely disdained. But the need for social approval did not even come close to the levels of the 1950s and 1960s—those days were gone forever.

A new movement dawned during the 1980s, however, a trend that Generation Me would take to new heights, leaving Boomers in the dust. Generation Me believes, with a conviction that approaches boredom because it is so undisputed, that the individual comes first. It's the trend that gives the generation its name, and I explore it in the next two chapters.

2

An Army of One: *Me*

O ne day when my mother was driving me to school in 1986, Whitney Houston's hit song "The Greatest Love of All" was warbling out of the weak speakers of our Buick station wagon with wood trim. I asked my mother what she thought the song was about. "The greatest love of all—it has to be about children," she said.

My mother was sweet, but wrong. The song does say that children are the future (always good to begin with a strikingly original thought) and that we should teach them well. About world peace, maybe? Or great literature? Nope. Children should be educated about the beauty "inside," the song declares. We all need heroes, Whitney sings, but she never found "anyone to fulfill my needs," so she learned to depend on (wait for it) "me." The chorus then declares, "learning to love yourself is the greatest love of all."

This is a stunning reversal in attitude from previous generations. Back then, respect for others was more important than respect for yourself. The term "self-esteem" wasn't widely used until the late 1960s, and didn't become talk-show and dinner-table conversation until the 1980s. By the 1990s, it was everywhere.

Take, for example, the band Offspring's rockingly irreverent 1994 riff "Self-Esteem." The song describes a guy whose girlfriend "says she wants only me . . . Then I wonder why she sleeps with my friends." (Hmmm.) But he's blasé about it—it's OK, really, since he's "just a sucker with no self-esteem."

By the mid-1990s, Offspring could take it for granted that most people knew the term "self-esteem," and knew they were supposed to have it. They also knew how to diagnose themselves when they didn't have it.

Offspring's ironic self-parody demonstrates a high level of understanding of the concept, the satire suggesting that this psychological self-examination is rote and can thus be performed with tongue planted firmly in cheek.

In the years since, attention to the topic of self-esteem has rapidly expanded. A search for "self-esteem" in the books section of amazon.com yielded 105,438 entries in July 2005 (sample titles: *The Self-Esteem Workbook, Breaking the Chain of Low Self-Esteem, Ten Days to Self-Esteem, 200 Ways to Raise a Girl's Self-Esteem*). Magazine articles on self-esteem are as common as e-mail spam for Viagra. *Ladies' Home Journal* told readers to "Learn to Love Yourself!" in March 2005, while *Parenting* offered "Proud to Be Me!" (apparently the exclamation point is required) in April, listing "5 simple ways to help your child love who he is." TV and radio talk shows would be immediately shut down by the FCC if "self-esteem" were on the list of banned words. The American Academy of Pediatrics guide to caring for babies and young children uses the word self-esteem ten times in the space of seven pages in the first chapter, and that doesn't even count the numerous mentions of self-respect, confidence, and belief in oneself.

How did self-esteem transform from an obscure academic term to a familiar phrase that pops up in everything from women's magazines to song lyrics to celebrity interviews? The story actually begins centuries ago, when humans barely had a concept of a self at all: your marriage was arranged, your profession determined by your parents, your actions dictated by strict religious standards. Slowly over the centuries, social strictures began to loosen and people started to make more choices for themselves. Eventually, we arrived at the modern concept of the individual as an autonomous, free person.

Then came the 1970s, when the ascendance of the self truly exploded into the American consciousness. In contrast to previous ethics of honor and duty, Baby Boomer ideals focused instead on meaning and self-fulfillment. In his 1976 bestseller, *Your Erroneous Zones*, Wayne Dyer suggests that the popular song "You Are the Sunshine of My Life" be retitled "I Am the Sunshine of My Life." Your love for yourself, he says, should be your "first love." The 1970 allegory, *Jonathan Livingston Seagull*, describes a bird bored with going "from shore to food and back again." Instead, he wants to enjoy flying, swooping through the air to follow "a higher meaning, a higher purpose for life," even though his actions get him exiled from his flock. The book, originally rejected by nearly every major publishing house, became a runaway bestseller as Americans came to agree with the idea that life should be fulfilling and focused on the needs of the self. The seagulls in the animated movie *Finding Nemo* were still on message almost twenty-five years later: all that comes out of their beaks is the word "Mine."

BOOMERS AND THEIR "JOURNEY" INTO THE SELF

But this book is not about Baby Boomers, and it's not about the 1970s. Because the Boomers dominate our culture so much, however, we have to understand them first so we can see how they differ from the younger Generation Me. Why aren't the Boomers—the Me Generation in the 1970s—the *real* Generation Me? It's about what you explore as a young adult versus what you're born to and take for granted.

For the Boomers, who grew up in the 1950s and 1960s, self-focus was a new concept, individualism an uncharted territory. In his 1981 book *New Rules: Searching for Self-Fulfillment in a World Turned Upside Down*, Daniel Yankelovich describes young Boomers struggling with new questions: How do you make decisions in a marriage with two equal partners? How do you focus on yourself when your parents don't even know what that means? The Boomers in the book sound like people driving around in circles in the dark, desperately searching for something. The world was so new that there were no road signs, no maps to point the way to this new fulfillment and individuality.

That's probably why many Boomers talk about the self using language full of abstraction, introspection, and "growth." New things call for this kind of meticulous thought, and require the idea that the process will take time. Thus Boomers talk about "my journey," "my need to keep growing," or "my unfulfilled potentials." Sixties activist Todd Gitlin called the Boomer quest the "voyage to the interior." Icky as they are to today's young people, these phrases drum with motion and time, portraying self-focus as a continuous project that keeps evolving as Boomers look around for true meaning. In a 1976 *New York Magazine* article, Tom Wolfe described the "new dream" as "remaking, remodeling, elevating and polishing one's very self . . . and observing, studying, and doting on it." Sixties radical Jerry Rubin wrote that he tried just about every fad of the 1970s (rolfing, est, yoga, sex therapy, finding his inner child); one of the chapters in his book *Growing (Up) at Thirty-Seven* is called "Searching for Myself."

Such introspection primarily surfaces today in the speech of New Agers, therapists who have read too much Maslow, and over-45 Boomers. When asked what's next in her life, Kim Basinger (born in 1953) replies, "Watching what the rest of my journey is going to be about." In answer to the same question, Sarah Ferguson, Duchess of York (born in 1959) says: "My coming to stay in America for a few months is like my blossoming into my true Sarah, into my true self. And I'm just coming to learn about her myself." Not all Boomers talk this way, of course, but enough do that it's an immediately recognizable generational tic. It's also a guaranteed way to get a young person to roll her eyes. She might also then tell you to lighten up.

Many authors, from William Strauss and Neil Howe in *Generations* to Steve Gillon in *Boomer Nation,* have noted that abstraction and spirituality are the primary hallmarks of the Boomer generation. Gillon describes Boomers as having a "moralistic style" and devotes a chapter to Boomers' "New Fundamentalism." Whether joining traditional churches or exploring meditation or yoga, Boomers have been fascinated with the spiritual for four decades.

Even Boomers who don't adopt New Age language seek higher meaning in the new religion of consumer products—thus the yuppie revolution. In *Bobos in Paradise,* David Brooks demonstrates that upper-class Boomers have poured their wealth into things like cooking equipment, which somehow feels more moral and meaningful than previous money sinks like jewelry or furs. Even food becomes "a barometer of virtue," Brooks says, as 1960s values are "selectively updated. . . . Gone are the sixties-era things that were fun and of interest to teenagers, like Free Love, and retained are all the things that might be of interest to middle-aged hypochondriacs, like whole grains."

The Boomers' interest in the abstract and spiritual shows up in many different sources. In 1973, 46% of Boomers said they "focused on internal cues." Only 26% of 1990s young people agreed. Thirty percent of Boomers said that "creativity comes from within," versus 18% of young people in the 1990s. Even stronger evidence comes from a national sur-

vey of more than 300,000 college freshmen. In 1967, a whopping 86% of
incoming college students said that "developing a meaningful philosophy of life" was an essential life goal. Only 42% of GenMe freshmen in
2004 agreed, cutting the Boomer number in half. I'm definitely a member of my generation in this way; despite being an academic, I'm not sure
I know what a "meaningful philosophy of life" even is. Jerry Rubin
does—if you can understand him. "Instead of seeking with the expectation of finding, I experience my seeking as an end in itself," he writes. "I
become one with my seeking, and merge with the moment." OK, Jerry.
Let us know when you've reentered the Earth's atmosphere.

While up there, maybe Jerry met Aleta St. James, a 57-year-old
woman who gave birth to twins in 2004. She explained her unusual
actions by saying, "My whole world is about manifesting, so I decided to
manifest children." It's not surprising that an enterprising GenMe member put together a list of books on amazon.com titled "Tired of Baby
Boomer Self-Righteousness?"

Boomers display another unique and somewhat ironic trait: a strong
emphasis on group meetings. Boomers followed in the footsteps of their
community-minded elders—they just joined the Weathermen instead of
the Elks Lodge. This is one of the many reasons why Boomers are not the
true Generation Me—almost everything they did happened in groups:
Vietnam protests, marches for feminism, consciousness raising, assertiveness training, discos, even seminars like est. Maybe it felt safer to explore
the self within a group—perhaps it felt less radical. No one seemed to
catch the irony that it might be difficult to find your own unique direction in a group of other people. Even Boomers' trends and sayings belied
their reliance on groups: "Don't trust anyone over 30" groups people by
age, as did the long hair many Boomer men adopted in the late 1960s and
early 1970s to distinguish themselves from older folks. In a 1970 song,
David Crosby says he decided not to cut his hair so he could "let my freak
flag fly." If you've got a flag, you're probably a group. Boomers may have
thought they invented individualism, but like any inventor, they were
followed by those who truly perfected the art.

Boomers took only the first tentative steps in the direction of self-
focus, rather than swallowing it whole at birth. Most Boomers never
absorbed it at all and settled down early to marry and raise families.
Those who adopted the ways of the self as young adults speak the lan-

guage with an accent: the accent of abstraction and "journeys." They had to reinvent their way of thinking when already grown, and thus see self-focus as a "process." In his book, Rubin quotes a friend who says, "We are the first generation to reincarnate ourselves in our own lifetime."

THE MATTER-OF-FACT SELF-FOCUS
OF GENERATION ME

Generation Me had no need to reincarnate ourselves; we were born into a world that already celebrated the individual. The self-focus that blossomed in the 1970s became mundane and commonplace over the next two decades, and GenMe accepts it like a fish accepts water. If Boomers were making their way in the uncharted world of the self, GenMe has printed step-by-step directions from Yahoo! Maps—and most of the time we don't even need them, since the culture of the self is our hometown. We don't have to join groups or talk of journeys, because we're already there. We don't need to "polish" the self, as Wolfe said, because we take for granted that it's already shiny. We don't need to look inward; we already know what we will find. Since we were small children, we were taught to put ourselves first. That's just the way the world works—why dwell on it? Let's go to the mall.

GenMe's focus on the needs of the individual is not necessarily self-absorbed or isolationist; instead, it's a way of moving through the world beholden to few social rules and with the unshakable belief that you're important. It's also not the same as being "spoiled," which implies that we always get what we want; though this probably does describe some kids, it's not the essence of the trend (as I argue in Chapter 4, GenMe's expectations are so great and our reality so challenging that we will probably get less of what we want than any previous generation). We simply take it for granted that we should all feel good about ourselves, we are all special, and we all deserve to follow our dreams. GenMe is straightforward and unapologetic about our self-focus. In 2004's *Conquering Your Quarterlife Crisis*, Jason, 25, relates how he went through some tough times and decided he needed to change things in his life. His new motto was "Do what's best for Jason. I had to make *me* happy; I had to do what was best for myself in every situation."

Our practical orientation toward the self sometimes leaves us with a distaste for Boomer abstraction. When a character in the 2004 novel *Something Borrowed* watched the 1980s show *thirtysomething* as a teen, she wished the Boomer characters would "stop pondering the meaning of life and start making grocery lists." The matter-of-fact attitude of GenMe appears in everyday language as well—a language that still includes the abstract concept of self, but uses it in a very simple way, perhaps because we learned the language as children. We speak the language of the self as our native tongue. So much of the "common sense" advice that's given these days includes some variation on "self":

- Worried about how to act in a social situation? "Just be yourself."
- What's the good thing about your alcoholism/drug addiction/ murder conviction? "I learned a lot about myself."
- Concerned about your performance? "Believe in yourself." (Often followed by "and anything is possible.")
- Should you buy the new pair of shoes, or get the nose ring? "Yes, express yourself."
- Why should you leave the unfulfilling relationship/quit the boring job/tell off your mother-in-law? "You have to respect yourself."
- Trying to get rid of a bad habit? "Be honest with yourself."
- Confused about the best time to date or get married? "You have to love yourself before you can love someone else."
- Should you express your opinion? "Yes, stand up for yourself."

Americans use these phrases so often that we don't even notice them anymore. Dr. Phil, the ultimate in plainspoken, no-nonsense advice, uttered both "respect yourself" and "stop lying to yourself" within seconds of each other on a *Today* show segment on New Year's resolutions. One of his bestselling books is entitled *Self Matters*. We take these phrases and ideas so much for granted, it's as if we learned them in our sleep as children, like the perfectly conditioned citizens in Aldous Huxley's *Brave New World*.

These aphorisms don't seem absurd to us even when, sometimes, they are. We talk about self-improvement as if the self could be given better drywall or a new coat of paint. We read self-help books as if the self could receive tax-deductible donations. The *Self* even has its own magazine. Psychologist Martin Seligman says that the traditional self—responsible,

THE SELF ACROSS THE GENERATIONS

Baby Boomers	Generation Me
Self-fulfillment	Fun
Journey, potentials, searching	Already there
Change the world	Follow your dreams
Protests and group sessions	Watching TV and surfing the Web
Abstraction	Practicality
Spirituality	Things
Philosophy of life	Feeling good about yourself

hardworking, stern—has been replaced with the "California self," "a self that chooses, feels pleasure and pain, dictates action and even has things like esteem, efficacy, and confidence." Media outlets promote the self relentlessly; I was amazed at how often I heard the word "self" used in the popular media once I started looking for it. A careful study of news stories published or aired between 1980 and 1999 found a large increase in self-reference words (I, me, mine, and myself) and a marked decrease in collective words (humanity, country, or crowd).

Young people have learned these self-lessons very well. In a letter to her fans in 2004, Britney Spears, 23, listed her priorities as "Myself, my husband, Kevin, and starting a family." If you had to read that twice to get my point, it's because we take it for granted that we should put ourselves first on our list of priorities—it would be blasphemy if you didn't (unless, of course, you have low self-esteem). Twenty-year-old Maria says her mother often reminds her to consider what other people will think. "It doesn't matter what other people think," Maria insists. "What really matters is how I perceive myself. The real person I need to please is myself."

Smart marketers have figured this out, too. In the late 1990s, Prudential replaced its longtime insurance slogan "Get a Piece of the Rock" with the nakedly individualistic "Be Your Own Rock." The United States Army, perhaps the last organization one might expect to focus on the individual instead of the group, has followed suit. Their standard slogan, adopted in 2001, is "An Army of One."

CHANGES IN SELF-ESTEEM: WHAT THE DATA SAY

The data I gathered on self-esteem over time mirror the social trends perfectly. My colleague Keith Campbell and I looked at the responses of 65,965 college students to the Rosenberg Self-Esteem Scale, the most popular measure of general self-esteem among adults. I held my breath when I analyzed these data for the first time, but I needn't have worried: the change was enormous. By the mid-1990s, the average GenMe college man had higher self-esteem than 86% of college men in 1968. The average mid-1990s college woman had higher self-esteem than 71% of Boomer college women. Between the 1960s and the 1990s, college students were increasingly likely to agree that "I take a positive attitude toward myself" and "On the whole, I am satisfied with myself." Other sources verify this trend. A 1997 survey of teens asked, "In general, how do you feel about yourself?" A stunning 93% answered "good." Of the remainder, 6% said they felt "not very good," and only 1% admitted they felt "bad" about themselves. Another survey found that 91% of teens described themselves as responsible, 74% as physically attractive, and 79% as "very intelligent."

Children's self-esteem scores tell a different but even more intriguing story. We examined the responses of 39,353 children, most ages 9 to 13, on the Coopersmith Self-Esteem Inventory, a scale written specifically for children. During the 1970s—when the nation's children shifted from the late Baby Boom to the early years of GenX—kids' self-esteem declined, probably because of societal instability. Rampant divorce, a wobbly economy, soaring crime rates, and swinging singles culture made the 1970s a difficult time to be a kid. The average child in 1979 scored lower than 81% of kids in the mid-1960s. Over this time, children were less likely to agree with statements like "I'm pretty sure of myself" and "I'm pretty happy" and more likely to agree that "things are all mixed up in my life." The individualism that was so enthralling for teenagers and adults in the 1970s didn't help kids—and, if their parents suddenly discovered self-fulfillment, it might have even hurt them.

But after 1980, when GenMe began to enter the samples, children's self-esteem took a sharp turn upward. More and more during the 1980s and 1990s, children were saying that they were happy with themselves. They agreed that "I'm easy to like" and "I always do the right thing." By the mid-1990s, children's self-esteem scores equaled, and often exceeded, children's scores in the markedly more stable Boomer years before 1970. The average kid in the mid-1990s—right in the heart of GenMe—had higher self-esteem than 73% of kids in 1979, one of the last pre-GenMe years.

This is a bit of a mystery, however. The United States of the 1980s to mid-1990s never approached the kid-friendly stability of the 1950s and early 1960s: violent crime hit record highs, divorce was still at epidemic levels, and the economy had not yet reached its late-1990s boom. So without the calm and prosperity of earlier decades, why did children's self-esteem increase so dramatically during the 1980s and 1990s?

THE SELF-ESTEEM CURRICULUM

The short answer is that they were taught it. In the years after 1980, there was a pervasive, society-wide effort to increase children's self-esteem. The Boomers who now filled the ranks of parents apparently decided that children should always feel good about themselves. Research on programs to boost self-esteem first blossomed in the 1980s, and the number of psychology and education journal articles devoted to self-esteem doubled between the 1970s and the 1980s. Journal articles on self-esteem increased another 52% during the 1990s, and the number of books on self-esteem doubled over the same time. Generation Me is the first generation raised to believe that everyone should have high self-esteem.

Magazines, television talk shows, and books all emphasize the importance of high self-esteem for children, usually promoting feelings that are actually a lot closer to narcissism (a more negative trait usually defined as excessive self-importance). One children's book, first published in 1991, is called *The Lovables in the Kingdom of Self-Esteem*. "I AM LOVABLE. Hi, lovable friend! My name is Mona Monkey. I live in the Kingdom of Self-Esteem along with my friends the Lovable Team," the book begins. On the next page, children learn that the gates of the kingdom will swing open if you "say these words three times with pride: *I'm lovable! I'm lovable! I'm lovable!*" (If I hear the word "lovable" one more time, I'm going to use my hefty self-esteem to pummel the author of this book.)

Another example is the "BE A WINNER Self-Esteem Coloring and Activity Book" pictured in this chapter. Inside, children find activities and pictures designed to boost their self-esteem, including coloring a "poster

Parents are encouraged to raise their children's self-esteem even when kids are simply coloring. Even the cat has high self-esteem on this coloring book cover. However, the dog lacks a self-esteem boosting ribbon. He probably has low self-esteem—after all, he drinks out of the toilet.

for your room" that reads "YOU ARE SPECIAL" in yellow, orange, and red letters against a purple background. Another page asks kids to fill in the blanks: "Accept y_ur_e_f. You're a special person. Use p_si_iv_ thinking." A similar coloring book is called "We Are All Special" (though this title seems to suggest that being special isn't so special). All of this probably sounds like Al Franken's *Saturday Night Live* character Stuart Smal-

COLOR THIS POSTER FOR YOUR ROOM –

· Dot color Purple   ·· Dots color Yellow
··· Dots color Orange   ···· Dots color Red

Remember, everyone is special. Maybe if you color the whole poster you can catch the irony.

ley, an insecure, sweater-vest-wearing man who looks in the mirror and unconvincingly repeats, "I'm good enough, I'm smart enough, and doggone it, people like me." It sounds like it because it's exactly the type of thing Franken was parodying. And it's everywhere.

Many school districts across the country have specific programs designed to increase children's self-esteem, most of which actually build self-importance and narcissism. One program is called "Self-Science: The Subject Is Me." (Why bother with biology? *I'm* so much more interesting!) Another program, called "Pumsy in Pursuit of Excellence," uses a dragon character to encourage children to escape the "Mud Mind" they experience when feeling bad about themselves. Instead, they should strive to be in the "Sparkle Mind" and feel good about themselves. The Magic Circle exercise designates one child a day to receive a badge saying "I'm great." The other children then say good things about the chosen child, who later receives a written list of all of the praise. At the end of the exercise, the child must then say something good about him- or herself. Boomer children in the 1950s and 1960s gained self-esteem naturally from a stable, child-friendly society; GenMe's self-esteem has been actively cultivated for its own sake.

One Austin, Texas, father was startled to see his five-year-old daughter wearing a shirt that announced, "I'm lovable and capable." All of the kindergarteners, he learned, recited this phrase before class, and they all wore the shirt to school on Fridays. It seems the school started a bit too young, however, because the child then asked, "Daddy, all the kids are wondering, what does 'capable' mean?"

Some people have wondered if the self-esteem trend waned after schools began to put more emphasis on testing during the late 1990s. It doesn't look that way. Parenting books and magazines stress self-esteem as much as ever, and a large number of schools continue to use self-esteem programs. The mission statements of many schools explicitly announce that they aim to raise students' self-esteem. A Google search for "elementary school mission statement self-esteem" yielded 308,000 Web pages in January 2006. These schools are located across the country, in cities, suburbs, small towns, and rural areas. "Building," "improving," "promoting," or "developing" self-esteem is a stated goal of (among many others) New River Elementary in New River, Arizona; Shady Dell Elementary in Springfield, Missouri; Shettler Elementary in Fruitport, Michigan; Baxter Elementary in Baxter, Tennessee; Rye Elementary in Westchester County, New York; Copeland Elementary in Augusta, Georgia; and Banff Elementary in Banff, Alberta, Canada. Private religious schools are not immune: St. Wendelin Catholic Elementary in Fostoria, Ohio, aims to "develop a feeling of confidence, self-esteem, and self-worth in our students." Andersen Elementary in Rockledge, Florida, raises the bar, adding that students will "exhibit high self-esteem." So self-esteem must not just be *promoted* by teachers, but must be actively *exhibited* by students.

As John Hewitt points out in *The Myth of Self-Esteem*, the implicit message is that self-esteem can be taught and should be taught. When self-esteem programs are used, Hewitt notes, children are "encouraged to believe that it is acceptable and desirable to be preoccupied with oneself [and] praise oneself." In many cases, he says, it's not just encouraged but required. These exercises make self-importance mandatory, demanding of children that they love themselves. "The child *must* be taught to like himself or herself. . . . The child *must* take the teacher's attitude himself or herself—'I am somebody!' 'I am capable and loving!'—regardless of what the child thinks."

Most of these programs encourage children to feel good about themselves for no particular reason. In one program, teachers are told to discourage children from saying things like "I'm a good soccer player" or "I'm a good singer." This makes self-esteem contingent on performance, the program authors chide. Instead, "we want to anchor self-esteem firmly to the child . . . so that no matter what the performance might be, the self-esteem remains high." In other words, feeling good about yourself is more important than good performance. Children, the guide says, should be taught "that it is who they are, not what they do, that is important." Many programs encourage self-esteem even when things go wrong or the child does something bad. In one activity, children are asked to finish several sentences, including ones beginning "I love myself even though . . ." and "I forgive myself for . . ."

Teacher training courses often emphasize that a child's self-esteem must be preserved above all else. A sign on the wall of one university's education department says, "We Choose to Feel Special and Worthwhile No Matter What." Perhaps as a result, 60% of teachers and 69% of school counselors agree that self-esteem should be raised by "providing more unconditional validation of students based on who they are rather than how they perform or behave." Unconditional validation, to translate the educational mumbo-jumbo, means feeling good about yourself no matter how you act or whether you learn anything or not. A veteran second-grade teacher in Tennessee disagrees with this practice but sees it everywhere. "We handle children much more delicately," she says. "They feel good about themselves for no reason. We've given them this cotton-candy sense of self with no basis in reality."

Although the self-esteem approach sounds like it might be especially popular in liberal blue-state areas, it's common in red states as well, perhaps because it's very similar to the ideas popularized by fundamentalist Christian churches. For example, the popular Christian children's book *You Are Special* promotes the same unconditional self-esteem emphasized in secular school programs. First published in 1997, the book notes, "The

Calvin knows exactly why the notion of unconditional
self-esteem is so popular: It feels good and requires little work.

world tells kids, 'You're special if . . . you have the brains, the looks, the talent.' God tells them, 'You're special just because. No qualifications necessary.' Every child you know needs to hear this one, reassuring truth." Traditional religion, of course, did have "qualifications" and rules for behavior. Adults hear this message as well. In an article in *Ladies Home Journal*, Christian author Rick Warren writes, "You can believe what others say about you, or you can believe in yourself as does God, who says you are truly acceptable, lovable, valuable, and capable."

Even programs not specifically focused on self-esteem often place the utmost value on children's self-feelings. Children in some schools sing songs with lyrics like "Who I am makes a difference and all our dreams can come true" and "We are beautiful, magnificent, courageous, outrageous, and great!" Other students pen a "Me Poem" or write a mock TV "commercial" advertising themselves and their good qualities. An elementary school teacher in Alabama makes one child the focus of a "VIP for a week" project. The children's museum in Laramie, Wyoming, has a self-esteem exhibit where children are told to describe themselves using positive adjectives.

Parents often continue the self-esteem lessons their children have learned in school, perhaps because more children are planned and cherished. The debut of the birth control pill in the early 1960s began the trend toward wanted children, which continued in the early 1970s as abortion became legal and cultural values shifted toward children as a choice rather than a duty. In the 1950s, it was considered selfish not to have kids, but by the 1970s it was an individual decision. As a result, more and more children were born to people who really *wanted* to become parents. Parents were able to lavish more attention on each child as the average number of children per family shrank from four to two. Young people often say that their parents believed in building self-esteem. "My mom constantly told me how special I was," said Natalie, 19. "No matter how I did, she would tell me I was the best." Kristen, 22, said her parents had a "wonderful" way of "telling me what a great job I did and repeatedly telling me I was a very special person." Popular media has also promoted this idea endlessly, offering up self-esteem as the cure for just about everything. In one episode of the family drama *7th Heaven*, one young character asks what can be done about war. The father on the show, a minister, says, "We can take a good look in the mirror, and when we see peace, that's when we'll have peace on earth." The rest of the episode featured each character smiling broadly to himself or herself in the mirror. In other words, if we all just loved ourselves enough, it would put an end to war. (Not only is this tripe, but wars, if anything, are usually rooted in too *much* love of self, land, and nation—not too little.) But, as TV and movies have taught us, loving yourself is more important than anything else.

These efforts have had their intended impact. Don Tapscott, who interviewed hundreds of people for his book *Growing Up Digital*, notes, "Chat moderators, teachers, parents, and community workers who spend time with [young people] invariably told us that they think this is a confident generation who think highly of themselves." In a CBS News poll, the high school graduates of 2000 were asked, "What makes you feel positive about yourself?" The most popular answer, at 33%, was the tautological "self-esteem." School performance was a distant second at 18%, with popularity third at 13%. Yet this is not surprising: Saying that having self-esteem makes you feel positive about yourself—forget any actual reason—is exactly what the self-esteem programs have taught today's young generation since they were in kindergarten.

Yet when everyone wears a shirt that says "I'm Special," as some of the programs encourage, it is a wide-open invitation to parody. The 1997 premiere episode of MTV's animated show *Daria* featured a character named Jane, who cracked, "I like having low self-esteem. It makes me feel special." Later in the episode, the teacher of a "self-esteem class" asks the students to "make a list of ten ways the world would be a sadder place if you weren't in it." "Is that if we'd never been born, or if we died suddenly and unexpectedly?" asks one of the students. Wanting to get out of the rest of the class, Daria and Jane recite the answers to the self-esteem "test": "The next time I start to feel bad about myself [I will] stand before the mirror, look myself in the eye and say, 'You are special. No one else is like you.'"

By the time GenMe gets to college, these messages are rote. Hewitt, who teaches at the University of Massachusetts, says his students are very excited when they begin discussing self-esteem in his sociology class. But once he begins to question the validity of self-esteem, the students' faces become glum and interest wanes. Hewitt compares it to what might happen in church if a priest suddenly began questioning the existence of

God. After all, we worship at the altar of self-esteem and self-focus. "When the importance of self-esteem is challenged, a major part of the contemporary American view of the world is challenged," Hewitt writes.

GIRLS ARE GREAT

It is no coincidence that the *Daria* episode parodying self-esteem programs features two girls. Feminist Gloria Steinem, who spent the 1970s and 1980s fighting for practical rights like equal pay and maternity leave, spent the early 1990s promoting her book *Revolution from Within: A Book of Self-Esteem*. In 1991, a study by the American Association of University Women (AAUW) announced that girls "lose their self-esteem on the way to adolescence." This study was covered in countless national news outlets and ignited a national conversation about teenage girls and how they feel about themselves. *Reviving Ophelia*, a bestselling book on adolescent girls, popularized this idea further, documenting the feelings of self-doubt girls experience as they move through junior high and high school. Apparently, girls' self-esteem was suffering a severe blow when they became teenagers, and we needed to do something about it.

Before long, programs like the Girl Scouts began to focus on self-esteem through their "Girls Are Great" program. Girls could earn badges like "Being My Best" and "Understanding Yourself and Others." Amanda, 22, says that her Girl Scout troop spent a lot of time on self-esteem. "We did workshops and earned badges based around self-esteem building projects," she says. "We learned that we could do anything we wanted, that it was good to express yourself, and being different is good."

In 2002, the Girl Scout Council paired with corporate sponsor Unilever to launch "Uniquely ME!" a self-esteem program to "address the critical nationwide problem of low self-esteem among adolescent and preadolescent girls." The program includes three booklets for girls ages 8 to 14, each including exercises on "recognizing one's strengths and best attributes" and "identifying core values and personal interests."

However, there is little evidence that girls' self-esteem dives at adolescence. The AAUW study was seriously flawed, relying on unstandardized measures and exaggerating small differences. In 1999, a carefully researched, comprehensive study of sex differences in self-esteem was published in *Psychological Bulletin*, the most prestigious journal in the field. The study statistically summarized 216 previous studies on more than 97,000 people and concluded that the actual difference between adolescent girls' and boys' self-esteem was less than 4%—in other words, extremely small. Exaggerating this difference might be unwise. "We may create a self-fulfilling prophecy for girls by telling them they'll have low self-esteem," said University of Wisconsin professor Janet Hyde, one of the study authors.

When my colleague Keith Campbell and I did a different analysis of 355 studies of 105,318 people, we also found that girls' self-esteem does not fall precipitously at adolescence; it just doesn't rise as fast as boys' self-esteem during the teen years. There was no large drop in girls' self-esteem, and by college the difference between men's and women's self-esteem was very small. Another meta-analysis, by my former student Brenda Dolan-Pascoe, found moderate sex differences in appearance self-esteem, but no sex differences at all in academic self-esteem. Girls also scored *higher* than boys in behavior self-esteem and moral-ethical self-esteem. The achievements of adolescent girls also contradict the idea that they retreat into self-doubt: girls earn higher grades than boys at all school levels, and more go on to college.

In other words, adolescent girls don't have a self-esteem problem—there is no "critical nationwide problem of low self-esteem among adolescent and preadolescent girls" as the Girl Scouts claimed. But in a culture obsessed with feeling good about ourselves, even the hint of a self-esteem deficit is enough to prompt a nationwide outcry. The Girl Scout program premiered three years after the 1999 comprehensive study found a minuscule sex difference in self-esteem. Why let an overwhelming mass of data get in the way of a program that sounded good?

SELF-ESTEEM AND ACADEMIC PERFORMANCE

There has also been a movement against "criticizing" children too much. Some schools and teachers don't correct children's mistakes, afraid that this will damage children's self-esteem. One popular method tells teachers not to correct students' spelling or grammar, arguing that kids should be "independent spellers" so they can be treated as "individuals." (Imagine reading a nuespaper wyten useing *that* filosofy.) Teacher education courses emphasize that creating a positive atmosphere is more important

Many Generation Me students would instead believe that their substandard work deserved an A. Trudeau's comment on grade inflation
in the service of self-esteem mirrors the views of many psychologists
and education experts critical of the self-esteem movement.

than correcting mistakes. In 2005, a British teacher proposed eliminat-
ing the word "fail" from education; instead of hearing that they have
failed, students should hear that they have "deferred success." In the
United States, office stores have started carrying large stocks of purple
pens, as some teachers say that red ink is too "scary" for children's papers.
Florida elementary schoolteacher Robin Slipakoff said, "Red has a negative connotation, and we want to promote self-confidence."
    Grade inflation has also reached record highs. In 2004, 48% of Amer-

ican college freshmen—almost half—reported earning an A average in high school, compared to only 18% in 1968, even though SAT scores decreased over this time period. "Each year we think [the number with an A average] can't inflate anymore. And then it does again. The 'C' grade is almost a thing of the past," noted Andrew Astin, the lead researcher for the study. These higher grades were given out even though students were doing less work. Only 33% of American college freshmen in 2003 reported studying six or more hours a week during their last year of high school, compared to 47% in 1987. So why are they still getting better grades? "Teachers want to raise the self-esteem and feel-good attitudes of students," explains Howard Everson of the College Board. We have become a Lake Wobegon nation: all of our children are above average.

The results of these policies have played out in schools around the country. Emily, 8, came home from school one day proud that she got half of the words right on her spelling test (in other words, a grade of 50). When her mother pointed out that this wasn't very good, Emily replied that her teacher had said it was just fine. At her school near Dallas, Texas, 11-year-old Kayla was invited to the math class pizza party as a reward for making a good grade, even though she had managed only a barely passing 71. The pizza parties used to be only for children who made A's, but in recent years the school has invited every child who simply passed.

This basically means that we don't expect children to learn anything. As long as they feel good, that seems to be all that's required. As education professor Maureen Stout notes, many educational psychologists believe that schools should be "places in which children are insulated from the outside world and emotionally—not intellectually—nourished. . . . My colleagues always referred to the importance of making kids feel good about themselves but rarely, if ever, spoke of achievement, ideals, goals, character, or decency." The future teachers whom Stout was educating believed that "children shouldn't be challenged to try things that others in the class are not ready for, since that would promote competition, and competition is bad for self-esteem. Second, grading should be avoided if at all possible, but, if absolutely necessary, should be done in a way that avoids any indication that Johnny is anything less than a stellar pupil."

Grade inflation and lack of competition may be backfiring: in 2003, 43% of college freshmen reported that they were frequently bored in class during their last year of high school, up from 29% in 1985. This is not surprising: how interesting could school possibly be when everyone gets an A and self-esteem is more important than learning?

Perhaps as a result of all of this self-esteem building, educational psychologist Harold Stevenson found that American children ranked very highly when asked how good they were at math. Of course, their *actual* math performance is merely mediocre, with other countries' youth routinely outranking American children. Every year, news anchors solemnly report how far American kids are falling behind. The emphasis on self-esteem can't be blamed entirely for this, of course, but one could easily argue that children's time might be better spent doing math than hearing that they are special. In 2004, 70% of American college freshmen reported that their "academic ability" was "above average" or "highest 10%," an amusing demonstration of American youths' self-confidence outpacing their ability at math.

What kind of young people does this produce? Many teachers and social observers say it results in kids who can't take criticism. In other words, employers, get ready for a group of easily hurt young workers. Peter Sacks, author of *Generation X Goes to College*, noted the extraordinary thin-skinnedness of the undergraduates he taught, and my experience has been no different. I've learned not to discuss test items that the majority of students missed, as this invariably leads to lots of whiny defensiveness and very little actual learning. The two trends are definitely related:

research shows that when people with high self-esteem are criticized, they became unfriendly, rude, and uncooperative, even toward people who had nothing to do with the criticism.

None of this should really surprise us. Students "look and act like what the [self-esteem] theories say they should look and act like," notes Hewitt. "They tend to act as though they believe they have worthy and good inner essences, regardless of what people say or how they behave, that they deserve recognition and attention from others, and their unique individual needs should be considered first and foremost." And, of course, this is exactly what has happened: GenMe takes for granted that the self comes first, and we often believe exactly what we were so carefully taught—that we're special.

But this must have an upside; surely kids who have high self-esteem go on to make better grades and achieve more in school. Actually, they don't. There is a small correlation between self-esteem and grades. However, self-esteem does not cause high grades—instead, high grades cause higher self-esteem. So self-esteem programs clearly put the cart before the horse in trying to increase self-esteem. Even much of the small link from high grades to high self-esteem can be explained by other factors such as income: rich kids, for example, have higher self-esteem and get better grades, but that's because coming from an affluent home causes both of these things, and not because they cause each other. This resembles the horse and the cart being towed on a flatbed truck—neither the cart nor the horse is causing the motion in the other even though they are moving together. As self-esteem programs aren't going to make all kids rich, they won't raise self-esteem this way either.

Nor does high self-esteem protect against teen pregnancy, juvenile delinquency, alcoholism, drug abuse, or chronic welfare dependency. Several comprehensive reviews of the research literature by different authors have all concluded that self-esteem doesn't cause much of anything. Even the book sponsored by the California Task Force to Promote Self-Esteem and Personal and Social Responsibility, which spent a quarter of a million dollars trying to raise Californians' self-esteem, found that self-esteem isn't linked to academic achievement, good behavior, or any other outcome the Task Force was formed to address.

ARE SELF-ESTEEM PROGRAMS GOOD OR BAD?

Psychologist Martin Seligman has criticized self-esteem programs as empty and shortsighted. He argues that self-esteem based on nothing does not serve children well in the long run; it's better, he says, for children to develop real skills and feel good about accomplishing something. Roy Baumeister, the lead author of an extensive review of the research on self-esteem, found that self-esteem does not lead to better grades, improved work performance, decreased violence, or less cheating. In fact, people with high self-esteem are often more violent and more likely to cheat. "It is very questionable whether [the few benefits] justify the effort and expense that schools, parents and therapists have put into raising self-esteem," Baumeister wrote. "After all these years, I'm sorry to say, my recommendation is this: forget about self-esteem and concentrate more on self-control and self-discipline."

I agree with both of these experts. Self-esteem is an outcome, not a cause. In other words, it doesn't do much good to encourage a child to feel good about himself just to feel good; this doesn't mean anything. Children develop true self-esteem from behaving well and accomplishing things. "What the self-esteem movement really says to students is that their achievement is not important and their minds are not worth developing," writes Maureen Stout. It's clearly better for children to value learning rather than simply feeling good.

So should kids feel bad about themselves if they're not good at school or sports? No. They should feel bad if they didn't work hard and try. And even if they don't succeed, sometimes negative feelings can be a motivator. Trying something challenging and learning from the experience is better than feeling good about oneself for no reason.

Also, everyone can do *something* well. Kids who are not athletic or who struggle with school might have another talent, like music or art. Almost all children can develop pride from being a good friend or helping someone. Kids can do many things to feel good about themselves, so self-esteem can be based on something. If a child feels great about himself even when he does nothing, why do anything? Self-esteem without basis encourages laziness rather than hard work. On the other hand, we shouldn't go too far and hinge our self-worth entirely on one external goal, like getting good grades. As psychologist Jennifer Crocker documents, the seesaw of self-esteem this produces can lead to poor physical and mental health. A happy medium is what's called for here: don't feel bad about yourself because you made a bad grade—just don't feel good about yourself if you didn't even study. Use your bad feelings as a motivator to do better next time. True self-confidence comes from honing your talents and learning things, not from being told you're great just because you exist.

The practice of not correcting mistakes, avoiding letter grades, and discouraging competition is also misguided. Competition can help make learning fun; as Stout points out, look at how the disabled kids in the Special Olympics benefit from competing. Many schools now don't publish the honor roll of children who do well in school and generally downplay grades because, they falsely believe, competition isn't good for self-esteem (as some kids won't make the honor roll, and some kids will make C's). But can you imagine not publishing the scores of a basketball game because it might not be good for the losing team's self-esteem? Can you imagine not keeping score in the game? What fun would that be? The self-esteem movement, Stout argues, is popular because it is sweetly addictive: teachers don't have to criticize, kids don't have to be criticized, and everyone goes home feeling happy. The problem is they also go home ignorant and uneducated.

Kids who don't excel in a certain area should still be encouraged to keep trying. This isn't self-esteem, however: it's self-control. Self-control, or the ability to persevere and keep going, is a much better predictor of life outcomes than self-esteem. Children high in self-control make better grades and finish more years of education, and they're less likely to use drugs or have a teenage pregnancy. Self-control predicts all of those things researchers had hoped self-esteem would, but hasn't.

Cross-cultural studies provide a good example of the benefits of self-control over self-esteem. Asians, for example, have lower self-esteem than Americans. But when Asian students find out that they scored low on a particular task, they want to keep working on that task so they can improve their performance. American students, in contrast, prefer to give up on that task and work on another one. In other words, Americans preserve their self-esteem at the expense of doing better at a difficult task. This goes a long way toward explaining why Asian children perform better at math and at school in general.

Young people who have high self-esteem built on shaky foundations might run into trouble when they encounter the harsh realities of the real world. As Stout argues, kids who are given meaningless A's and promoted when they haven't learned the material will later find out in college or the working world that they don't know much at all. And what will *that* do to their self-esteem, or, more important, their careers? Unlike your teacher, your boss isn't going to care much about preserving your high self-esteem. The self-esteem emphasis leaves kids ill prepared for the inevitable criticism and occasional failure that is real life. "There is no self-esteem movement in the work world," points out one father. "If you present a bad report at the office, your boss isn't going to say, 'Hey, I like the color paper you chose.' Setting kids up like this is doing them a tremendous disservice."

In any educational program, one has to consider the trade-off between benefit and risk. Valuing self-esteem over learning and accomplishment is clearly harmful, as children feel great about themselves but are cheated out of the education they need to succeed. Self-esteem programs *might* benefit the small minority of kids who really do feel worthless, but those kids are likely to have bigger problems that self-esteem boosting won't fix. The risk in these programs is in inflating the self-concept of children who already think the world revolves around them. Building up the self-esteem and importance of kids who are already egocentric can bring trouble, as it can lead to narcissism—and maybe it already has.

CHANGES IN NARCISSISM

Narcissism is one of the few personality traits that psychologists agree is almost completely negative. Narcissists are overly focused on themselves and lack empathy for others, which means they cannot see another person's perspective. (Sound like the last clerk who served you?) They also feel entitled to special privileges and believe that they are superior to other people. As a result, narcissists are bad relationship partners and can be difficult to work with. Narcissists are also more likely to be hostile, feel anxious, compromise their health, and fight with friends and family.

Unlike those merely high in self-esteem, narcissists admit that they don't feel close to other people.

All evidence suggests that narcissism is much more common in recent generations. In the early 1950s, only 12% of teens aged 14 to 16 agreed with the statement "I am an important person." By the late 1980s, an incredible 80%—almost seven times as many—claimed they were important. Psychologist Harrison Gough found consistent increases on narcissism items among college students quizzed between the 1960s and the 1990s. GenMe students were more likely to agree that "I would be willing to describe myself as a pretty 'strong' personality" and "I have often met people who were supposed to be experts who were no better than I." In other words, those other people don't know what they're talking about, so everyone should listen to me.

In a 2002 survey of 3,445 people conducted by Joshua Foster, Keith Campbell, and me, younger people scored considerably higher on the Narcissistic Personality Inventory, agreeing with items such as "If I ruled the world it would be a better place," "I am a special person," and "I can live my life anyway I want to." (These statements evoke the image of a young man speeding down the highway in the world's biggest SUV, honking his horn, and screaming, "Get out of my way! I'm important!") This study was cross-sectional, though, meaning that it was a one-time sample of people of different ages. For that reason, we cannot be sure if any differences are due to age or to generation; however, the other studies of narcissism mentioned previously suggest that generation plays a role. It is also interesting that narcissism scores were fairly high until around age 35, after which they decreased markedly. This is right around the cutoff between GenMe and previous generations.

Narcissism is the darker side of the focus on the self, and is often confused with self-esteem. Self-esteem is often based on solid relationships with others, whereas narcissism comes from believing that you are special and more important than other people. Many of the school programs designed to raise self-esteem probably raise narcissism instead. Lillian Katz, a professor of early childhood education at the University of Illinois, wrote an article titled "All About Me: Are We Developing Our Children's Self-Esteem or Their Narcissism?" She writes, "Many of the practices advocated in pursuit of [high self-esteem] may instead inadvertently develop narcissism in the form of excessive preoccupation with oneself." Because the school programs emphasize being "special" rather than encouraging friendships, we may be training an army of little narcissists instead of raising kids' self-esteem.

Many young people also display entitlement, a facet of narcissism that involves believing that you deserve and are entitled to more than others. A scale that measures entitlement has items like "Things should go my way," "I demand the best because I'm worth it," and (my favorite) "If I were on the *Titanic*, I would deserve to be on the *first* lifeboat!" A 2005 Associated Press article printed in hundreds of news outlets labeled today's young people "The Entitlement Generation." In the article, employers complained that young employees expected too much too soon and had very high expectations for salary and promotions.

Teachers have seen this attitude for years now. One of my colleagues said his students acted as if grades were something they simply deserved to get no matter what. He joked that their attitude could be summed up by "Where's my A? I distinctly remember ordering an A from the catalog." Stout, the education professor, lists the student statements familiar to teachers everywhere: "I need a better grade," "I deserve an A on this paper," "I *never* get B's." Stout points out that the self-esteem movement places the student's feelings at the center, so "students learn that they do not need to respect their teachers or even earn their grades, so they begin to believe that they are entitled to grades, respect, or anything else . . . just for asking."

Unfortunately, narcissism can lead to outcomes far worse than grade grubbing. Several studies have found that narcissists lash out aggressively when they are insulted or rejected. Eric Harris and Dylan Klebold, the teenage gunmen at Columbine High School, made statements remarkably similar to items on the most popular narcissism questionnaire. On a videotape made before the shootings, Harris picked up a gun, made a shooting noise, and said "Isn't it fun to get the respect we're going to deserve?" (Chillingly similar to the narcissism item "I insist upon getting the respect that is due me.") Later, Harris said, "I could convince them that I'm going to climb Mount Everest, or I have a twin brother growing out of my back. I can make you believe anything" (virtually identical to the item "I can make anyone believe anything I want them to"). Harris and Klebold then debate which famous movie director will film their story. A few weeks after making the videotapes, Harris and Klebold killed thirteen people and then themselves.

Other examples abound. In a set of lab studies, narcissistic men felt less empathy for rape victims, reported more enjoyment when watching a rape scene in a movie, and were more punitive toward a woman who refused to read a sexually arousing passage out loud to them. Abusive husbands who threaten to kill their wives—and tragically sometimes do—are the ultimate narcissists. They see everyone and everything in terms of fulfilling their needs, and become very angry and aggressive when things don't go exactly their way. Many workplace shootings occur after an employee is fired and decides he'll "show" everyone how powerful he is.

The rise in narcissism has very deep roots. It's not just that we feel better about ourselves, but that we even think to ask the question. We fixate on self-esteem, and unthinkingly build narcissism, because we believe that the needs of the individual are paramount. This will stay with us even if self-esteem programs end up in the dustbin of history, and it is the focus of the next chapter.

3

You Can Be Anything
You Want to Be

Beginning in May 2005, high school students faced a completely revamped SAT college entrance exam. Its most prominent feature is an essay portion designed to measure students' writing ability. Instead of asking for a balanced treatment of a topic, however, the test asks the student to "develop your point of view on this issue." This means that to get a high score, it's necessary to argue only one side of the question: yours. As the test-prep book *Kaplan New SAT 2005* advises, "What's important is that you take a position and state how you feel. It is not important what other people might think, just what you think."

Generation Me has always been taught that our thoughts and feelings are important. It's no surprise that students are now being tested on it. Even when schools, parents, and the media are not specifically targeting self-esteem, they promote the equally powerful concepts of socially sanctioned self-focus, the unquestioned importance of the individual, and an unfettered optimism about young people's future prospects. This chapter explores the consequences of individualism that go beyond self-esteem, and all of the ways that we consciously and unconsciously train children to expect so much out of life. High school senior Scot, a contestant on the reality show *The Scholar,* captured this notion when he said, "I feel it's very important to be your own hero." So forget presidents, community leaders, even sports figures—it's more important to look up to *yourself*.

Like self-esteem, self-focus and individuality have been actively promoted in schools. When I was in sixth grade in Irving, Texas, our fall assignment in Reading was a project called "All About Me." We finished

A page from my "All About Me" project in 6th grade Reading class,
fetchingly illustrated with cutouts from magazine ads. The project
promoted the idea that thinking about yourself is very important—
apparently more important than reading and writing,
given the uncorrected spelling mistake.

sentences like "I feel angry when . . ." and "Something special I want you
to know about me is . . ." We were also asked to include pictures of ourselves. Many of my classmates spent hours on this project, mulling over
their answers and making elaborate albums with their best photographic
self-portraits. In effect, we were graded on how well we could present our
opinions and images of ourselves. Later that year, our assignment was to
make a personal "coat of arms" that illustrated our interests and hobbies.
In the past, a coat of arms was the symbol of an entire extended family,
so an individual coat of arms—particularly one created by an eleven-
year-old—is an interesting cultural construct.

My school was not the only one to value and promote children's individual feelings and thoughts. The popular school program called Quest has students keep track of their feelings for a day on an "Emotion Clock" or a "Mood Continuum." Andrea, 22, told me that her junior high and high school English classes included weekly "free writing." She notes, "This not only encouraged writing but pushed expressing yourself." Even employers are getting in on the game: Xerox's new recruiting slogan is "Express Yourself."

The growing primacy of the individual appears in data I gathered on 81,384 high school and college students. These young people completed questionnaires measuring what psychologists call agency—a personality trait involving assertiveness, dominance, independence, and self-promotion. Between the 1970s and the 1990s, both young men's and women's agency increased markedly, with the average 1990s college student scoring higher than 75% of college Boomers from the 1970s. I had expected women's agency to increase over this time, but men's feelings of agency also rose, suggesting that the trend went beyond gender roles. As the Boomers gave way to GenMe, more and more young people were saying that they stood up for their individual rights, had a "strong personality," and were "self-sufficient" and "individualistic." So GenMe not only has high self-esteem, but we take pride in being independent actors who express our needs and wants.

The focus on the needs of the individual self begins when children are very young, sometimes before they are born or even conceived. Advertising convinces parents to spend lots of money on the perfect nursery, since the room should "reflect" the child's personality and individuality. (Yet, as The Mommy Myth by Susan Douglas and Meredith Michaels points out, "remember, kid not born yet, personality unknown.") One of the most popular nursery decorations right now is 12-inch-tall letters spelling out the child's name, an obvious bow to individualism. Douglas and Michaels refer to the trends toward perfection and individuality in nurseries as our "narcissism around our kids . . . a hyperindividualized emphasis on how truly, exquisitely unique and precious our child is, the Hope diamond, more special than the others."

We also promote individuality and self-importance by giving our children choices. One of my psychology colleagues called me one day and said, "You know, I just realized how kids learn this self stuff so quickly. I just asked my 1-year-old if she wanted apple juice or milk. Earlier today I asked her if she wanted to wear her red dress or her blue one. She can't even talk and I'm asking her what she wants!" My friend is not alone in asking his daughter such questions; most American parents begin asking their children their preferences before they can answer. When kids get a little older, many parents think it's important to let their children pick out the clothes they wear in the morning—the kid might end up wearing red polka dots with green and blue stripes, but it's OK because they are "expressing themselves" and learning to make their own choices.

Culture Shock! USA, a guidebook to American culture for foreigners, explains: "Often one sees an American engaged in a dialogue with a tiny child. 'Do you want to go home now?' says the parent. 'No,' says an obviously tired, crying child. And so parent and child continue to sit discontentedly in a chilly park. 'What is the matter with these people?' says the foreigner to himself, who can see the child is too young to make such decisions." It's just part of American culture, the book says: "The child is acquiring both a sense of responsibility for himself and a sense of his own importance." We expect our kids to have individual preferences and would never dream, as earlier generations did, of making every single decision for our children and asking them to be seen and not heard. Not coincidentally, this also teaches children that their wants are the most important.

This can sometimes cause problems when children get older. One mother says she treated her daughter "as if she had a mind of her own ever since she was a baby," asking her what she wanted to do next and what she wanted to wear. "But now that she's 4, sometimes I really want her to mind me. The other day I told her, 'Alexis, you're going to do this right now because I say so!' She looked up at me astounded, as if to say, 'What's going on here? You're changing the rules on me!'" And just wait until she's 14.

Perhaps as a result, some experts maintain that more kids these days are behaving badly. Psychologist Bonnie Zucker, interviewed for a People magazine article on "Kids Out of Control," saw a 10-year-old whose parents let him decide whether or not to go to school—if he didn't want to go, he didn't go. Another mother didn't make her son do homework because it made him "unhappy." Other children scream at their parents when their oatmeal is lumpy or openly call their parents "freak" or "retard." Writer Martin Booe recently devoted an entire column to overindulgent parents who "let their kids run roughshod over themselves and other adults . . . they're rampant." Says educational psychologist Michele Borba: "Too many parents subscribe to the myth that if you discipline children, you're going to break their spirit. . . . The 'Me Generation' is raising the 'Me-Me-Me Generation.'"

Douglas and Michaels argue that because mothers are now expected to understand their child's inner feelings and wants, the child comes to believe "that he's the center of the universe, his thoughts and feelings the only ones worth considering, the ones that cut in line before everyone else's." Gone are the days, they say, when parents were told to "disabuse [their child] of the notion that he or she is the Sun King." These days, watch *Supernanny* or *Nanny 911* and you'll see a screen full of screaming and defiant Sun Kings.

Paula Peterson's two kids, Abby and Joey, throw temper tantrums when they don't get the toys they want. And why does she put up with such behavior? Well, as the *People* article explains, "the same spark that sets off the kicking and screaming may also give Abby and Joey what they need to excel in a culture that rewards outspokenness and confidence." Peterson says she'd rather have kids who are "strong-willed and say what they want" than "kids who are bumps on logs." Another parent says of his son, "I don't want Holden to just be a well-behaved child. I want him to feel he has control and choices." As *Culture Shock! USA* explains, "In most of the countries of the world, parents feel that their obligation is to raise an obedient child who will fit into society. The little ego must be molded into that of a well-behaved citizen. Not so here [in the U.S.]. . . . the top priority is to raise an individual capable of taking advantage of opportunity."

It's easy to see how these values can quickly lead to disaster. A recent article in *Time* magazine asked, "Does Kindergarten Need Cops?" After being told to surrender a toy, one kindergartner screamed, knocked over her desk, and threw books at the other kids. Another 6-year-old told his teacher to "Shut up, bitch." A report from the Tarrant County, Texas, school district found that 93% of 39 schools agreed that kindergartners have "more emotional and behavioral problems" than they did five years ago. While it's difficult to tell if this can be traced back to kids having their own way at home, it's certainly one possibility. The youngest members of GenMe are, apparently, taking self-importance to a whole other level.

Sometimes the flip side of this equation occurs when a child ends up fending for herself because a parent has to work long hours, or is depressed about a divorce. This situation, obviously, does not lead to the narcissistic self-centeredness that overindulgence does. Instead, it leads to an independent, self-reliant individualism, but individualism nonetheless. Jerry's parents divorced when he was 11. As a consequence, he says in *Emerging Adulthood*, "I grew up on my own. I mean, my mom was there, but when you deal with things, you have to take care of yourself. . . . I always know that I can count on myself, and that's what it comes down to. You've got to be able to count on yourself, and then you can count on others." Dealing with a parental divorce was a pretty common experience for much of GenMe—more of us have divorced parents than any other generation in history. Another large segment of the generation grew up (or is growing up) with a single parent, usually the mother. These family compositions often create very independent, self-sufficient children, confident in their ability to get by on their own. This can be useful, but it also results in self-importance. What kind of environment leads to less self-important children? The happy medium, where kids aren't self-reliant miniadults, but are also not overindulged or taught to think that the world revolves around them.

ANYTHING IS POSSIBLE: NEVER GIVE UP ON YOUR DREAMS

In his book *What Really Happened to the Class of '93*, Chris Colin notes that his classmates were constantly told "You can be whatever you want to be" and "Nothing is impossible." His interviewees mention this time and time again. "I was told, growing up, that I could do whatever I wanted, and I fully believed I could," said one. Alexandra Robbins and Abby Wilner, authors of *Quarterlife Crisis*, agree: "For all of their lives, twentysomethings have been told that they can be whatever they want to be, do whatever they want to do." Lia Macko, the coauthor of a similar book (*Midlife Crisis at 30*), dedicates the work to her mother, "for truly instilling in me the belief that Anything Is Possible," which she describes as "the unqualified mantra of our youth."

These messages begin early. When the boy band 'N Sync appeared on the kids' show *Sesame Street*, they sang a song called "Believe in Yourself." Some people might tell you there are things you can't do, the song says. But you can be whatever you want to be, as long as you "believe in yourself." (What if they want to be brats?) One of the most popular Barney (the annoying purple dinosaur) videotapes for toddlers promotes a similar message: it's called *You Can Be Anything!*

And so it goes, into high school as well. Joey, a character in the teen soap *Dawson's Creek*, was usually portrayed as realistic and disillusioned; after all, her mother died a few years ago and her father is in prison. But after she paints a mural for the high school hallway in a 1998 episode, she says, "We could all use a daily reminder that, if you believe in yourself, even when the odds seem stacked against you, anything's possible." So much for realism. (Notice, too, the automatic connection between "anything's possible" and "believe in yourself.") It's not surprising, though, because the logical outcome of every kid having high self-esteem is every kid thinking that he can achieve anything. In a recent survey, a stunning 98% of college freshmen agreed with the statement, "I am sure that one day I will get to where I want to be in life."

One professor encountered this GenMe attitude quite spectacularly in an undergraduate class at the University of Kansas. As she was introducing the idea that jobs and social class were based partially on background and unchangeable characteristics, her students became skeptical. That can't be right, they said: you can be anything you want to be. The professor, a larger woman with no illusions about her size, said, "So you're saying that I could be a ballerina?" "Sure, if you really wanted to," said one of the students.

This ethos is reflected in the lofty ambitions of modern adolescents. In 2002, 80% of high school sophomores said they expected to graduate from a four-year college, compared to 59% just twelve years before in 1990. In the late 1960s, by comparison, only 55% of high school seniors thought they would attend college at all, much less graduate. High schoolers also predict they will have prestigious careers. Seventy percent of late-1990s high school students expected to work in professional jobs, compared to 42% in the 1960s. Unfortunately, these aspirations far outstrip the need for professionals in the future. In *The Ambitious Generation*, sociologists Barbara Schneider and David Stevenson label these "misaligned ambitions." In other words, the kids have learned the lesson "you can be whatever you want to be" a little too well, as there probably won't be enough desirable jobs for everyone to be whatever he wants to be.

Ambitions grow stronger once young people enter college. In 2003, an incredible 3 out of 4 American college freshmen said that they wanted to earn an advanced degree (such as a master's, Ph.D., M.D., or law degree). For example, 39% say they will earn a master's degree, 19% a Ph.D., and 12% an M.D. Grand ambitions indeed, since the number of Ph.D.'s granted each year is only 4% of the bachelor's degrees given, and M.D.'s only 1%. Thus about 4 in 5 aspiring Ph.D.'s will be disappointed, and a whopping 11 in 12 would-be doctors will not reach their goals. And that's if you finish your bachelor's degree at all; figures are hard to nail down, but the discrepancy between college enrollment and bachelor's degrees suggests that less than 50% of entering college students finish their degrees within 5 years. During the next decade, we are going to see a lot of young people who will be disappointed that they cannot reach their career goals.

Young people also expect to make a lot of money. In 1999, teens predicted that they would be earning, on average, $75,000 a year by the time they were 30. The average income of a 30-year-old that year?—$27,000, or around a third of the teens' aspirations. Ray, 24, recently got his masters' degree and expects to land a high-paying job right away. "I don't want to have all those years of education and make only $60,000 a year," he scoffs. Of course, most starting salaries are much lower than that, even with a master's. Overall, young people predict a bright future for themselves. Sixty-five percent of high school seniors in 2000 predicted that their lives would be better than their parents'; only 4% thought their lives would be worse. Adults surveyed at the same time were much less optimistic, with only 29% saying that high school seniors would have better lives, and 32% predicting a worse outcome. One young employee told a startled manager that he expected to be a vice president at the company within three years. When the manager told him this was not realistic (most vice presidents were in their sixties), the young man got angry with him and said, "You should encourage me and help me fulfill my expectations."

Even the vice presidency of the company might not be good enough if the job is not "fulfilling." *Financial Times* writer Thomas

Barlow notes that "the idea has grown up, in recent years, that work should not be just . . . a way to make money, support a family, or gain social prestige but should provide a rich and fulfilling experience in and of itself. Jobs are no longer just jobs; they are lifestyle options." Many twentysomethings interviewed in *Quarterlife Crisis* agreed, like one young woman, that if "she wasn't both proud of and fulfilled by her job, then it was not a job worth having." Several interviewees were looking to quit their jobs, including one young man who wanted to quit his "dream" job working on Capitol Hill because "it's not ful- filling." Shannon, 27, sees this as an obvious sign of generational change. "Most of my friends would like a 'calling' to do something they are passionate about. But I can't imagine a 1950s businessman worked up about whether his job fulfilled him."

Rosa, 24, interviewed in the book *Emerging Adulthood*, thinks she would not like either of her parents' professions (her mother is an opti- cian and her father travels around the world doing maintenance on large ships). "I knew I wanted to be somewhere that I would grow as a person, and I don't see [my parents] growing as individuals," she said. The book also tells the story of Charles, 27, a Princeton graduate who thought about becoming a psychologist or a lawyer but instead is in a band called the Jump Cats, which he describes as "a rock band without instruments." "Music is where my heart is," he says. "I didn't want to regret not going for something that would ultimately bring me more satisfaction." In the future, he also expects to pursue other avenues, such as writing novels and screenplays.

Related to "you can be anything" is "follow your dreams"—like self- focus, a concept that GenMe speaks as a native language. An amazing number of the young people interviewed in *Quarterlife Crisis* adhered fiercely to this belief. Derrick, struggling to be a comedy writer in Holly- wood, says, "Never give up on your dreams. If you're lucky enough to actually have one, you owe it to yourself to hold onto it." Robin, a 23- year-old from Nebraska, says, "Never give up on your dreams. Why do something that won't bring about your dreams? Life is short enough— don't waste it working in a job that doesn't drive you." I was pretty well indoctrinated myself: the title of my high school valedictory speech was "Hold Fast to Dreams."

Why are dreams so important to GenMe? It's the self, as usual. "I want

No wonder kids have such big dreams—even cheese is supposed
to make them sports stars. The ad might be more accurate if the
kid were standing on a hypodermic needle filled with steroids.

to write for sitcoms," says Brandon, 24. "I wouldn't be satisfied with
myself if I didn't try to do something I'm passionate about," Lara, 29,
posted on an Internet board for mothers (she has a toddler and is expecting her second child). She says that someday she would like to be a college professor and teach English literature. "I think I need to start putting
myself first and start making my dreams a reality," she wrote.

Some people might argue that this is just youthful hope—after all,
hasn't every generation dreamed big during adolescence? Maybe, but
GenMe's dreams are bigger. While our parents may have aimed simply to
leave their small town, or to go to college, we want to make lots of money

at a career that is fulfilling and makes us famous. *American Idol* contestant David Brown, 20, has a bet with his mother and younger brother on which of them will become a millionaire first. "I'm about to win [the bet]," he said in February 2005. A few weeks later, Brown was voted off the show, finishing seventeenth out of twenty-four finalists.

"Following your dreams" sounds like a good principle, until you realize that every waiter in L.A. is following his or her dreams of becoming an actor, and most of them won't succeed. Most people are not going to realize their dreams, because most people do not dream of becoming accountants, social workers, or trash collectors—just to name three jobs that society can't do without but nevertheless factor into few childhood fantasies. And few dream of the white-collar jobs in business that many of us have or will have. "No one at my company is following his dream," says one of my friends who works in marketing.

The most common dreams of young people are acting, sports, music, and screenwriting. In 2004, a national survey found that more college freshmen said they wanted to be an "actor or entertainer" than wanted to be a veterinarian, a dentist, a member of the clergy, a social worker, an architect, or work in the sales department of a business. Music was just as popular as acting, and even more said they wanted to be artists. Almost 1 out of 20 college students expects to become an actor, artist, or musician, more than want to be lawyers, nurses, accountants, business owners, journalists, or high school teachers.

GenMe also holds on to dreams more fiercely, and in a way that makes you wonder how we will react if we don't achieve our lofty goals. Sharon, 22, began her graduate school application essay by writing, "On my 70th birthday, I want to be able to reflect on my life and say 'I followed my dreams and lived for my passions.' In other words, I will not be discouraged by closed doors, and will not be denied the opportunity to live to my fullest potential." Emily, 22, apparently believes that denial will solve all problems. Interviewed in *Quarterlife Crisis*, she says that if a young person "never gives up, then he or she will never have to admit to failure." Uh-huh. But you might have to live in your car.

The book does discuss one young person who "decided to change his dream rather than accept failure." Mark, 29, tried for years to make it as an actor in New York; he realizes now he should have moved to L.A.

sooner, where "I bet I would have been cast on a soap opera." He finally decided to give up on acting and pursue another career. His new, and presumably more realistic, choice? To be a movie director. (I am not making this up, and the book's authors, both twentysomethings themselves, present this story without comment or irony.)

Mark's story illustrates another change from previous generations: the length of time GenMe has to pursue dreams. Because we expect to marry and have children later, it's more acceptable to spend your entire twenties pursuing "dream" careers like music, screenwriting, or comedy. Jeffrey Arnett calls that period emerging adulthood, a time when "no dreams have been permanently dashed, no doors have been firmly closed, every possibility for happiness is still alive." That period is getting longer and longer for people who spend years trying to make it in Hollywood or attempting to get their first novel published. Many twentysomethings struggle with the decision to keep pursuing their dream, or to cut their losses and go home. More and more young people are going to find themselves at 30 without a viable career, a house, or any semblance of stability.

Although some dreams can be beneficial, others are clearly thwarting more realistic goals. Arnett describes Albert, who works in an ice-cream store but says he really wants to play professional baseball. Yet he did not play baseball in high school and does not play on a team right now either. So how will he make this happen? "I don't know," he says. "I'll see what happens." Adrianne, 16, dreamed of being on *American Idol*. But, her mother says, "Unfortunately she was so focused on it that she didn't care for school too much." Some dreams are not just big but huge. "My big goal is to have a shoe named after me, like Michael Jordan or LeBron James," says Corvin Lamb, 13, interviewed in *People* magazine. "I want to be something in life."

Even staid publications like *Kiplinger's Personal Finance* promote the pursuit of dreams. In 1996, 2002, and 2004, the magazine ran articles on "Dream Jobs," with the 2004 article adding "(and How to Get One)." Among other enviable professions, the article profiles a batting-practice pitcher for the San Francisco Giants, a Harry Winston Jewelry employee who lends diamond necklaces to celebrities like Gwyneth Paltrow, and a guy who gets paid to play with Legos as a builder for Legoland Park. The article advises, "People who love their work don't just sit around, waiting to get lucky. . . . Sometimes they happen to be in the right place to take advantage of an opportunity. More often, however, they take the initiative to put themselves in the right place so they can create their own opportunities." So if you can't get one of these jobs, you're just not trying hard enough. A sidebar offers tips on how to do this; the suggestions include a networking club with a $600 initiation fee and an image makeover firm that charges $150 an hour.

Movies have latched onto "never give up on your dreams" with a vengeance. I like to say that modern movies have only four themes: "Believe in yourself and you can do anything," "We are all alike underneath," "Love conquers all," and "Good people win." (*Do* try this at home; almost every recent movie fits one of the four.) All of these themes tout the focus on the self so common today; in fact, it is downright stunning to realize just how well movies have encapsulated the optimistic, individualistic message of modern Western culture. Romantic love with a partner of one's choice (often opposed by one's parents) always wins in the end; intolerance is always bad; and when you believe in yourself, you can do anything. Sure enough, people who pursue an impossible dream in a movie almost always succeed: *Rudy* gets to play Notre Dame football, formerly broke single mother *Erin Brockovich* wins her million-dollar lawsuit, and the underdog 1980 U.S. hockey team achieves the *Miracle* of beating the Russians. Former Hollywood producer Elisabeth Robinson tried to get the classic and very sad story of Don Quixote made into a movie, but the studio insisted he win the duels he loses in the book and that "he dies in his bed because he's an old man—who lived his dream and now *can* die—*not* because his dreams have been crushed or 'reality' has killed him." It wouldn't be a movie if it wasn't an "inspirational" story of people never giving up—so what if it cuts the heart out of the world's first novel? No one wants to watch a movie more like real life, where people try hard but fail more often than they succeed.

At least GenMe doesn't want to watch this type of movie; previous generations liked them just fine. Take the 1946 film *It's a Wonderful Life*, where George Bailey gives up on his dreams of making it big to stay in his small town and run the local bank. After one particularly bad day, he decides to kill himself, but an angel stops him by showing him how all of his good deeds have benefited others. Many people love this movie for its message that self-sacrifice can lead to good outcomes. I saw *It's a Wonderful Life* for the first time when I was 18, and I hated it, probably because it violated the conventions of every other movie I had ever seen: Why should he have to give up his dreams? He should be able to pursue his ambitions, and—modern movies had taught me well—he could have won if he had tried hard enough.

The message comes across even in somewhat unlikely sources. In a 2004 episode of *7th Heaven*, one of the few relatively conservative, G-rated shows on television, 21-year-old Lucy gives a sermon to the young women in the congregation. "God wants us to know and love ourselves," she says. "He also wants us to know our purpose, our passion. . . . So I ask you . . . 'What have you dreamt about doing?' . . . What you are waiting for is already inside of you. God has already equipped us with everything we need to live full and rich lives. It is our responsibility to make that life happen—to make our dreams happen." So if you want to do it, you can make it happen. But what if your dream is to be a movie star or an Olympic athlete? Or even a doctor? What if we're not actually equipped with absolutely everything we need—say, a one-in-a-million body, Hollywood connections, or the grades to make it into med school?

A website sponsored by the National Clearinghouse on Families and Youth (a division of the U.S. Department of Health and Human Services) also displays this trend toward flagrantly unrealistic optimism. In "Express Yourself: A Teenager's Guide to Fitting In, Getting Involved, Finding Yourself," teens are told that their experiences will differ depending on their background, since some kids don't have support from family and live in neighborhoods without "opportunities." "But no matter what your experience, you can still figure out how to be happy, it states in bold print. (While living in the ghetto with no support from your family?! Sure.) After some useful advice about youth organizations and friends, the website says cheerily, "Believe in yourself. You can't compare yourself to others." Really? Everyone else will, from college admissions to job interviews, so you might as well start now. The website concludes with a statement that leaves no doubt about its individualistic message: "YOU ARE UNIQUE!" it emphasizes in all caps.

Though I'm sure some teens gain hope from such advice, I worry that many others will emerge with little armor to protect themselves when things aren't so sugarcoated. Real life will intervene sometime. The kids whom the website is trying to reach the most—those without good family support who come from underprivileged backgrounds—probably realized that a long time ago. Learning to believe in yourself doesn't help much when your mom is addicted to crack and you're afraid to walk home from school. And as the research presented earlier shows, believing in yourself might not even help you get better grades or stay out of trouble.

THE BRIEF BUT HILARIOUS REIGN OF WILLIAM HUNG

One of the more humorous products of this system has to be William Hung, the UC Berkeley engineering student who stretched his fifteen minutes of fame to almost an hour in early 2004 with his spectacularly bad and uproariously funny rendition of Ricky Martin's "She Bangs." Hung's singing was tuneless, but it was his jerky, utterly uncoordinated dancing that caused the *American Idol* judges to hide discreetly behind their ratings sheets as they choked back their laughter. When judge Simon Cowell stopped him from finishing, Hung looked surprised and hurt. Cowell chided him: "You can't sing; you can't dance. What do you want me to say?" Hung replied, "I already gave my best. I have no regrets at all."

Judge Paula Abdul praised him, saying, "That's good, that's the best attitude yet." (Rule of the modern world: Doing your best is good enough, even if you suck.) Hung then attempted to explain: "I have no professional training." "There's the surprise of the century," Cowell shot back.

In a later interview with *Star* magazine, Hung said he hopes to make a career out of being a singer. This was after the poor guy had become a national joke for *not* being able to sing. It's especially ironic since he probably has a perfectly good career ahead of him as an engineer. But he had done his best and had learned the lesson that "you can be anything." Sure enough, when asked if he had any advice for his fans, Hung said, "I want to say something to the public: Always try your best, and don't give up on your dreams." William, please, for the sake of all of us, give up on your dream of being a singer.

Simon Cowell, the British *American Idol* judge who first gave Hung this advice, sees unflinching criticism as his personal mission. TV critic James Poniewozik notes that Cowell "has led a rebellion against the tyranny of self-esteem that is promoted on talk shows and in self-help books—the notion that everyone who tries deserves to win." Although Cowell admittedly takes things a little far, Americans think he's mean mostly because he bursts contestants' bubbles of unsubstantiated self-esteem. Even the nicer *American Idol* judges are surprised by the hubris of many of the hopefuls. "It's mind-boggling how horrific some of them are, [especially those] with unbelievably healthy egos [thinking] they are all that," said Paula Abdul. "Kenny [Loggins] said, 'Is it sick or healthy to walk around believing in yourself so much?' I said, 'Well, it's delusional.'" It sure is, but it's also young people doing precisely what they have been taught.

WE WILL ALL BE FAMOUS

Hung is not very unusual: much of GenMe expects to be famous. Many kids today grow up thinking that they will eventually be movie stars, sports figures, or at least rich. These are the adults they see on television; hardly anybody on TV works in a white-collar job in an office like most kids will do someday. A lot of young people also assume that success will come quickly. One of my students, who wasn't more than 22, noted during a class presentation that "there are lots of people our age who are CEOs of their own companies." He probably read a profile or two of one of these rare beasts in a magazine and, fueled by the "you can be anything" mythos, decided that this was commonplace.

These attitudes are pervasive and have been for a while. When I was in high school, one of my friends decided to collect items from each of the talented people in our class—a tape of one student playing the piano, a mathematical proof from another, a set of handwritten poems from me. He was sure we would all become famous one day and these would then be worth money (and this was *before* eBay). The three of us have done fine, but none of us is famous. Somehow no one ever told us that this was unlikely to happen. Given the choice between fame and contentment, 29% of 1990s young people chose fame, compared to only 17% of Boomers.

Many reality TV shows feed on this obsession with celebrity and fame. Flip channels for a few minutes during prime time, and you'll see *Survivor* contestants barely getting enough food, *Fear Factor* participants with bugs crawling all over them, and *Rebel Billionaire* CEO wannabes falling off cliffs. Why do people do these crazy things? Ostensibly, it's for the challenge and the money, but everyone knows the real attraction: You get on TV. For many people—particularly GenMe—instant fame is worth eating bugs.

In August 2005, the trend got its own cable channel, called Current TV. Aimed specifically at the 18 to 34 demographic, the channel airs video segments sent in by young viewers. The idea is that young people will watch something that offers the tantalizing possibility of attaining their fifteen minutes of fame—and lets them define the news. Al Gore, one of the network's founders, says that the channel aims to move away from the model of only a few people making programming to "a democratized medium where everybody has a chance to learn how to make television." Or to be heard and be famous. As a *New York Times* article about the channel put it, "Reality television has spawned a generation of viewers who feel entitled to be on camera."

Musician Nellie McKay, 19, illustrates this GenMe trend. Although she flunked out of music college, she said in 2004, "I've been telling [my friends] for years that I'm going to be famous. When I look at me in the mirror, I see someone on the front cover of *Us Weekly.*" Even with a first album that sold moderately well, this is the quest for fame at its most bald and unrealistic. "Apparently everyone else sees a regular girl. I'm very disappointed in that," McKay continues. "I want them to see me as Frank Sinatra or Bill Clinton." Apparently, this fame is also supposed to happen overnight. "It tends to get on my nerves when people say, 'Wow, can you believe this is happening to you?'" says McKay. "I say 'Yeah, I've worked hard for this.'" Perhaps, but how hard, for how many years, can you have possibly worked when you are nineteen years old?

In *What Really Happened to the Class of '93,* Chris Colin relates the story of his most accomplished classmate, Alo Basu, who went to Harvard and MIT and was a science prodigy in high school. Their senior year, she was voted most likely to appear on the cover of *Time* magazine. "Ten years after leaving high school, Alo has yet to grace *Time,*" he notes, with no sarcasm that I could detect. Um, yes: Most people—even most geniuses—won't *ever* be on the cover of *Time* magazine, much less before the age of 28.

The quest for fame may explain the recent fascination with over-the-top weddings, and why, in general, Americans still have weddings when living together is so popular. Having a dress fit specifically for you, having someone else apply your makeup, having everyone admire your beauty—as author Carol Wallace points out, these are experiences usually shared by only two groups of women: celebrities and brides. Wedding vendors often emphasize that this is your one chance to be a "princess for a day," and we believe it. One bride said, "Finally, I got center stage in something." Finally. As Wallace writes, "Having 'center stage,' being the focus of all eyes is so highly prized in today's culture that many of us, relegated to the background, feel diminished until we get our turn in the spotlight." Gwyneth Paltrow said that for many women "the whole wedding fantasy [is] their day at the Oscars."

Ordinary people can also find a taste of fame on the Internet. Anyone can put up a Web page, start a LiveJournal (LJ), or post to message boards. Blogs are built around the idea that everyone wants to hear your thoughts. Had a bad day? Tell the world about it on LJ. Proud of your athletic ability, your family, your hobbies, your witty writing? Create your own Web page. Allison Ellis, who moderates a chat room for teenagers, says, "I think everyone deserves a chance to express themselves and be important." At least Web pages can't sing.

Perhaps because of our comfort with the spotlight, today's young people are more confident in their social interactions. As part of my dissertation, I gathered data on 16,846 college students who completed a questionnaire measuring extraversion, or being outgoing and talkative. This trait rose markedly, with the average 1990s college student scoring as more extraverted than 83% of students in the 1960s. Compared to Boomers, GenMe is more comfortable talking to people at parties and social occasions, more confident when meeting new people, and accustomed to being surrounded by bustle and excitement. This makes sense: GenMe is more likely to have gone to day care, to have worked in a service job, or to meet new people on a regular basis. High levels of extraversion have been our adaptation: We are a generation with few shrinking violets.

YOU MUST LOVE YOURSELF
BEFORE YOU CAN LOVE OTHERS

This is one of the most widely accepted of our cultural aphorisms. After *20/20* aired a segment on self-esteem programs in schools, anchor Hugh Downs asked, "Could it be that self-esteem, real self-esteem, comes from esteeming other people and not thinking so much about yourself, to begin with?" Barbara Walters clearly thought he was deluded. "Oh, Hugh!" she exclaimed, as if he had just said the silliest thing in the world. "First of all, you have to like yourself before you can like others."

The *7th Heaven* episode mentioned previously also promoted the "love yourself first" message. Lucy, 21 and just named associate pastor, uses the example of the woman from the Song of Solomon. "She loves who she is and she doesn't care what anybody thinks of her," she preaches. "She has self-love and self-esteem." So many of us, she goes on to say, make "loving ourselves dependent on something outside of ourselves. But it's not someone else's job to make us happy. It's your job to make yourself happy. And to know who you are. And if you don't know yourself, or love yourself, how can you expect someone else to?"

There are a number of problems with this. First, if you truly don't care what anybody thinks of you, you're probably not relationship material. And if we could all be happy alone, why be in a relationship at all? Also, plenty of people in earlier generations loved their spouses and children quite a bit, even though they never worried much about loving themselves. Lower rates of divorce in previous decades might even suggest that they were better at relationships than we are. Maybe we love ourselves a little too much.

But pop psych teaches us otherwise. "No person can be happy with others until they are happy with themselves," says Lindsay, 19. It is now commonly accepted that you should have your own life and develop your own identity first, before you settle down with someone. You're supposed to date lots of people and find out who's right for you before you marry someone. As Jeffrey Arnett notes in *Emerging Adulthood*, "finding a love partner in your teens and continuing in a relationship with that person through your early twenties, culminating in marriage, is now viewed as unhealthy, a mistake, a path likely to lead to disaster." Anyone who considers this will hear "Why marry the first guy you date? You should have fun first," "Don't you want your own identity first?" and "How do you know he's the one if you've never dated anyone else?" This might be good advice, but these are new questions, rarely asked just two decades ago. Even compromises made later in one's twenties are scrutinized. One article describes Kathryn, 29, who, to the consternation of her friends, moved to England to be with her boyfriend. "We're not meant to say: 'I made this decision for this person.' Today, you're meant to do things for yourself," she says. "If you're willing to make sacrifices for others—especially if you're a woman—that's seen as a kind of weakness."

Even breaking up is supposed to be good for us—after all, then we can focus on ourselves. "Women in relationships tend to lose a piece of themselves, and when they move out on their own, they tend to find themselves," says psychotherapist Dr. Karen Gail Lewis, quoted in *Us Weekly*. "It's common to get a huge amount of energy, feel better about yourself and take on new things." A huge amount of research soundly refutes this—breakups lead to depression, not "energy"—but it's classic "you must love yourself first" pop psychology. Maybe Dr. Lewis has watched too much TV. On a 1998 episode of the teen soap *Dawson's Creek*, Joey broke up with Dawson because, she says, "You make me so happy, but I have to make myself happy first." On MTV's *Real World: Philadelphia* in 2005, Shavonda got caught cheating on her boyfriend, and they broke up. "I know I'm going to be by myself. That's the price I'm paying to figure out who I am right now," she says. "I just want to start working on, you know, being there for myself, rather than seeking a man to be there for me."

This is the dirty little secret of modern life: We are told that we need to know ourselves and love ourselves first, but being alone sucks. Our ultimate value is not to depend on anyone else. "Commitments imply dependency," writes Jerry Rubin in *Growing (Up) at Thirty-Seven*. "A lover is like an addiction. . . . [I will] learn to love myself enough so that I do not need another to make me happy." But the truth is that human beings *do* need other people to be happy—this is just the way we are built. Yet say this at a cocktail party, and someone will probably say yes, sure, but it's better not to *need* someone. That's co-dependent, the resident psychotherapy expert will say, and will repeat the modern aphorism "You can't expect someone else to make you happy—you have to make yourself happy." Actually, you *can* expect this: having a stable marriage is one of the most robust predictors of happiness. We gain self-esteem from our relationships with others, not from focusing on ourselves. In other words, Hugh Downs was right. Study after study shows that people who have good relationships with friends and family are the happiest—these things consistently trump money or job satisfaction as predictors of happiness and life satisfaction. Even Abraham Maslow, the favorite psychologist of New Agers, says that belonging and love needs must be satisfied before esteem needs. And we know this, which is why we continue to get married, have children, and make friends. Despite the idea that you can *Be Your Own Best Friend*, as the title of a popular self-help book claims, we know it's better to have real friends and real relationships.

Research by Sandra Murray and her colleagues does show that people with low self-esteem appreciate their partners less and feel less secure in their relationships. If you truly don't like yourself, you may feel insecure about the other person's affection. Insecurity doesn't mean you don't love your partner, however, and this same research finds no evidence that low-self-esteem people choose bad partners. In addition, talk of loving yourself, making yourself happy first, and being there for yourself crosses the line from self-esteem into narcissism. And narcissists—people who *really* love themselves—are not very good at getting along with others. As Keith Campbell shows in his recent book *When You Love a Man Who Loves Himself*, narcissists are spectacularly bad relationship partners: they cheat, they are unsupportive, they play games, and they derogate their partners to make themselves look better. They also tend to lie, manipulate other people, and exert control and power. Campbell begins his book by relating a story told by one of his students, a woman who was dating a narcissistic man. One evening, they went to his fraternity's spring formal dance, where several awards were announced. To the woman's surprise, her boyfriend of a year won the prize for "the most hook-ups during Spring Break." Instead of looking ashamed, he looked proud and commented on how hot the girls were. When his girlfriend got upset, he blamed her for "ruining his formal." Clearly, a man who loved himself, but maybe not someone good at loving another.

Despite their self-aggrandizing tendencies, narcissists freely say that they are not as moral or as likable as other people. They think they are better than others at most things, but are also fully aware that they're not very good at relationships. And no, it's not because narcissists are actually insecure underneath—there's no evidence for that. They act this way because they put themselves first. As Campbell points out matter-of-factly, "If I were to name the top 10 things that are important for a good relationship, loving yourself wouldn't make the list." When asked what traits they value in a partner, most people name things like kindness or consideration—in other words, loving and caring for other people, not yourself.

There's also the obvious danger of getting too accustomed to being on your own. If you learn to love yourself and your solitude, it will be a lot harder to adjust once you do find someone to share your life with. It's difficult to adapt to another person's needs when you're used to putting your own needs first and doing things your way. Many of the fights Gen Me'ers have with our partners can be traced back to this fundamental assumption that we are special. In her book *Narcissism and Intimacy: Love and Marriage in an Age of Confusion*, therapist Marion Solomon says that an increasing number of her patients have trouble in their relationships because they are too focused on themselves. "When the focus of life is on determining one's own needs and finding another who can fill those needs and wishes, any relationship is in danger of being flawed by narcissistic expectations," she writes. There is, she says, "an increasing demand for effective independent functioning without emotional reliance on others. The result is an inability to invest freely in deep feelings for others." If these trends continue—and it appears that they will—the divorce rate will probably remain high.

One young woman, interviewed in the book *Flux*, broke up with her boyfriend not because she was unhappy, but because she thought she might be happier with someone else. "I'm not inspired by you. Don't you think I deserve to be inspired?" she said to the hapless young man. Even if you haven't faced this kind of narcissism (and count yourself lucky if you haven't), we all face little tugs of war in our relationships on occasion: Should we go to his favorite restaurant or hers? Who does the dishes tonight? Who gets the rights to the TV? And who has to watch the children this evening?

This last question really brings the focus on the self crashing down to earth. In an analysis of data from 47,692 respondents, Keith Campbell, Craig Foster, and I found that childless married couples were, on average, more satisfied with their marriages than those with children. This effect has rapidly accelerated in recent decades. Compared to previous generations, Generation X and Generation Me experience a 42% greater drop in marital satisfaction after having children. Researchers at the National Marriage Project found similar results and concluded that "children seem to be a growing impediment for the happiness of marriages."

Although economic pressures may partially explain this change, it is likely rooted in the radical shift away from the self that parenthood requires. Having a baby suddenly means that you have little control over your life—the freedom to which you were accustomed vanishes, and your individual accomplishments are not as valued anymore. Parenthood has always been a difficult transition, but it's even more difficult for GenMe. When you're used to calling the shots, and then the baby dictates everything, it's hard to keep your sanity, much less get along with your spouse. The idea of individual choice also makes things more difficult; in previous generations, having children was a duty rather than a choice. Now that we "choose" parenthood, we presumably have no one to blame but ourselves when the baby has kept us up for two months in a row.

OUTCOMES OF THE FOCUS ON THE SELF

The appearance obsession

More and more people every year get nose jobs, breast implants, facelifts, and a long list of less invasive procedures like Botox injections and lip plumping. Eyebrow waxing has become a near requirement for women, and today's body-hugging fashions are enough to make women long for the big-shirt-and-leggings days of the early 1990s. With the rise of the metrosexual, more men are focusing on their own physical appearance as well. Many young men prize their workout-produced muscles and even resort to steroid use; in 2004, 8% of twelfth-grade boys admitted to using steroids.

We have come to equate looking good with feeling good, and to say that we should do whatever makes us feel good or makes us happy. Fox's controversial show *The Swan* justified the expensive, painful surgeries of its contestants by claiming that the women now felt better about themselves. MTV has a show called *I Want a Famous Face*, in which young people undergo plastic surgery so they can look like their favorite

A sunless tan as individual as you are.

Introducing Banana Boat® Summer Color™.

An ad clearly aimed at Generation Me: the product is "unique,"
"individual," and "yours alone." Plus, it makes you look hot.

celebrity. Crystal, 23, underwent a breast enlargement and liposuction,
ostensibly to resemble actress Brooke Burke. Immediately after the surgery, Crystal was in so much pain, she said, "I just want to die right now."
A few months later, however, she's confident that her surgically enlarged
breasts will help her reach her goal of becoming a bikini model. She says
that the surgery "definitely built up my self-esteem." Her boyfriend, who
thought she looked great before, says he's fine with it as long as "you're
happy with yourself."

In October 2004, *People* magazine interviewed several celebrities about their views on plastic surgery. All of those who supported it said almost exactly the same thing. "If it makes you happy, if it makes you feel good, you should do whatever that is," said Julia Roberts. "Anything that makes you feel better, go for it," said Jennifer Aniston. But it was the youngest interviewee—Hilary Duff, then 17—who summed it up the best: "If it's going to boost their self-esteem and make them feel better about themselves, then I don't see a problem with it." This is pure GenMe: Do whatever it takes to feel better about yourself, because that's the most important thing in the world. More important, apparently, than keeping a scalpel off your face.

Tattoos, nose piercings, and God-knows-where piercings

Unless you've been in a cave for the past fifteen years, you've probably noticed that young people today are much more likely to adorn themselves in unconventional ways. Tattoos are no longer the sole province of bikers and sailors, but a trendy self-decoration employed by large numbers of young people, including the rich and famous. Young people pierce regions that older generations won't even mention in polite—or any—conversation. Lips, tongues, belly buttons, and eyebrows are adorned with metal rings and studs. A recent exchange on a pregnancy message board addressed the best way to remove your belly button ring before your swelling abdomen made it pop out.

I didn't think piercings and tattoos had anything to do with psychological changes over the generations until Jay, 20, told me a story about his tattoos and his reasons for getting them. Jay went to his grandparents' house one day and took off his shirt before jumping in the pool. His grandmother, shocked to see his heavily tattooed upper back, gasped audibly and expressed her disappointment in him, since he'd always been "the good grandkid." Jay tried to enlighten his grandmother: "I explained to her that to me my tattoos are an expression of who I am and how I view myself. My tattoos show the different sides of who I am," he wrote. It turns out that Jay's motivations are representative. In a 1999 survey of 766 college students with tattoos or body piercings, the most common reason given for their choices was "self-expression." Eighty-one percent of tattooed college students named self-expression, independence, or uniqueness as a motivation. Sixty-nine percent of students with body piercings named self-expression or "to be different" as their reasons. Natasha, 25, has several tattoos and piercings, including several studs at the nape of her neck. During a class presentation on the topic, another student asked Natasha why people get unusual piercings when they so often elicit negative comments and appalled looks from other people. "They do it to express themselves and be different," Natasha said. "Most people who get piercings don't care what other people think. They do it to make themselves happy, and that's what's most important to them."

So tattoos and nose rings might not be just random fashion trends after all. Instead, they are a medium for self-expression and the communication of individuality. They fit the generational trend perfectly: they are outward expressions of the inner self. They allow you to be different and unique. It's so important to be an individual, and to communicate that fact to others, that young people routinely tattoo it onto their skin.

Extending adolescence beyond all previous limits

When Daniel finally finished college at 24, he wasn't sure what career to pursue. So he moved back in with his parents and stayed there, unemployed, for two and a half years. His brother John lived at home for three years while attending community college. After moving away to attend a four-year university, he finally earned his college degree at age 26. Six months later, he was back to living at home when he couldn't find a job. This postponement of adulthood is not limited to men, either: Tina, 26, plans to drive around the country in a van for several years after she finishes her Ph.D. She has no idea when, or if, she will "settle down."

Ask someone in GenMe when adulthood begins, and a surprising number will say 30. For this generation, your early twenties—and often your late twenties—are a time to move around, try different things, and date different people. "In the past, people got married and got a job and had kids, but now there's a new 10 years that people are using to try and found out what kind of life they want to lead," says Zach Braff, 29, the actor and screenwriter of the 2004 GenMe hit movie *Garden State*. The movie plays off these ideas: Braff's character works as a waiter in L.A. and is trying to break into acting. His friends back home in New Jersey live with their parents and work dead-end jobs, one quite literally as a gravedigger, and another as a knight-waiter, in full metal body armor, at the restaurant-cum-festival Medieval Times. The only guy with any money made it by inventing something ridiculous ("silent Velcro"), and spends his time getting laid, taking Ecstasy, and riding around his giant house on a four-wheeler.

GenMe marries later than any previous generation, at 27 for men and 25 for women (and in many European countries, it's 30 for men and 27 for women). In 1970, when the Boomers were young, these figures were 23 and 21—so much for Free Love. What's even more surprising are the number of young people who do not achieve financial independence; for example, the percentage of 26-year-olds living with their parents has almost doubled since 1970, from 11% to 20%. In 2002, 57% of men and 43% of women aged 22 to 31 lived with their parents. Young people are also taking longer to finish college: only 37% of students complete their degrees in four years. Even at prestigious schools like UCLA, less than half of students finish in the previously customary four years.

In a 2005 cover story on the phenomenon, *Time* magazine labeled these young people "Twixters"; others label this new area between adolescence and adulthood "youthhood" or "adultesence." Some of the forces behind these trends are economic, and I'll address those further in Chapter 4. But many young people interviewed in the article say that the reason they are postponing adult roles is, you guessed it, their desire to put themselves first. "I want to get married but not soon," said Jennie Jiang, 26. "I'm enjoying myself. There's a lot I want to do by myself still." Marcus Jones, 28, says he won't marry for a long time. "I'm too self-involved. I don't want to bring that into a relationship now," he admits. Maroon 5 singer Adam Levine, 25, echoed this in an *Us Weekly* profile: "I'm all about getting married in my thirties, but right now I'm enjoying my selfish twenties!"

The same motivations appear in career choices. Many young people don't want to commit to a career and stay with it because they'd like to find exactly the right job for them. Jeffrey Arnett, author of *Emerging Adulthood*, says: "They're not just looking for a job. They want something that's more like a calling, that's going to be an expression of their identity." Overall, it's the pursuit of individual wants at its most undiluted. As the Twixters article explains, young people are "making sure that when they do settle down, they do it the right way, *their* way." Their individual way.

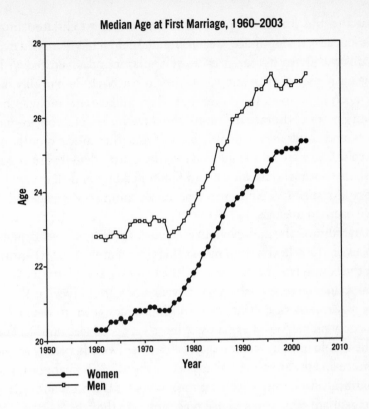

Median Age at First Marriage, 1960–2003

Generation Me'ers marry considerably later than their
Boomer counterparts did in the 1960s and 1970s.

Materialism

GenMe's brand of self-importance also shows up as materialism. In 1967, when the Boomers were in college, 45% of freshmen said it was important to be well-off financially. By 2004, 74% embraced this life goal. Another survey found that 1990s high school students were twice as likely as their 1970s counterparts to say that "having lots of money" was "very important." Olivia Smith, interviewed for the CBS Class of 2000 project, says, "I basically just want to grow up safe and luxurious and have lots of money."

Some of this is probably due to necessities like housing being more expensive—it takes more money to get by now. However, GenMe has always lived in a time when possessions were valued. Boomers were exposed to the nascent beginnings of marketing to children in the 1950s, but advertising aimed specifically at children has increased exponentially within the last few decades. If it's plastic and advertised on TV, kids want it. As Juliet Schor documents in her book *Born to Buy*, kids have much more spending power these days, and parents include them in many more consumer decisions. Advertising is common in many schools, and children can identify brands when they are 18 months old. College students are fully engrained into these attitudes—the new trend is designer dorm rooms with coordinated bedding and new couches. College kids spend $2.6 billion a year on decorating their spaces, about $1,200 each on average.

Materialism is the most obvious outcome of a straightforward, practical focus on the self: you want more things for yourself. You feel entitled to get the best in life: the best clothes, the best house, the best car. You're special; you deserve special things. Seventeen-year-old Jocelyn Bower's uncle, Kevin Arnett, bought her a $8,275 Versace gown to wear to her high school prom. Arnett explains, "She's a very good girl, one of a kind, and she should have it." Next year, Jocelyn says, "We'll hopefully go back to Versace and get an even more expensive dress!" This might be unusually extravagant, but it's clear that the days of a $100 dress and a dance in the gym are over. *Prom Guide* magazine says that the average high school couple spends $800 for their prom night, up from $300 per couple five years ago.

A Sears ad for girls' clothing ties it all together: "You gotta believe in your dreams. You gotta stand up for yourself. You gotta be there for your friends. But, hey, *first* you gotta have something to wear. You *gotta* have the *clothes*." And the clothes the model is wearing? The outfit costs $267. This continues into adulthood as well. "I have a six-year-old house with four bedrooms, I have a nice big garage. I'm about to get a new car, and I already had one before the current one. I'm able to purchase what I like," says Marcus Groenig, 28, interviewed in *What Really Happened to the Class of '93*. "Physical possessions are a way to measure happiness," he concludes.

And it's not to "keep up with the Joneses" as it was in previous generations. The virtue of expensive things is comfort, enjoyment, and getting what you want. In the past, many people wanted a big house to impress people. GenMe wants a big house so each family member can have as much personal space as possible, consistent with the needs of the individual. Kids don't want to share rooms anymore, and parents like to have "retreats" off the master bedroom where they can relax away from the kids. Plus we need places to put all of the stuff we buy, like our computers and our game systems. And everyone wants to move out of the apartment where he can smell his neighbor's food and hear his neighbor's music. SUVs serve much the same purpose, building an impenetrable fortress around the individual even when driving to the grocery store. We also shun used things and hand-me-downs; in the pursuit of individualism, we want something made just for us that's shiny and new. "Why go on your honeymoon with the same old luggage?" asks an ad. (I dunno—because your old luggage is just fine?) It's a long way from my father's and grandfather's favorite phrase, "Use it up, wear it out, make it do or do without."

So many products now cater to the tastes of the individual. Instead of listening to the radio and hearing what everyone else does, we program our own special mix on our iPod, put in the headphones, and enter an individually created world. We even choose unique ring tones for our cell phones. Instead of three or four network stations, we can watch cable channels dedicated to our own interests. Instead of watching TV live with everyone else in our time zone, we TiVo it and watch it when we want to. "I want to do things that conform to my time frame, not someone else's," says UCLA senior Matthew Khalil on why he rarely goes to the movie theater anymore but instead watches DVDs at home.

Individualism has driven the increasingly large universe of consumer choice in other things as well. Within a few decades, cream and sugar became decaf skim cappuccino grande to go. The coffee choices at Starbucks amount to 19,000 combinations—what better way to feel like an individual? From clothing to cars to jewelry, consumer products are designed to exhibit the wants of the unique self. "Shopping, like everything else, has become a means of self-exploration and self-expression," writes David Brooks.

It's also taken for granted that everyone who is someone is rich, and that materialism is not only desirable but practically orgasmic in its pleasure. Almost half of the shows on MTV the last few years featured rich people and their lifestyles: *Meet the Barkers, The Osbournes, Newlyweds: Nick and Jessica, Cribs, My Super Sweet 16.* The last show is especially egregious, focusing on teenagers whose parents spend half a million dollars on 16th birthday parties. The trips to Vegas to shop, the New York dancers brought in for the party, and the thousands on the invitation list are all presented without comment, making these extravagances seem normal. There's certainly some parody intended in the way the rich kids whine, but this subtlety is likely to slide past the average 15-year-old watching the show. A show on the cable channel Home & Garden TV is actually called *I Want That!* It's described by *Life & Style Weekly* as a new series that "focuses on modern must-haves for the home. Tonight: a rain- and snow-resistant outdoor TV." Yep, a TV you can watch in the snow is definitely a must-have—particularly if your list of "musts" includes subjecting your neighbors to the noise from your indestructible television.

It reminds me of my first Halloween as a home owner, just a few years ago. Most of the trick-or-treaters were both very cute and polite, but then a boy who looked about 10 came to the door, dressed in an unidentifiable costume. I gave him two pieces of candy. He stood there with his bag open, looked at me, and said, "More."

This is where self-esteem crosses over into entitlement: the idea that we deserve more. And why shouldn't we? We've been told all of our lives that we are special.

So are there any upsides to the confidence and optimism of GenMe? Maybe—*if* this confidence is based in reality, and *if* it does not cross over into narcissism and entitlement. It is fine for children to be encouraged to try many different things and to be praised for doing well. It's also great that young people have been taught not to limit their career choices based on their sex or race; this was the original intent behind "you can be anything." Sooner or later, however, everyone has to face reality and evaluate his or her abilities. It is good for young people to believe that they can succeed, but only if they have the tools to do so. When based on real skills, the high aspirations of GenMe can propel young people into volunteer projects, college, and desirable jobs. Even then, however, bright young people may be disappointed that their jobs are not as fantastically fulfilling, high-paying, or fame-producing as they would have liked. Focusing on individual goals can be an asset, but only up to a point.

The individualistic ethos of America also explains a lot of negative trends that we see around us every day. A trip to the grocery store, as just

one example, often involves aggressive drivers, sullen clerks, and screaming children. Then there's that ultimate modern annoyance: the people
who talk loudly on their cell phones, oblivious to their effect on others.
GenMe didn't pioneer this trend—it's popular among middle-aged people as well—but young people are certainly continuing it. It's not the
technology that causes the problem, but the attitude that comes with it,
an attitude that captures the trend toward self-importance better than
almost anything else. "Years ago, cell phones were the province of the
powerful, but now that they are mass-market items, everyone has delu-
sions of grandeur," says Eric Cohen, editor of *The New Atlantis*. "Now
there are 280 million masters of the universe in America."

4

The Age of Anxiety
(and Depression, and Loneliness):
Generation Stressed

I n most ways, Kim looks like a well-adjusted college student. She dates her high school sweetheart and is studying psychology at a university in the Midwest. For the past five years, however, Kim has struggled with severe depression. When it was at its worst, she could not force herself to get out of bed to go to class. After hours of therapy and courses of antidepressant drugs, Kim was stable and ready to graduate; then she had a relapse. Now it will take her another year to finish college as she tries to manage her depression.

Jason, 22, appeared from the outside to have everything: he had just graduated with honors from an Ivy League university and was starting his first job at a leading investment banking firm. But he soon found that his job was not what he had imagined—the bosses doled out constant criticism and expected sixteen-hour days. The work itself was boring. Jason hated it, so after three months, he quit. Suddenly uncertain about what he wanted to do with his life, he sank into depression. He was devastated that a lifetime of achieving his goals had not brought him happiness.

Beth, 19, became severely depressed in high school and seriously considered suicide. "My parents thought I was just a grumpy teenager," she says. "They didn't realize there were demons inside my head that screamed at me and ripped my life apart." Although her parents were opposed to the idea, she eventually saw a therapist and began to take antidepressant medication. "I have so many more opportunities now that I can control the depression and the crippling panic attacks," she says.

Being young has not always carried such a high risk of being anxious, depressed, suicidal, or medicated. Only 1% to 2% of Americans born before 1915 experienced a major depressive episode during their life-times, even though they lived through the Great Depression and two world wars. Today, the lifetime rate of major depression is ten times higher—between 15% and 20%. Some studies put the figure closer to 50%. In one 1990s study, 21% of teens aged 15 to 17 had already experi-enced major depression. Although some of this trend might be due to

The ubiquitous sad blob of Zoloft. Correct your chemical
imbalances and you might become a happy blob.

more frequent reporting of mental illness, researchers have concluded that the change is too large and too consistent across studies to be explained solely by a reporting bias. In addition, these studies use a fairly strict definition, counting only depression severe enough to warrant medication or long-term therapy. If more mild depression were included, the vast majority of young people would raise their hands in recognition.

Depression is oddly commonplace in today's society. In a ubiquitous TV commercial, a frowning, oval-shaped blob becomes happy and smiling after taking the antidepressant medication Zoloft. Panic attacks are the subject of cocktail party conversation and episodes of HBO's *The Sopranos*. Almost every high school and college student knows someone who committed suicide or tried. In past generations, suicide and depression were considered afflictions of middle age, as it was unusual for a young person to be depressed, but for Generation Me, these problems are a rite of passage through adolescence and young adulthood. Karen, 23, became depressed during college, as did her brother. One thing that helped, she said, was realizing that for young people, "going through a time of depression is normal."

It wasn't always "normal," but it is certainly heading in that direction. The number of people being treated for depression more than tripled in the ten-year period from 1987 to 1997, jumping from 1.8 million to 6.3 million. During 2002 alone, 8.5% of Americans took an antidepressant at some time, up from 5.6% just five years before in 1997.

Depression now arrives at younger and younger ages. The number of children on mood-altering drugs tripled between 1987 and 1996. A recent cover of *Time* magazine featured a picture of Jamari, 8, who is taking medication for a mood disorder. The article described numerous cases of children suffering from anxiety disorders, depression, and obsessive-compulsive disorder. A 2003 government survey asked high school students if, during the past year, they ever "felt so sad and hopeless almost every day for two weeks or more in a row that they stopped doing some usual activities" (an accepted definition of depression). A stunning 29% of teenagers said yes, including 36% of girls (more than 1 out of 3). At the Kansas State University counseling center, the number of students treated for depression doubled between 1988 and 2001, and the number who were suicidal tripled.

I wanted to find out if this trend extended to feelings of anxiety, which often lead to depression as well as to intestinal problems, relation-ship dysfunction, and low life satisfaction. If anxiety had increased, this would truly be bad news for young people. As part of my doctoral disser-tation, I gathered data on 40,192 college students and 12,056 children aged 9 to 17 who completed measures of anxiety between the 1950s and the 1990s. I was stunned by the size of the changes I found. Anxiety increased so much that the average college student in the 1990s was more anxious than 85% of students in the 1950s and 71% of students in the 1970s. The trend for children was even more striking: Children as young as 9 years old were markedly more anxious than kids had been in the 1950s. The change was so large that "normal" schoolchildren in the 1980s reported higher levels of anxiety than child psychiatric patients in the 1950s.

This study had another surprising finding: *when* you were born has more influence on your anxiety level than your individual family envi-ronment. Previous research found that family environment explains only about 5% of variations in anxiety (much of the rest is a combination of genetics, peer influence, and unknown factors). Generational differences explained about 20% of the variation in anxiety—thus four times more than family environment. So even if you come from a stable, loving fam-ily, growing up amidst the stress of recent times might be enough to make you anxious.

Other studies have confirmed that younger generations experience more anxiety and stress. Twice as many people reported symptoms of panic attacks in 1995 compared to 1980, and 40% more people said they'd felt an impending nervous breakdown in 1996 than had in 1957. The number of teens aged 14 to 16 who agreed that "Life is a strain for me much of the time" quadrupled between the early 1950s and 1989. A 2001 poll found that almost 75% of teenagers said they felt nervous or stressed at least some of the time; half said they often felt this way. One out of three college freshmen reported feeling "frequently overwhelmed" in 2001, twice as many as in the 1980s.

I know this trend toward depression and anxiety firsthand. Among my ten closest friends (most in their early thirties, and living across the country), seven have been in therapy at least once, two suffer from panic attacks, one is manic-depressive, and another recently had a nervous breakdown. These are college-educated, successful, and usually well-adjusted people, but loneliness, relationship breakups, and career pressures have taken their toll.

Many young people shared their stories of depression and anxiety with me through my website. Several confessed to being suicidal in their early teens. Clarissa, now 20, became depressed when she was 11. At 13, she locked herself in her room for a week and refused to speak to anyone. She took apart a plastic razor, thinking "about slicing my wrist open and watching the life drain away, taking the pain and loneliness with it." Fortunately, she realized what she was doing, and soon began counseling. Matt, 28, stood at the top of a rock quarry when he was 13 and thought of "ending it all by jumping." He didn't, but only because he wondered what the future would bring: "even though that day and the preceding days basically sucked, tomorrow may suck in a novel way." Debbie, 20, says that when she was 13, "I became unable to see that people around me cared. I was confused and unsure of how to get through the transition of child to young adult. I contemplated suicide, but when it came to it, I couldn't actually cut my flesh because I thought about my family and how awful they would feel if they buried me."

Someone commits suicide every eighteen minutes in the United States. While the suicide rate for middle-aged people has declined steeply since 1950, the suicide rate for young people has more than doubled (though it has, fortunately, declined since its peak in the early 1990s). The suicide rate for children under age 14 has doubled just since 1980. Suicide is the third leading cause of death for people aged 15 to 24. In 2003, 16.9% of high school students admitted that they had seriously considered attempting suicide during the past year, and most of those said they had made a plan about exactly how they would kill themselves. These suicidal thoughts are often brought on by depression. Miranda, an 18-year-old from the Midwest, tried to commit suicide by overdosing on drugs. "Depression tends to grab people and suck them in," she says.

The year before I moved into my college dorm at the University of Chicago, a freshman from Ohio named Jay lived on the first floor. When no one had seen Jay for a while, the resident head opened the door to his room, calling his name. After a brief glance in, the resident head quickly shut the door, blocking the view of the other students huddled behind him: Jay had hanged himself on his closet door with a belt. He had been dead for two days.

In 2003, three students committed suicide at NYU within a month of each other, two by jumping off a balcony at the campus library. Three more NYU suicides followed in 2004. In *What Really Happened to the Class of '93*, Chris Colin describes his high school classmate Sean Bryant, a Rhodes scholar nominee whose goal was to become governor of Virginia. In an incident eerily similar to that in my dorm, the resident head and a friend opened Sean's door when no one answered repeated knocks. As Colin describes it, "The two stepped in and then stepped back out. Sean was hanging over his bed, from a belt looped to his bicycle hook. He was twenty-one years old."

BUT SHOULDN'T WE BE HAPPIER NOW?

At first, it seems paradoxical that GenMe feels so much anxiety and pain. After all, the lives of people born from the 1970s to the 1990s have been remarkably free of traumatic historical events. Except for a few recessions here and there, economic prosperity has reigned. There have been no world wars, and since the early 1990s, no real worries of nuclear war. (The threat of terrorism did not emerge until after the rise in depression was well established.) GenMe has never been drafted. Advances in health care and safety mean that more kids live longer and better lives. More students graduate from high school, and fewer are involved in crime than were so in the early 1990s. Teen pregnancy rates have also declined markedly over the last decade.

In many ways, there's no better time to be alive than right now. Think of all of the advantages we have that earlier generations did not: television, cell phones, better medical care, computers, more education, less physical labor, the freedom to make our own choices, the ability to move to a more desirable city. These last two, however, begin to hint at the underlying problem. Our growing tendency to put the self first leads to unparalleled freedom, but it also creates an enormous amount of pressure on us to stand alone. This is the downside of the focus on the self—when we are fiercely independent and self-sufficient, our disappointments loom large because we have nothing else to focus on. But it's not just us: Generation Me has been taught to expect more out of life at the very time when good jobs and nice houses are increasingly difficult to obtain. All too often, the result is crippling anxiety and crushing depression.

LONELINESS AND ISOLATION

My friend Peter moved to an apartment on the North Side of Chicago after graduating from college. He did not seem happy when I visited him that fall. He had several hellish stories about going out on dates through personal ads, including one woman who told him outright that he was not good-looking enough. His friends from college were either still living near campus or had scattered to graduate schools around the country. In his apartment, he showed me the feature on his cable TV that allowed him to buy movies. "This is what I do most weekends," he said, a sad smile on his face.

He's not the only one. More than four times as many Americans describe themselves as lonely now than in 1957. In *Bowling Alone,* Robert Putnam documents the steep decline in all kinds of social connections: we're less likely to belong to clubs and community organizations, less likely to have friends over for dinner, and less likely to visit our neighbors. Our social contacts are slight compared to those enjoyed by earlier generations.

It's almost as if we are starving for affection. "There is a kind of famine of warm interpersonal relations, of easy-to-reach neighbors, of encircling, inclusive memberships, and of solid family life," argues political scientist Robert Lane. To take the analogy a little further, we're malnourished from eating a junk-food diet of instant messages, e-mail, and phone calls, rather than the healthy food of live, in-person interaction.

It helps explain a new kind of get-together that's popping up in cities around the country: cuddle parties. It's a deliberately nonsexual (though usually coed) gathering where pajama-clad people can enjoy the hugs and touch of others, overseen by a "cuddle lifeguard on duty" who keeps things friendly and nonthreatening. One 26-year-old participant called it "rehab for lonely people." As the official website (www.cuddleparty. com, of course) explains, "In today's world, many of us aren't getting our Recommended Daily Allowance of Welcomed Touch." Most cuddle party participants are young and single. As the website notes, "It's okay to touch the one you're dating or married to . . . but what about the single people? . . . We are touch-and-snuggle deprived."

For many in GenMe, the instability in close relationships began at an early age with their parents' divorce. In *Prozac Nation,* her memoir of adolescent depression, Elizabeth Wertzel describes her father's departure from her life and her mother's subsequent struggle to raise her. When Wertzel told her therapists about her background, they would say, "No wonder you're so depressed." She was not as sure. "They react as if my family situation was particularly alarming and troublesome," she writes, "as opposed to what it actually is in this day and age: perfectly normal." And she's right: almost half of GenMe has seen their parents divorce, or have never known their father at all. This has a clear link to the rise in depression, as children of divorce are more likely to be anxious and depressed. Beyond the statistics, the personal stories of children of divorce—painted in books such as *The Unexpected Legacy of Divorce*—vividly illustrate the lifetime of pain, cynicism, and uncertainty that divorce can create among young people. Ashley, 24, attended a group counseling session at her elementary school, unofficially known as the "divorce club," where she and the other kids would "share our feelings of anger, sadness and confusion and listen to our peers who were sharing the same."

GenMe's own romantic relationships often don't go much better. Although a little extreme, the situations faced by the four characters on *Sex and the City* are right on the mark; the young women I know describe similar dating pitfalls of strange behavior and dashed hopes. Even when the date goes well and becomes a relationship, there is no guarantee it will last. The cycle of meeting someone, falling in love, and breaking up is a formula for anxiety and depression. This often begins in high school. Maggie, now 20, broke up with her boyfriend of a year and a half when she was 17. "I honestly thought I loved him, and I wasn't sure how I would get through the pain and loneliness," she says. In college, many people find that their romantic relationships are a lifeline in an otherwise lonely place—until the relationship ends. Leslie, 20, went through a breakup a month ago. "He was basically my whole life besides school and family," she says. "Now I am very lonely and depressed because I don't have many friends and the friends I do have are all away at their colleges."

The situation is so dire that some young people think there has to be a better way. One day in a graduate class on cultural differences, I was surprised when the students—almost all Americans from the Midwest and West—expressed their approval of arranged marriage. Two women in their mid-twenties were particularly adamant: they hated dating, living alone sucked, and they wanted to settle down. The men in the class agreed. Arranged marriage is probably not the solution, but the students' attraction to the idea is telling—young people clearly feel that something is missing in the current dating scene. The Broadway musical *Avenue Q* includes a song that sums up dating in the modern era pretty well: "There's a fine, fine line between love—and a waste of time."

Dating websites are one recent development that has made it easier to meet people, though they, too, can often lead to anxiety. You write a profile, post your picture, and wait. About half the time, no one e-mails you; often the people who do e-mail are not your type. If you e-mail other people, most of them don't write back—some as a passive form of rejection, but many others because they have let their accounts lapse. My own two months of Internet dating were fraught with worry about what I must be doing wrong and will-he-write-me-back-please-let-him-write-me-back high anxiety. I have never checked my e-mail so obsessively in my life. Fortunately, my story has a happy ending: the man who would become my husband e-mailed me on match.com (asking me, in a particularly deft generational move, what my favorite John Hughes movie was). We went out on our first date two weeks later, and married two years after that. A month later, his best friend married a woman he had met on eharmony.com.

Typical for our generation, both men were in their early thirties by this time. GenMe marries later than any other previous generation. Though later marriage has some advantages, it also means that many in GenMe spend their twenties (and sometimes thirties) in pointless dating, uncertain relationships, and painful breakups. Many relationships last several years and/or involve living together, so the breakups resemble divorces rather than run-of-the-mill heartbreak (as if there were such a thing). By the age of 24, my friend June had been involved in five serious relationships. All had lasted more than a year, and all resulted in a wrenching breakup (often because she or her boyfriend was moving to a new city for college, graduate school, or a career). I have other friends who dated or lived with someone for seven years or more before breaking up. Divorce after only a few years of marriage has become so common that Pamela Paul wrote a book called *The Starter Marriage*. It is the rare member of GenMe who has not experienced the breakup of a serious romantic relationship (or two, or five, or ten).

Many people think of single women when they imagine lonely young people. Watch a TV show about single women, such as *Ally McBeal,* and the enormous wave of anxiety will practically knock you out of your chair. On *Sex and the City,* Carrie compares the Catholic Church to "a desperate 36-year-old single woman, willing to settle for anything it can get." (Let's hear it for a statement that manages to insult both the Catholic Church and single women in the same breath.) Yet there is a grain of truth in the media hype. The deadline for having children— somewhere between 35 and 40—makes life extremely anxious for many single women. They constantly perform the calculation I call "woman math": "If we get married next year, I'll be 32; we'll want a year or two to be married without kids and it might take a year to get pregnant, so I'll be 34 or 35 before I'm pregnant and probably 36 when the child is born. Then if we wait until the first kid is two years old before we try for another one, I'll be trying to get pregnant at 38. Crap."

Even—or especially—women who are living with their boyfriends hear the loud ticking of the biological clock as years go by and no proposal is imminent. The new equation of premarital sex and living together before marriage might be liberating, but it has major downsides. Waiting for a guy to pop the question can be almost as anxiety-producing as being alone. Laurie, interviewed in *Emerging Adulthood,* says that during the five years she lived with the man she eventually married, "I was really stressed, because I didn't know exactly whether or not I was going to be with him or if I was wasting that much time in my life." Another couple described in the book has been living together for eighteen months. Jean, 26, wants to be engaged by Christmas. When the author interviews her boyfriend Trey, 28, however, "It becomes clear that Jean can forget about getting engaged by Christmas. . . . Trey says he might get married—'possibly someday . . . I'm not ready to settle down yet.'" Men have the advantage of a biological clock set at a later time. As Jake puts it, "I could be 35 and marry someone who's 23. I mean, I've got all the time in the world." (Women have a word for guys like this, and it ends with hole.)

But there are plenty of lonely guys out there, too. There are actually thousands more single young *men* than women—between the ages of 25 and 39, for every 1 unmarried woman there are 1.2 unmarried men. Even when you look only between the ages of 35 and 39, there are thousands more unmarried men. I can hear women immediately yelling that all of the good ones are taken, but the truth is that it's single men who should be anxious and complaining. Men get lonely too, though we rarely see that addressed on TV or in the movies. For a noteworthy exception, check out the great movie *Swingers*, which features a fairly realistic look at young men talking about loneliness and their anxiety around dating. For GenMe, loneliness is an equal-opportunity experience.

As a result of modern dating, later marriage, and the higher divorce rate, a lot of people spend a great deal of time living alone. Twice as many 15-to-24-year-olds are in one-person households now compared to 1970, as are almost three times more 25-to-34-year-olds. More than 1 out of 3 people aged 25 to 29 lives alone or with roommates. A recent in-depth study found that Chicago residents, on average, spend half of their adult lives single. Being single does not have to be lonely, but for many people it often is, especially if they have been moving around and don't have friends who live close to them.

That's the other sad reality: not only is GenMe single for longer, but we often don't stay in one place long enough to make friends. More than 1 out of 4 people aged 25 to 29 moved between 2002 and 2003. It is shocking to consider the number of professions that require frequent moves for advancement. This is definitely true in academia: I have lived in six states, my friend Kathleen has lived in all four North American time zones, and few of my friends live within 500 miles of where they grew up. Doctors must move to medical school and to a residency before looking for a city in which to practice. The economic downturn in Silicon Valley in 2000 and 2001 sent many young technology employees looking for work in other cities. Even professions that don't require an advanced degree often involve frequent moves. I recently met a group of people who work in sales for a hotel chain. All had worked at more than four locations, requiring them to move every few years. Author Chris Colin, 28, sums it up: "Since high school I've had five lines of work, . . . eight street addresses, two bad trips, and one cat. I had a lousy breakup with doors slamming—house doors, car doors. I lived in New York and California and Chile. . . . I worry, but really I'm happy, though I worry."

Even if you stay in the same place, just having *time* to date and make friends is difficult. With the workweek expanding from relatively sane

9-to-5 hours into countless evenings and weekends, it's often impossible to find the time and energy to be with other people. "A decade after high school, that which most impacts my classmates' love lives might be busyness," says Colin. Seventy-five percent of women aged 25 to 35 say that their work lives interfere with their personal lives, and 35% say that the conflict is extreme. This goes for men as well—my brother works so many hours that it's no coincidence he met both his first New York girlfriend and his wife at work. When I visited him when he was single, he spent so many hours at work that his refrigerator contained nothing but a bottle of water ("I bought that for you," he said helpfully). I started to make a grocery list and then stopped short, wondering if I needed to buy more than food. "Do you even have any bowls?" I asked. "I have *bowl*," he quipped, opening the cabinet to reveal his lone dish.

Friends of mine who are lawyers and accountants often find it difficult to spare the time for a movie, a phone call to a long-distance friend, or a casual chat with a neighbor. In *The Costs of Living*, Barry Schwartz describes a former student who says his friendships "were not that *close*. Everyone was too busy. He thought twice about burdening friends with his life and his problems because he knew how consumed they were with their own, and what a sacrifice it would entail for them to spend the time required to listen to him and to help him out." I put a Post-it note on that page and wrote, "This is a very familiar story."

Isolation and loneliness readily lead to anxiety and depression. A mountain of scientific evidence links loneliness (and being alone) with negative mental health outcomes. Single and divorced people are significantly more likely to become depressed or suffer other mental health problems. Even people in unhappy marriages are happier than those who divorce. Of course, in many situations divorce is necessary and best in the long run, but even then it is painful and can lead to depression. When you consider the loneliness felt by many young people today, it's surprising that more of us aren't depressed. I often feel that many of us are one breakup or one move away from depression—our roots are not deep enough, our support systems too shallow.

The sadness of being alone is often the flip side of freedom and putting ourselves first. When we pursue our own dreams and make our own choices, that pursuit often takes us away from friends and family. An independence-minded society such as ours would never accept rules that encouraged arranged marriage or multigenerational households. Even marriage before a certain age—these days, around 25—is viewed as unwise and overly restricting. There is nothing wrong with individual freedom, of course; this is the advantage of the social change of the last few decades. But there are consequences, and loneliness is often one of them. Janis Joplin captured the GenMe dilemma with her famous line "Freedom's just another word for nothing left to lose."

One of the strangest things about modern life is the expectation that we will stand alone, negotiating breakups, moves, divorces, and all manner of heartbreak that previous generations were careful to avoid. This may be the key to the low rate of depression among older generations: despite all the deprivation and war they experienced, they could always count on each other. People had strong feelings of community; they knew the same people all their lives; and they married young and stayed married. It may not have been exciting, and it stymied the dreams of many, but it was a stable life that avoided the melancholy that is so common now.

STRESS IN COLLEGE ADMISSIONS AND JOBS

We live in an increasingly competitive world, and nowhere is this more evident than in college admissions. Many high school students determined to attend an Ivy League university strive for perfect grades, perfect SAT scores, and a long list of extracurricular activities. But even perfection is not enough these days: each year, Harvard rejects 50% of applicants who have perfect SAT scores. Many Ivy League schools admit only 10% of applicants overall. This stringent selectivity extends beyond the Ivy League: in 2003, Swarthmore rejected 62% of applicants with a perfect 800 verbal SAT score and 58% of students with a perfect 800 math score. In the same year, Notre Dame rejected 39% of high school valedictorians who applied. Public universities have become more discerning as well. In 2004, the majority of freshmen at the University of Wisconsin graduated in the top 10% of their high school class. Their average SAT total was 1264, a score above the 85th percentile (the national average was 1026). San Diego State University, where I teach, used to be a party school almost anyone could get into, but these days the average undergraduate earned a 3.5 GPA in high school and scored around the 67th percentile on her SATs. Young people realize just how competitive things are: in a 2000 survey, young people were 50% more likely than older people to say that working hard was "the most important [thing] for a child to learn to prepare him or her for life."

A 2002 *Washington Post* article titled "These Teens Are at the Top in Everything, Including Stress," describes a valedictorian who was rejected by Princeton. Though the student says it doesn't matter, "during a one-hour conversation, she mentions the rejection four times," the reporter notes. Given the complete dedication shown by many of these driven young teens, that's not surprising. The article describes students who load their schedules with every Advanced Placement (AP) class available, and then pile on three or four extracurricular activities and hours of community service, all in pursuit of getting into the right college. "Being repudiated by the college you wanted (or worse, your parents wanted) can be the ultimate disappointment because getting into that college has been what the previous four, eight—maybe even 12—years were all about," notes the article.

At the same time, young people and their parents are increasingly aware that a college education—sometimes the *right* college education—is a virtual necessity for securing a good job. In a recent survey, an amazing 97% of parents said that going to college was "absolutely necessary" or at least "helpful" for succeeding in life. Erica, 18, felt this pressure during high school: "I have gotten down on myself for not trying as hard or doing as well as I should have," she says. "I put all the pressure on myself. I knew I needed to do well to get into a good college. It seems to be very difficult to get a decent paying job nowadays without a college education." And although the local state university might be fine for most jobs, for others only the right school will do. Many New York investment banks, for example, focus their recruiting on Ivy League universities, and many graduate schools favor applicants from prestigious schools.

The new level of competition means that more and more high school students are going to great lengths to stand out. The number of high school students who took Advanced Placement (AP) exams in 2004 was 1.1 million, twice as many as in 1994 and six times as many as in 1984. *Time* magazine interviewed Marielle Woods, 17, who participates in twelve extracurricular activities and keeps up a 4.0 average. This can lead to a lot of stress. Jill, 23, describes her overachieving family as "a recipe for quiet terror." Although she's done very well in school, "always, ALWAYS before those grades come out, I struggle under the weight of a cloud of fear and depression," she says. "Every year I'm silently convinced that this will be the one—this time I'll actually screw it all up. It's a scary way to live."

The battle is not over after college, either. Medical schools and law schools, especially those with prestigious reputations, admit only a small fraction of applicants. Yale Law School lets in only 7% of applicants; the University of Maryland law school, 13%. Medical schools are even more competitive—Harvard Medical School admitted only 4.9% of applicants last year, UCLA only 4.5%, and the University of Wisconsin 11.4%. In 2004, more than half of medical school applicants were not admitted to any program. Other fields are fiercely competitive as well: graduate schools in clinical psychology often admit less than 10% of hopefuls. For example, the SDSU/UCSD joint doctoral program in clinical psychology at my school lets in only 4% of those who apply. In 2004, one of my brightest, hardest-working masters students applied to six Ph.D. programs in counseling psychology, which are usually easier to get into than clinical programs. Nevertheless, she wasn't admitted to a single program. MBA acceptance rates are a little higher, though at the best schools they hover around 15% to 20%. And these decisions are crucial: many economists say that a graduate degree is now the key to "making it," in the same way a college degree used to be.

Young college graduates who bypass graduate school often find the job market difficult even during boom times, particularly if they majored in the liberal arts. Even business graduates can have a hard time. "When I graduated from college, I thought getting a job would be a snap, because that's the impression we got from the career counselors and everyone around us. Boy, was I wrong," says Kristina, a business major interviewed in *Quarterlife Crisis*. "For the first six months after school, I couldn't even get an administrative position."

Academia is also not a guaranteed career path anymore. The majority of people who earn Ph.D.'s in English and history cannot find a university teaching job and consequently drop out of the field. Those in scientific fields must often complete several two- or three-year-long postdocs (temporary research jobs) after obtaining their Ph.D's—and then still might not find a job. A National Science Foundation study found that the number of science and engineering jobs at universities dropped by 1,800 between 1991 and 1995, at the same time that the number of postdocs swelled to 7,000. A recent *New York Times* article described a Harvard physics Ph.D. who had four postdocs in ten years and still could not find a faculty position. At 43, he finally left the field. He's not unusual; many young scientists are 35 or 40 by the time they've finished enough postdocs to get a job. One friend of mine was a postdoc for six years before he had a nervous breakdown that landed him in the university medical center.

There is also a pervasive uncertainty about finding the right profession. It's great to have the freedom to be whatever you want, but what exactly is that? I remember making a list of all the possible college majors and crossing them off one by one, as if the process of elimination would help me figure out what to do with my life. Settling on a career goal is even more challenging, and many people continue to struggle with this question throughout their twenties. It's particularly difficult because good information about professions is hard to come by—it's hard to know what being a lawyer, an accountant, or an engineer is really like day-to-day. So you might go through four or seven years of school only to find out you hate it. Or you might settle on a lucrative profession but then wonder if you're really doing the world any good by practicing it. "Am I living it right?" John Mayer repeats over and over in his 2001 hit song "Why Georgia," saying he wonders about how his "still verdictless life" will turn out. We worry about making the right choice, and we have no one else to blame when our choices go wrong. Personal freedom, the hallmark of our times, is a glorious thing, but too often we stand alone with our self-doubt about our own choices.

It's often difficult for young people to make the transition from the more certain world of college to the working world—or even graduate school—where "doing your best" isn't always enough and choices aren't always clear. Drew Lichtenberger, 28, whom I met on a generations chat board, calls the pervasive malaise of his generation "The Twenties Beat-Down." When he was starting his first job in business and his then-girlfriend was in law school, they talked frequently about how their twenties were turning out to be much more challenging than they expected. Even his friends who were successful wondered about fulfillment, asking, "Is this what I want to do with my life? Is it meaningful enough?" His summary of his friends' twenties experiences was "They used to be supersuccessful people, and now they're just freshmen in life." And sometimes they're freshmen who can't find good jobs. "I have one friend who graduated with a law degree and found herself working at a restaurant alongside MBA grads," says Drew.

THE NEW ECONOMICS

This is the scenario for young people today: To get a decent job, you must have a college degree, preferably from a good school. It is harder to get into a good college, and more expensive to pay for it. Once you get in and graduate, it is difficult to get into graduate school and sometimes even more difficult to find a job. Once you find a job, corporate downsizing and restructuring create the constant threat of layoffs. By the time you're in your thirties, career pressures are compounded by the demands of raising children when both of you have to work to pay the bills.

It is easy to say that this is just GenMe whining; things have always been tough—stop complaining and deal with it. Looked at objectively, however, things really are harder now. It was once possible to support a family on one middle-class or even working-class income. No longer. Many blue-collar jobs with good wages have been shipped overseas, and many white-collar jobs don't pay that well either. "You need a college degree now just to be where blue-collar people the same age were 20 or 30 years ago," says sociologist James Cote. Anne, 20, has experienced this firsthand. "When my parents were growing up, all they really needed was a high school degree to get by, but now things are so much harder, and the pressure is put on you to go to college and get a degree," she says. "It seems more people in today's generation are depressed because they can't achieve their dream of owning their own house because the world has become so much more competitive."

And although materialism has increased, as I noted in Chapter 3, that's not why things are so financially depressing now. These days, even the essentials are astronomically expensive: housing, health care, day care, and education costs have all far outstripped inflation. Between 1997 and 2002, the amount Americans aged 25 to 34 spent on mortgage interest went up 24%. The amount they spent on property taxes went up 15%, and on home maintenance and repairs, 24%. (And these numbers are likely to increase even more, given the spike in housing prices since 2002.) The amount that young adults spent on health insurance increased 18%. At the same time, young people's spending on discretionary items went down: clothing spending decreased 9%, entertainment decreased 3%, furniture decreased 11%, and alcohol decreased 7%. You'd think we'd need more alcohol to numb ourselves against the size of our mortgages, but the money had to come from somewhere. So we're not wasting our paychecks on luxuries; we're just trying to afford health insurance and a decent place to live.

That's getting increasingly difficult. In June 2005, the median house in the United States sold for $219,000, a 14.7% jump from prices just a year before and the largest one-year jump in twenty-five years. In 2004, a record sixty-two housing markets experienced double-digit (10% or more) increases. In 2004 alone, the cost of the average house in Las Vegas, Nevada, rose 47%. Houses in Los Angeles's San Fernando Valley, once an affordable place to live, shot up $96,000 in just one year, to a median price of $512,000. "Since I didn't get a $96,000 raise this year, I will continue to put quarters into a washer and dryer," says NPR commentator and L.A. resident Brian Unger, who says he expects to rent forever.

In the spring of 2005, the median house sold for $362,800 in West Palm Beach, Florida, $243,800 in Chicago, $689,200 in the San Francisco Bay Area, $398,300 in Boston, $198,900 in Milwaukee, Wisconsin, and $379,700 in Newark, New Jersey (yes, *that* Newark). In 2004, the average apartment in Manhattan sold for over $1,000,000—that's a million bucks—up from $450,000 in 1994.

This is great if you already own a house, particularly if you bought it a long time ago and are now seeking to downgrade for retirement. But for young people buying their first houses, or looking to upgrade as their families grow, the hot housing market is creating an enormous economic squeeze. The benefit for the Boomers and older folks is being paid out of the pockets of young people; it's generational warfare by mortgage.

Where I live in San Diego, only 11% of households have enough income to buy the median-priced home; in Los Angeles the number is an infinitesimal 5%. Even these numbers are deceptive, since the median price often doesn't buy you a house in a safe neighborhood with good schools; for that, you often have to spend quite a bit more. Unger comments that it's a good thing that people in their twenties and thirties can shop for caskets on the Internet, since "a casket, for some, is the only shelter they can afford to own."

Kelly, 27, and her husband looked for a house for a year. "We were getting so frustrated," she wrote on a message board. "The homes we saw in our price range near Chicago were so awful—little shacks with tons of problems." Jennifer, 29, is a teacher near Boston. Scanning the newspaper for houses, she would read the ad if the price was under $250,000 (this was a few years ago when homes were a little more affordable). "Usually, I would get only a few syllables into it and would ultimately hit one of the following words: condo, duplex, mobile home, fixer-upper, or handyman special," she says. When she and her husband went to see the few homes in their price range, she says that the ads should have read: "This pile of rotted wood offers 4 rooms and resembles a double wide trailer. You can store all kinds of crap that you don't care about in the musty, damp cellar that looks like something out of a horror movie" or "Very small house just a few miles into the ghetto. You'll be the envy of your neighbors as they push their shopping cart homes by your overpriced dump."

Many young people comment that their parents were able to buy a house when they were much younger, and on much less income. For example, my parents bought their first house in the early 1970s, when they were in their mid-twenties. It cost $23,000—a little more than their combined annual income at the time. In contrast, my husband and I bought our first house in 2003 when we were both 31. The house is smaller than my parents' first house, has a tiny yard, and cost $390,000—four times our annual income, even though we both work full-time at professional jobs. Two years later, the house was worth a staggering $550,000. Midwesterners are not immune: in July 2005, my 30-year-old cousin and her husband paid $300,000 for a 1930s-era, 1,450-square-foot house in Minneapolis, Minnesota.

Some social critics have pointed out that homes are larger now on average than they were in the 1950s and 1960s. However, this has been driven by "McMansions" at the high end of the market, not the ridiculously expensive—and often small—houses GenMe is buying. Even though houses are larger on average, even one-bedroom condos are out of reach for many people in many cities.

The amount of the family budget that went to the mortgage increased 69% between 1975 and 2000, a number that is likely even higher now.

A tale of two housing markets. Top: A young couple poses outside their newly purchased house in Minneapolis, Minnesota, about 1,450 square feet and built in the 1930s. Price tag: $300,000.

Below: A housing development in San Diego, California. Despite their close proximity, each of these three 1,300 to 1,700 square feet houses is worth at least $500,000.

The rule of thumb used to be that your house should not cost more than two times your annual income, and that you should spend about 25% of your income on housing. What a joke. Mortgage lenders now regularly increase this percentage to 40%, and in a lot of markets people do everything they can to exceed this figure: borrowing down payments, taking out interest-only loans, using adjustable-rate mortgages. That's usually not so they can afford mansions, but just to buy into the market while they still can. At the same time that family incomes have risen due to more women in the workforce, the number of middle-class families who paid over 35% of their income toward the mortgage more than quadrupled between 1975 and 2001. With the median home now selling for $219,000 and the median family income at around $43,000, the average American family would need to spend 5 times their income to buy this home, or around 37% of their *before*-tax income (assuming zero down on a 30-year fixed-rate mortgage with an interest rate of 6%). And that's just for an average home, presumably in an average school district and an average neighborhood (which often means not very good on either count).

Renters don't have it much easier. Affordable housing is increasingly scarce even as wages for service workers remain low. In *Nickel and Dimed*, Barbara Ehrenreich reports that the service industry workers she met often lived in their cars because they couldn't afford even a small apartment. Even borderline-affordable apartments were difficult to find, so during much of her yearlong experiment as a service worker, Ehrenreich lived in fleabag motels. "Something is wrong, seriously wrong, when a single person in good health . . . can barely support herself by the sweat of her brow," writes Ehrenreich. "You don't need a degree in economics to see that wages are too low and rents too high."

Middle-class renters can usually find an apartment, but the rent still eats up most of their money. Most people I know pay around 50% of their take-home pay for rent—I always did when I was renting. It was usually the only way to live in a safe neighborhood within any reasonable distance of where I was working. And we're not talking about luxury living here—one Michigan apartment featured an oven too small to hold a pizza pan and worn blue carpet apparently installed in the 1960s. My apartment near Cleveland, where I lived from 1999 to 2001, had a rusted-out parking garage and was in a poor neighborhood with a mall that was half vacant. One morning, I awoke to find three maintenance men in work boots standing at my bedroom door—a neighbor had smelled gas, and they wanted to make sure I wasn't dead or unconscious. Sure enough, the 1970s-era oven was leaking gas. I'm just grateful I didn't have children living with me like most of my neighbors. I got all this for about half of my take-home pay.

At the same time that rents and home prices have increased, earnings have gone *down* for many groups. How can this be when we're always hearing about rich people spending so much money? It's because the rich really have gotten richer, and the poor—or actually the middle-class— has gotten poorer. Over the last twenty-five years, the share of the wealth held by the very richest Americans (the top one-thousandth) has doubled, whereas the lower 90% has lost income and wealth. The income of men ages 25 to 34 with full-time jobs dropped 17% from 1971 to 2002. So where does the extra money for housing come from? Primarily from women's salaries. Most families have been able to stay afloat mostly because both adults are in the workforce. Summarizing data from several large studies, political scientist Robert Putnam concludes, "Virtually all of the increase in full-time employment of American women over the last twenty years is attributable to financial pressures, not personal fulfillment."

The dual-income formula works—until the woman (or the man) wants to take some time off to care for a child. With today's housing prices, this is becoming a virtual impossibility for many families. Several couples I know live in apartments or commute two hours from their jobs because that's all they can afford on one income. My childless friends wonder how they will be able to stay in their homes (or buy one) after they have children, given that they both have to work to afford the mortgage payment and the prohibitive cost of full-time day care for an infant (usually $1,000 a month or more—for *each* kid). When I told my undergraduate class the price of day care, they were stunned; most guessed it cost about $500 a month. I heard a woman in the back row exhale audibly. "I'm not having kids," she said ruefully.

A year of full-time day care is now significantly more expensive than in-state tuition at a public university. (Somewhat of a paradox given that day-care workers are paid very little, but that's the going rate.) It's difficult to underestimate just how stressful looking for—and paying for—day care is on young families. It is a frequent topic of discussion among pregnant women on message boards like those on constantchatter.com. Over and over, women expressed surprise and shock at the outrageous price of day care; most had no idea how expensive it was before they made a few calls. Words like "nightmare," "insane," "freaked out," and "scary" were frequent. Describing a day care facility that charged $845 a month, Lauren, 23, wrote, "I nearly choked." Alexandra, 27, responded, "I want to live where you live," explaining that day care was at least $1,000 a month in her city. Many also found long waitlists and numerous day cares that didn't take infants under six months, or even two years old. With most paid maternity leaves lasting only six *weeks* (and that's if you even *get* paid maternity leave), this is a big problem.

Lisa, 28, is pregnant with her first child; she found out that day care in Denver will cost $1,000 a month, more than a third of her take-home pay even though she is a lawyer. "And we have been having trouble getting by on what we make now without an extra expense like that. I have no clue what we're going to do," she writes. Jenny, 32, lives in Kansas. "Just thinking of all the costs associated with a baby (medical copays and deductibles even with insurance, higher medical insurance premiums, day care, diapers, maybe formula) makes me wonder how we will make it," she says.

And don't forget to save for college for those kiddos! In Oregon, colleges and universities cost 34% of the average family's income, up from 25% in 1994. Four years at an Ivy League school now tops $160,000; the average private college, $110,000. Even four years at most public universities will run you at least $40,000 (for example, it's over $60,000 for four years at San Diego State, including room and board). And these are *today's* prices—I can't imagine what they will be in twenty years when my future children are heading off to college, since college costs outstrip inflation almost every year. A woman on a message board for mothers put it well: "Maybe we'll win the Powerball."

The price of education has an immediate effect on young people as well, who often have staggering amounts of debt when they graduate. Today's young people are the most highly educated generation ever—more than 30% of people between the ages of 25 and 39 have a college degree. But all of that education comes at a price. Average student loan debt has increased 85% in the last ten years alone; 66% of recent college graduates owe more than $10,000, and 5% owe more than $100,000. The average is about $15,000. And that's just undergrad; add graduate or professional school loans and things get even worse. Sarah, 29, wrote, "I have a TON of debt from my law school loan. Think six digits."

This is the flip side of the Twixter equation of delayed adulthood. Some GenMe'ers may put off settling down to pursue their individual desires, but many others simply can't afford to become full-fledged adults.

"I graduated from college with honors in three years but could not find a job that allowed me to become financially independent," wrote Tricia Engelhardt in a letter to *Time*. "So I moved back in with my parents. I was surprised to find that the majority of my high school class had done the same thing." Between college loans, the astronomical price of housing, and low entry-level salaries, pretty soon GenMe'ers (and post-GenMe'ers) are going to be living with our parents until we're 30.

Health care costs are also astoundingly high. Even people with good jobs often find themselves paying $500 a month or more for their family's health care premiums—if they have health care at all. The self-employed can lay out over $1,000 a month for just a basic health care plan. And the cost keeps going up: health care premiums surged 11.2% in 2004, five times the increase in wages or general inflation that year. It was the fourth year in a row that premiums had increased 10% or more. Perhaps as a result, almost 1 out of 3 people ages 18 to 24 has no health insurance; for people ages 25 to 34, the figure is 1 out of 4. Even people who have coverage can run into serious financial trouble if they or their family members develop major health problems. *People* profiled several families, even some with health insurance, who went bankrupt after unexpected medical crises. Bankruptcies caused by illness or medical debt increased a whopping 22 times over (2,200%) between 1981 and 2001.

The need for job-based health care can often mean some difficult choices. For example, many women find that they are required to return to their jobs immediately after a six-week maternity leave. If they go even one day over, they can be forced to pay "COBRA" rates on their health care plans, which can top $1,200 a month—or more, if you're covering your whole family. And having just given birth, what a perfect time to lose your health care or incur another staggering bill.

With the new baby often comes unrealistic advice from outside sources—advice that is straight out of the 1950s in its economic assumptions *and* its sexual stereotypes. The current trend is toward attachment parenting, which involves "wearing" your baby in a sling, breast-feeding for at least a year, and sleeping in the same bed with your child. Some of this is still possible if you're working, but William and Martha Sears, the high priest and priestess of attachment parenting, make it clear that this is not desirable. In *The Baby Book*'s 2003 edition, the Searses recommend that couples get accustomed to living on one income before the baby arrives so they don't get too accustomed to having two salaries. (Is he kidding? I'm "accustomed" to the mortgage payment eating up one entire salary.) Mothers should stay at home if at all possible, they say, and children under a year should not go to day care centers because of the risk of infectious diseases. Their subheading "I Have to Work—We Need the Income" is placed in quotes, as if to question its veracity, and it's followed by advice on how this might not be true—you probably only need that second income for "desired luxuries," they say.

When I read this, I wondered how the authors could be so clueless about housing costs. I turned to the back of the book to scan the "About the Authors" blurb, thinking perhaps the Searses lived in Dallas, Indianapolis, or another undervalued housing market. Nope. They live and practice in San Clemente, California, where (as of March 2005) the least expensive two-bedroom *condo* was going for $400,000, and the least expensive single-family house cost $580,000 (and this winner looked like it needed *a lot* of work and had no real yard). Three-bedroom houses in San Clemente regularly sell for over $700,000. Yes, this is an especially expensive place to live, but more and more housing markets are heading in this direction. Unless you've married someone making well over $100,000 a year when you're ready to have kids, learning to live on one income is going to mean learning to raise a family in a rented apartment (and even that will set you back $1,500 a month in their town). So when the Searses talk about doing without "desired luxuries," do they mean a place to live? What a great idea for the new century—let's all quit work, wear our babies, and live in a cardboard box on the street. (C'mon, kids, it'll be fun!) At least we'd be "attached" to our children, though I bet they'd get a few more infectious diseases than they would have caught at day care.

The Two-Income Trap, coauthored by a Harvard economist, provides a summary of the balance sheet. Fixed costs like housing, health insurance, and child care have *doubled* for the average family since the early 1970s, while discretionary income has gone down. (The gap, of course, has been filled by more women working.) Home foreclosures have more than tripled in twenty-five years, and car repossessions have doubled in five years. Families with children are significantly more likely to go bankrupt than childless couples, probably because living in a safe neighborhood with good schools is very expensive. Bankruptcy is more common now, they argue, because fixed costs like housing are higher, so there is no way to "cut back" when things get tough. Even more alarming, *The Two-Income Trap* was published in 2003, before the huge housing run-up of 2004 and early 2005. More and more families will declare bankruptcy in the next few years. Even if housing prices dip—and that's anyone's guess—a decrease of 5% or even 15% is still going to leave housing costs considerably higher than they were in previous generations. We're probably stuck with the situation.

To sum up: we're supposed to have one parent stay at home, but to afford a house—and sometimes even the rent—both parents have to work. You "choose" between expensive, difficult-to-find day care and renting an apartment where your child has no space to run around and you hear your neighbors' music all the time. Even if you don't have children, you face huge bills just for the necessities of life: housing, health care, and paying for those student loans. More and more people are filing for bankruptcy, or on the verge of it. We're screwed no matter what we do—no wonder we're anxious.

HIGHER EXPECTATIONS

So in this world where essentials like housing are so astronomically expensive, what messages has GenMe been fed? Save your money? Feel lucky to have a house even if it's not a mansion? Of course not. In the world of individualism and consumer longing, we've been taught to expect more. Perhaps because of media exposure, we want to be millionaires, to be famous, to live in a large house and drive fancy cars. It's all we've seen on TV and in movies since we were babies. In the 1999 movie *Fight Club*, the character Tyler Durden captures this perspective with searing accuracy: "Our generation has had no Great Depression, no Great War," he says. "Our depression is our lives . . . We were raised on television to believe that we'd all be millionaires, movie gods, rock stars, but we won't. And we're starting to figure that out. And we're very, very, pissed off."

These movie lines are ironic; after all, they are delivered by Brad Pitt, a "movie god" if there ever was one. But that's the point: not everyone can grow up to be Brad Pitt, or Michael Jordan, or Bill Gates, or Jennifer Lopez. It has always been normal for kids to have big dreams, but the dreams of kids today are bigger than ever. By the time kids figure out that they're not going to be celebrities or sports figures, they're well into adolescence, or even their twenties. Brian, a character in *Avenue Q*, says that as a kid he thought he'd "grow up to be a comedian on late-night TV." Ten years out of college, he's broke and unemployed. Before long the entire cast is singing a song called "It Sucks to Be Me."

High expectations can be the stuff of inspiration, but more often they set GenMe up for bitter disappointment. *Quarterlife Crisis* concludes that twentysomethings often take a while to realize that the "be whatever you want to be, do whatever you want to do" mantra of their childhoods is not attainable. When they do come to this harsh realization, they say, the feeling resembles Charlie Brown falling flat on his back after Lucy pulls away the ball.

Characters on TV shows and in movies rarely have boring jobs working for corporations, building houses, or working a cash register. Yet these are the jobs most young people will grow up to have. In between the shows, advertising constantly asks us if we are good enough, thin enough, rich enough. Writer Cathi Hanauer sums this up as "the ideas and belief—courtesy of a culture ever more mired in materialism, consumerism, and false advertising—that we should have it all, do it all, and be it all, and be Happy. And if we're not, by God, something is wrong." Lynn, 19, agrees that television has inspired many of these unrealistic expectations. "I think there is so much anxiety and depression because of the pressure the media is putting on the world to be perfect. On television, stars are portrayed as beautiful and worry-free. People are spending more and more time trying to make themselves a replica of what they see on TV." This is where "you can be anything" and reality collide—right at the intersection of anxiety and depression.

GenMe'ers are also often woefully unprepared for what we encounter in the "real world" of the workplace. Years of self-esteem instruction, of being told we are special and can do anything, leave us confused and hurt by the harsh realities of many jobs. In *Quarterlife Crisis*, Joanna says, "College doesn't prepare you for the real world emotionally, which definitely brought on depression." The environment in her first job, she says, was "sterile, not nurturing, and full of people who didn't care about my welfare or happiness or well-being." (To which I can only cynically reply, "Welcome to reality, kid.")

Young women in particular often feel that they have to "have it all," balancing primary responsibility for a family with lofty career aspirations.

In her book on eating disorders, Joan Jacobs Blumberg lists the goals of young women as "to be brainy and beautiful; to have an exciting $75,000-a-year job; to nurture two wonderful children in consort with a supportive but equally high-powered husband." To achieve such a perfect life, "young women must be extremely demanding of themselves. . . . The kind of personal control required to become the new Superwoman . . . parallels the single-mindedness that characterizes the anorexic." It's a tall order to do this and still maintain your sanity. As *Midlife Crisis at 30* puts it, "the 'you can do anything' promise has a tendency to transform into an unrealistic 'you should be everything' brand of guilt."

Even if we reach many of our goals, GenMe'ers are likely to remain unsatisfied unless we earn heaps of money. The average person is now much more aware of all of the things she can't have. Author Gregg Easterbrook calls this "catalog-induced anxiety" after the glossy pages of expensive things that land in our mailboxes. But it goes beyond that; we constantly see expensive things through TV, the Internet, movies, and magazines. Particularly if the show is set in New York, TV characters often live in apartments that would require about three times the income they're likely to earn as coffee shop waitresses or sporadically employed actors (such as the characters on *Friends*). Shows like VH1's *The Fabulous Life of . . .* display the expensive trappings of the famous; the details of indulgence are then followed by the cost, usually delivered in a riveting accelerating cadence: "the tile in the kitchen alone cost over two MILLION DOLLARS!" The Travel Channel regularly runs shows like *Millionaires' Hawaii*, which demonstrate how nice a place would be—*if only* you had a huge pile of money. Sure enough, research shows that the more television you watch, the more materialistic you are.

Magazines are no better. "Whose Ring Is Bigger?" asks *Us Weekly* in an article on celebrities' engagement rings, and of course none of them are worth under $50,000. The very next page shows Jennifer Lopez's new "swank 6.5 million estate!" A sidebar informs us that "One is never enough!" and describes J-Lo's other homes in New York, Miami, and Long Island. The last section of the magazine tells you exactly what makeup and clothes the stars wear ("Star Style"), including where to buy it and exactly how much it costs. (General answer: rip-off. How about $200 for a pair of pants or $2,400 for a casual dress?)

The Internet contributes to the problem as well. For example, the site realtor.com makes it possible to view pictures—and sometimes 360-degree video—of houses listed for sale. No matter how I try to look only at the houses I might conceivably buy, they just keep going up in price until suddenly I am drooling over a $1.2 million house I'll never be able to afford. I often feel anxious after looking at this site, trying to figure out how I can possibly make enough money to buy one of these houses. Mostly, though, the experience is just abjectly depressing.

Our perceptions are also skewed by modern life. Television wasn't always a world devoid of working-class people. Witness 1970s shows like *Sanford and Son* (father and son run a junkyard and live in a house apparently furnished from it), *All in the Family* (Archie Bunker's working-class family lives in a duplex in Queens), and *Good Times* (family of five lives in a Chicago housing project). And because fewer of us ride buses and subways, send our children to public schools, and live in mixed-income neighborhoods, middle-class people rarely rub shoulders with poor people in real life either, which prompted a *New York Times Magazine* article titled "The Invisible Poor." We're constantly exposed to people who have more than we do and rarely see those who have less—a lack of perspective that's a formula for dissatisfaction.

People whose primary motivations are financial are much more likely to be anxious and depressed than people who value strong relationships with others. And research consistently finds that money cannot buy happiness—after you reach a subsistence level, income is not significantly related to life satisfaction. Psychologist Ed Diener got many of the hundred wealthiest Americans (from a *Forbes* list) to fill out a happiness questionnaire, and they turned out to be only marginally happier than people with average incomes. This is probably due to the adjustment of expectations; you think you'll be happier when you get that raise, but a few months later you've adjusted to your new standard of living and want yet more. People who win the lottery are ecstatic at first but then, a year after their win, are no happier than other people.

We also have very high expectations for our romantic partners. Marriage was once seen as a practical partnership for raising children, but is now expected to fulfill our most romantic ideals. GenMe writer Chuck Klosterman says that the idealized media portrayal of love is unattainable but completely seductive, explaining "why almost everyone I know is either overtly or covertly unhappy . . . personally, I would never be satisfied unless my marriage was as good as Cliff and Claire Huxtable's." In a Gallup poll, 94% of single women in their twenties agreed that "when you marry, you want your spouse to be your soulmate, first and foremost." Norval Glenn, an expert on marital satisfaction, states bluntly: "People now believe that a relationship with one person should meet all of their emotional needs. In most cases, that isn't going to happen." The authors of *Midlife Crisis at 30* call this the "romantic expectation gap." They note, "Most of the women we interviewed insisted that they were not looking for a Prince Charming—then, without missing a beat, they described an equally unattainable ideal. It's ironic that we've developed such lofty expectations of our potential husbands at a time when nearly 50 percent of marriages still end in divorce."

Or maybe it's not so ironic—we might expect so much that we end up unhappy. In the mid-1970s, 69% of people described their marriage as "very happy." By 2002, however, only 62% said they had "very happy" marriages. This decline is especially striking because the divorce rate rose steeply during this same time, presumably weeding out many unhappy marriages. Married couples also fight more. Compared to those married between 1969 and 1980, people married between 1981 and 1992 reported significantly more marital problems, such as anger and jealousy, and more marital conflict, such as frequent fights. Couples also reported less interaction—they were less likely to shop together or eat dinner together. These figures held even when the researchers took age, length of marriage, number of children, education level, and many other variables into account. It will be interesting to see if GenMe continues this trend toward greater unhappiness in marriage.

Few people can reach the goal of the perfect life, so more are anxious and depressed. "It's as if some idiot raised the ante on what it takes to be a normal human being," Martin Seligman writes. In many ways, the higher expectations of GenMe are rooted in our focus on the self. We've been told all our lives that we're special, so we think we deserve to be famous and rich. We also have higher expectations for jobs and romantic partners, expecting fulfillment in all realms of life. It would be wonderful if these appetites could always be sated, but of course they can't. Not everyone can live in a huge house, and most people's jobs, by economic necessity, are not going to be fulfilling, at least not all of the time. You might be married to a great guy, but he's not going to be your perfect soulmate all the time. We focus so much on our individual wants, feeling empty inside, that depression is often the result.

But our dissatisfaction can't be solely blamed on individualism. It's not just that we expect more, it's that the necessities of life are so much more expensive. GenMe anticipates more at a time when it's more difficult to attain even the bare minimum. Movies are filled with people who have glamorous jobs, but it's harder and harder just to get into a good college. TV shows are set in mansions, yet even a small house is outside the reach of most people. It's like a cruel joke—we've been raised to expect riches, and can barely afford a condo and a crappy health care plan.

DANGERS AND THREATS

One of my colleagues is originally from Belgium, so he and his family often travel back to Europe. His 2½-year-old daughter absorbed the routine of modern airline travel quickly: if you say the words "security check" to her, she will stand with her arms stretched out and wait.

Even before the threat of terrorism made the world such a frightening place, there were many other dangers that were once unknown. Almost every high school (and some middle schools) now has metal detectors at its doors. Many of my students were in high school at the time of the Columbine shootings. When I ask them about what events shaped their view of the world, "Columbine" is usually the first answer, because after that they no longer felt safe at their own school. It isn't hard to see how this might lead to feelings of anxiety.

Increases in violent crime occurred everywhere in the United States, not just at schools. Even with the recent sharp downturn in violent crime, our cities and towns are still more than four times as dangerous as they were in the 1950s. Although I grew up in a fairly safe, middle-class suburb, one of my middle school classmates was murdered when burglars broke into his house. My math teacher's son was shot in the head and killed when he got into an argument with another motorist. A high school classmate was murdered when thieves arrived at the sporting goods store where she was locking up for the night. Such incidents are, of course, even more common in the inner city: one of my students, who grew up in urban East Los Angeles, has almost lost count of the relatives and friends who have been shot in gang warfare.

The role of the media is also important here. The evening news (particularly the local broadcast) portrays a world filled with dangers. The mantra in local news is "If it bleeds, it leads," which is why murders are often the top story. Sure enough, people who watch many hours of news coverage are more afraid of crime than people who do not watch much TV news. In the quest for ratings, many news programs focus on the terrible things that can happen to children, knowing that this is a natural source of anxiety for parents. (I often joke that the teaser for every TV news story is "And how will it affect *your* children?")

Most people, fortunately, will never be the victim of a violent crime. But the atmosphere created by crime is pervasive and painful. Living in a dangerous society can make people enormously anxious: Is it safe to walk down that street? What if I get raped? Will I get carjacked if I take a wrong turn? What if my child is abducted? Crime affects you even if you are never a victim. Even though the crime rate wasn't much different then compared to now, I often walked home alone from elementary school in the early 1980s, and rode my bike for miles around our suburb (without a helmet!). Now parents are afraid to let their children walk to school alone, and many don't allow their children to ride their bikes around their neighborhood for fear of kidnappers and child molesters. Magda, 24, has two little sisters. "Because of all the bad things that happen to children that are shown in the media," she says, her mother "feels worried that something is going to happen to my sisters. She feels the world is a much more unsafe place now than 20 years ago."

Parents' fears of child abduction have led many to tell their kids they should never, ever talk to strangers. Sometimes children absorb this lesson a little *too* well. In June 2005, Boy Scout Brennan Hawkins, 11, got lost in the Utah mountains. Rescuers finally found him four days later, alive but weak and dehydrated. Why did it take so long to find him, considering he was alive and walking around all of this time? Because he got off the trail and hid every time he saw someone. After all, never talk to strangers. "His biggest fear, he told me, was someone would steal him," said his mother. In other words, Brennan was so concerned about being abducted by the people who were trying to rescue him that he almost starved to death.

As Barry Glassner writes in *The Culture of Fear*, media reports often make us afraid of things that are very unlikely to occur, as small scares are turned into seemingly large dangers. Very few children are abducted by nonrelatives. Other scares are considerably sillier. A few years ago, forty people in San Diego got food poisoning from the salad lettuce at a restaurant chain. The local media covered this story endlessly. Kristina, 25, commented on this sarcastically in one of my classes: "Now we're supposed to be scared of lettuce?" And this was before the threat of terrorism scared us all out of our wits (is the alert level orange today, or yellow?).

On the other hand, dangers and threats are nothing new. Previous generations faced world wars without suffering from high rates of depression. Perhaps uniting against a common enemy inoculated that generation against depression; people knew who the enemy was, and set about saving scrap metal and planting Victory gardens in order to stop it. Now the violence is much more random, the enemy unseen: children are shot because they went to school; adults die because they went to work on a Tuesday morning in September. The random violence of crime and terrorism is somehow more frightening.

CONCLUSION

In some ways, the shift toward melancholy in young people seems paradoxical: Generation Me has so much more than previous generations—we are healthier, enjoy countless modern conveniences, and are better educated. But Generation Me often lacks other basic human requirements: stable close relationships, a sense of community, a feeling of safety, a simple path to adulthood and the workplace. Our grandparents may have done without television and gone to the bathroom in an outhouse, but they were usually not lonely, scared by threats of terrorism, or obsessing about the best way to get into Princeton. As David Myers argues in his book *The American Paradox*, the United States has become a place where we have more but feel worse. Technology and material things may make life easier, but they do not seem to lead to happiness. Instead, we long for the social connections of past years, we enter a confusing world of too many choices, and we become depressed at younger and younger ages.

5

Yeah, Right: The Belief That There's No Point in Trying

Seventeen-year-old Caitlin begins her day early, with a quick check of her e-mail to see if there's any news from the ten colleges she applied to. She hopes to be admitted to an Ivy League school, but with acceptance rates at only 10%, it's a long shot even with her stellar grades and numerous extracurricular activities. After a long day at school and soccer practice, she makes it home in time to watch some TV with her family. Flipping between CNN and FOX News, she watches coverage of the war in Iraq interspersed with stories on the victims of a train bombing in Europe. There's an election coming up, and her parents plan on voting in it. "Why are you going to vote?" Caitlin asks. "You're more likely to get into an accident on the way to the polling place than to have your vote affect the election." Her parents try to convince her otherwise, but Caitlin replies with the universal teenage expression of cool cynicism: "Yeah, right."

Most of Generation Me's days are like this: filled with events and circumstances that we can't control. So why should we try? Perhaps as a result, older people complain that the idea of personal responsibility has faded, that young people blame others for their problems, and that apathy is rampant. We're not just Generation Me; we're Generation Whatever. The young are the new cynics.

The days when young Americans marched in the streets to change the world are, for the most part, gone. Although some protests still draw crowds and collective action, the young person who believes that she can make a difference in world events, national politics, and sometimes even her own life is more and more rare. And despite the recent talk about young people getting involved in political campaigns through the Internet, the vast majority of young people couldn't care less about politics. Only about 1 in 4 people under the age of 25 votes, even in presidential elections. In 2004, I gave a talk at a conference attended by a diverse group of two hundred undergraduates and about twenty of their professors. I asked the audience members to raise their hands if they had ever participated in a social or political protest. Only one person raised her hand: a fiftysomething professor in the front row.

Young people are also cynical about their own prospects. "There are plenty of students who don't have goals," says Liz, 18, a student interviewed in *Generation X Goes to College*. "They feel it's no use to have goals, society will keep them from those goals anyway." Or take Ryan, the character from the other side of the tracks in the current teen soap *The O.C.*, who says, "Where I'm from, having a dream doesn't make you smart. Knowing it won't come true—that does." Typical of the mixed messages fed to GenMe, though, Ryan's unlikely dreams do come true. Even though he's just been arrested for stealing a car, he's taken in by a wealthy family and within a week is wearing a tuxedo to a debutante ball. Whatever.

THE DATA ON CYNICISM AND FEELINGS OF CONTROL

I became interested in youthful cynicism after I had been doing research on generational differences for several years. Up to that point, I had concentrated on personality traits, like anxiety or self-esteem. But I suspected there were also differences in how we see the world and what we believe. I came across a popular psychological scale that measures a fundamental belief: are you in control of what happens to you, or do other people, luck, and larger forces control your fate? People who believe they are in control are "internal" (and possess "internality"); those who don't are "external" (and have "externality"). When I read the internal items of the scale, I had a strong feeling that there would be big generational differences. Some of the items:

- By taking an active part in political and social affairs, the people can control world events.
- With enough effort we can wipe out political corruption.
- The average citizen can have an influence in government decisions.

Even though I was in my late twenties at the time, I reacted to these items like a teenager would: I snorted sarcastically and said, "Yeah, right!" I thought, "Who believes that pie-in-the-sky crap anymore?" It sounded like the kind of stuff Boomers believed in when they thought they could change the world, and not at all like my generation or anyone younger.

Then I read some of the items on the external side, which measure the opposite beliefs:

- The world is run by the few people in power, and there is not much the little guy can do about it.
- Getting a good job depends mainly on being in the right place at the right time.
- Who gets to be boss often depends upon who was lucky enough to be in the right place first.

"No kidding," I thought. These items sounded a lot more truthful to me than the idealistic statements measuring internality.

But this was just my own opinion. I wanted to know if college students' responses to these questions really did change over the generations. Liqing Zhang, Charles Im, and I found 97 studies reporting data from 18,310 college students who filled out the control questionnaire between 1960 and 2002.

The results showed a remarkably clear change: College students increasingly believed that their lives were controlled by outside forces. The correlation between scores on the scale and the year the data were collected was .70—a stunning number, as even the larger correlations in the social sciences usually hover around .40 or .50. The average GenMe college student in 2002 had more external control beliefs than 80% of college students in the early 1960s. External control beliefs increased about 50% between the 1960s and the 2000s.

These results also gel with polling data collected by other researchers. From the 1950s to the 1990s, adult Americans were increasingly likely to agree with cynical statements such as "The people running the country don't care what happens to people like me," "The rich get richer and the poor get poorer," and "What you think doesn't count very much anymore." In contrast, they were less likely to agree that "hard work always pays off." High school students increasingly believed that "planning only makes you unhappy since plans hardly ever work out anyway."

What's even more disturbing is how early in development these changes begin. After finding the large change for college students, I wondered if children would show the same results. Maybe only adolescents had become more cynical. As it turned out, kids were just as jaded—41 samples of 6,554 children aged 9 to 14 showed that kids are now more likely to believe that things are out of their control. The magnitude of the change was about the same as it was in college students, with the average GenMe child scoring more externally than 80% of his or her counterparts in the early 1970s. Kids as young as 9 have caught the rising wave of apathy and cynicism.

It's when you look at the items on the children's form of the control scale that things really get fun. Many speak in general terms about trying hard, or studying. But others hint at the kind of bad behavior I mentioned in Chapter 3, exemplified by the *People* magazine article "Kids Out of Control." The scale asks:

- Are you often blamed for things that just aren't your fault?
- Most of the time, do you feel that you have little to say about what your family decides to do?
- When you get punished, does it usually seem it's for no good reason at all?

More kids now agree with these statements, suggesting that they are more likely to blame their parents or teachers when things go wrong. I can just hear millions of kids yelling, "But it's not my fault!"

THE WANING APPEAL OF POLITICS, PROTESTS, AND VOTING

There are two parts to the trend in control: first, there's the declining belief in personal responsibility and the efficacy of hard work and sacrifice—I'll talk about that later in this chapter. Then there's the fading idea that collective action will have an effect on politics, society, and the world.

The Boomers' infamous Vietnam protests, university sit-ins, and free-dom marches are legend—and they're gone. Whether you think this is a good thing or a bad thing, the peak of campus activism is clearly far in the past. One professor at a "socially progressive" college said that students on his campus "whine about the lack of action in the classroom or on campus, then back down when challenged or encouraged to use the resources at their disposal." In 2004, only 6% of college freshmen said they expected to participate in protests or demonstrations during their college years. Even staying informed is now apparently too much work. In 1966, 60% of freshmen said that "keeping up to date with political affairs" was an important or essential life goal. Only 34% agreed with this statement in 2004, and this was up from the all-time low of 28% in 2000. Fewer freshmen reported that they discussed politics frequently—26% in 2004 compared to 33% in 1968.

High school students are similarly disinclined to get involved. Megan, 15, recently attended a leadership workshop at which students wrote down what they disliked about their high school. The teens had no trou-ble listing problems, but when it came to saying how to change things, most "just shrugged their shoulders," Megan says. "They said they wouldn't really put any effort into trying to change the problems at all, because there was no way working towards change would do anything—gossip and stealing are just what kids do and there's no reasoning with the teachers about homework, so why even bother with it? Nobody seemed to feel they had much impact or could change any of the problems with our school." So the main thing Megan got out of the leadership workshop was learning that her peers thought there wasn't any point in leading.

And if young people don't think they can change their schools, changes to the country and the world seem even more unlikely. A recent poll found that 53% of GenMe mothers agreed that a person's main responsibility is to themselves and their children, and not to making the world a better place. In contrast, only 28% of Boomers agreed with this statement. Alexis, 20, says that her generation's favorite phrases include "What can one person do?" and "If you can't beat them, join them."

Part of the reason young people are disengaged is that they don't pay much attention to the news. Less than 20% of young people read newspapers, and the average age of people watching CNN or the network evening news is around 60. (Have you noticed all the commercials for dentures and arthritis medications during these programs?) Young people may be getting some news from the Internet, but most use the Web for specific interests instead (what media expert Nicolas Negroponte calls "The Daily Me"). Only 32% of people aged 18 to 24 agree that they "need to get the news every day," compared to 62% of those ages 55 to 64.

As a result, young people know very little about news and politics. David Mindich, author of *Tuned Out: Why Americans Under 40 Don't Follow the News*, interviewed young people in 2002–2003. He found that 60% could not name a single Supreme Court justice, 48% did not know what *Roe v. Wade* was, and 62% could not name any of the three countries Bush identified as the "axis of evil" (Iraq, Iran, and North Korea). In a 2000 survey, only 4% of 18-to-24-year-olds knew that John McCain had sponsored a campaign finance bill (and this was when he was running for the Republican nomination for president). In February 2000, 47% of 18-to-24-year-olds could not name a single Republican party primary candidate. In another poll, high school seniors were asked to say, in their opinion, the most important problem facing the country. One in three could not name a single issue.

What about all the young people who got involved in Howard Dean's presidential campaign in 2004? They were a very, very small minority. More typical was the SDSU student body president who went on a local TV show panel to talk about her drive to get students registered to vote for the 2004 election. When the moderator asked if she thought Howard Dean had inspired young people, she said, "I'm not sure I know who that is."

If staying informed isn't on the priority list, neither is protesting. Many GenMe'ers believe that college is a great opportunity and don't feel comfortable squandering those years in political activism. Theresa, 22, attends a private college on scholarship and feels strongly about fighting for Hispanic rights. However, she says, "I quickly learned to fight the right battles. Participating in rallies and sit-ins was exhausting, causing my grades to suffer. I knew that I had to stand up for what is right, but I also knew that I was at Smith to gain the education [that other people in] my family never could attain."

Many young people feel that the problems of the modern world are impossible to solve anyway. "Modern society has become so complex that it's a complete headfuck to figure out what's connected to what, what attempts at a solution will result in what effects on other things, and so forth," says Richard Scalzo, interviewed in *What Really Happened to the Class of '93*. "Each [problem] seems to be one head of a hundred-headed hydra, and if you cut off one head, two grow back in their place. There are plenty of smart people that don't know how to solve these problems, and if they do, they are voices crying in the wilderness."

Boomers are often appalled by what they see as the apathy of the young. On a recent plane trip, I told an older man about young people's beliefs in the futility of action. "But it's essential for people to stay informed and active—that's what democracy is all about," he said, visibly upset. "If we don't, it might as well be a dictatorship." Young people have heard this so often that Tom, the twentysomething graduate student on 2004's *Jack & Bobby*, referred to it as "the Boomer speech . . . The apathy of my generation versus the passionate ideology of yours."

I remember the first time I saw the quintessential Baby Boomer movie, 1983's *The Big Chill*. To be honest, I didn't get it. Although some of the movie deals with the characters' realization of their own mortality, the rest centers on the their various levels of discomfort about having "sold out." After all, they once talked about changing the world, and now here they are in jobs in journalism, medicine, and law. Jeff Goldblum's character, for example, writes for *People* magazine, for which he receives ample ribbing from his friends. If someone my age or younger got a job writing for *People*, they'd be envied and revered, not teased. Same goes for getting a lucrative job in corporate America, or even doing endorsements. Reid and Marcia, the thirtysomething founders of www.cuddleparty.com, say on their website that they are "completely willing to sell themselves out, as long as it's to someone fun and makes us look even crazier and cooler than we already are! In particular, we would love to hear from Nutella, Apple Computers, Ben & Jerry's Ice Cream, and Bailey's Irish Cream." I got the feeling they were not kidding. For GenMe, there is no such thing as "selling out," since we never aspired to change the structure of society in the first place.

We also think there's little point in voting. Voter participation among 18-to-20-year-olds plummeted from 48% in 1972 to 28% in 2000. In other words, about half of Boomer youth born between 1952 and 1954 voted in their first election, whereas only about a quarter of GenMe youth born

Rock the Vote and MTV's *Choose or Lose* spend a great deal of
money and time encouraging voter registration among young
people. Despite these efforts, voter participation among the
young is down sharply from the late 1960s.

between 1980 and 1982 showed up at the polling place. Voter participation among those aged 21 to 24 also slid, from 51% in 1972 to 35% in
2000. Even 25-to-34-year-olds show a voting decrease larger than the average, declining from 60% in 1972 to 44% in 2000. At the same time, voter
participation for those aged 45 and older hardly changed at all. This is especially alarming because the 1972 election was a landslide victory for
Nixon, and 2000 was the closest presidential election in American history.

Youth voter turnout was, thankfully, up in 2004. Forty-one percent of
18-to-20-year-olds voted in that election, probably due to a massive get-
out-the-vote effort on college campuses. Twenty-one-to-24-year-olds also
increased their participation, to 43%, although 25-to-34-year-olds barely
changed from 2000 (going up to 47% from 44%). These rates still do not
equal Boomer voter participation during their youth in the early 1970s,
but the upswing suggests that the tide may be starting to turn toward more
voting among young people. Yet the older third of GenMe is still voting
at a consistently lower rate than previous generations did at the same ages.
If you believe that there's nothing you can do to change the government,
this behavior makes sense. Why vote? It's not going to make a difference,
and all politicians are liars anyway. As a study by People for the American
Way concluded, "Young people have learned only half of America's story.
[They value] notions of America's unique character that emphasize freedom and license . . . [but] fail to perceive a need to reciprocate by exercis-

ing the duties and responsibilities of good citizenship." Grace, the Boomer-age professor on *Jack & Bobby*, says that when she was young "we didn't need Rock the Vote or Drew Barrymore to get us to the polls. We went because it was important." A little self-righteous—we've heard that before from Boomers—but it's definitely true that young people today have a noticeable lack of motivation to vote.

We also lack faith in government and politicians. The days when people believed we could eliminate poverty and war are long gone, and every year of GenMe's life seems to bring a new political scandal. We are too young to remember a pre-Watergate world when politicians could be trusted. Instead, our views of politicians have been shaped by Iran Contra, the Clinton-Lewinsky scandal, and the futile search for weapons of mass destruction in Iraq. "I have been lied to all my life," says Ana, 17. "My government is corrupt and evil." Yet we don't believe we can do much to change that.

Nor do we have any faith that government institutions will come through for us. When I was in graduate school, I remember seeing a headline in the newspaper that said, "More Young People Believe in UFOs than in Social Security Surviving." That pretty much sums it up.

NO CONTROL ON THE BIG-SCREEN TV

Media exposure probably explains a large part of the increase in externality. News broadcasts in the early 1960s were confined to a fifteen-minute evening segment. Can you imagine—only fifteen minutes of TV news? Now, of course, four national cable channels cover the news twenty-four hours a day, and the networks have not only the daily thirty-minute broadcast but three-hour morning shows and several hours of local news every day.

Of course, a lot of news coverage has turned to fluff about celebrities, television shows (starring celebrities), and movies (sometimes starring celebrities playing celebrities). Yet the "big" news stories—the ones to which CNN, FOX News, and MSNBC will devote twenty-four hours a day—are almost always bad news, and they're almost always events that the average viewer cannot control. At the beginning of 2005, for example, the tsunami in Asia dominated news broadcasts; a viewer could, if he wished, watch giant waves sweeping people away almost twenty-four hours a day. Don't like that? You can also see pictures of the survivors, mostly cut and bruised children who are now orphans. The events of September 11, 2001, of course, produced similarly horrifying images, as did the aftermath of Hurricane Katrina. And it's not just these large disasters; media outlets' other favorite stories include plane crashes, murders of pregnant women, child abductions, stock market crashes. Sitting in their living rooms, modern citizens may increasingly feel that they belong to a huge, complex, confusing, and terrible world that is utterly beyond their control to change.

Media saturation has had an impact on GenMe. Not that long ago, many older folks thought that young people were idealistic and willing to believe the best of people. But that was before 8-year-olds wanted to know what oral sex was, since the president was being impeached for it. Or why some people hate Americans so much that they used airplanes to kill thousands of people, or why we went to war in Iraq when they had no weapons of mass destruction. It's not just that these events happened—sex scandals and wars have occurred in every generation—but that their every detail is exposed on television. As author Neil Postman notes, "From the child's point of view, what is mostly shown on television is the plain fact that the adult world is filled with ineptitude, strife, and worry."

It's just one part in the larger trend of "kids growing up too fast." Along with adult information and adult themes, they've also managed to absorb the cynicism that once came only with age. Some of this is simple self-protection brought on by information overload—much of it false and not to be believed. When we're not watching TV, we're on the Internet, sometimes on traditional news offshoots like cnn.com, but other times trolling through places where we have to wear our skepticism cap at every moment. We have learned not to forward the e-mail that says doing so will contribute money to help a child dying of cancer (it's a hoax). We know that e-mails with the subjects "I love you" or "Your prescription has expired" are a computer virus and spam for Viagra, respectively, and can be deleted without being opened. We know that your friend's aunt's hairdresser did not put her poodle in the microwave to dry it off (and if we believed it for a second, we confirmed it wasn't true on the Urban Legends reference pages on snopes.com). We are suspicious of anyone who calls on the phone and wants to sell us something. We don't believe for a second that the "tests" in laundry detergent ads are true (and haven't ever since third grade, when Carol Channing's piece in *Free to Be You and Me* informed us that the lady in the ad "is smiling because she's an *actress*, and she's earning *money* for learning those speeches"). Says Ryan Beckwith, interviewed in *What Really Happened to the Class of '93*: "We're constantly being bombarded with bullshit." Author Chris Colin concludes that this bombardment "now infects with such constancy, over so many channels, that it no longer even registers as sickness; through sheer proliferation, the bullshit bombardment gets reified into the norm."

Prime example: the "fake news" outlets like Jon Stewart's *Daily Show* or the satirical newspaper the *Onion* that are so popular among young people. We enjoy knowing that it's false—at least it's funny and entertaining. The fake aspect also allows us to flex the cynicism muscles we're so generationally proud of ("My mom saw that *Onion* story and thought it was true! Can you believe that?"). Then there's the other trend in journalism, the Paris Hilton beat, or what's generally known as "infotainment." We grew up on the "tabloid" shows of the 1990s like *Hard Copy* and *A Current Affair* (complete with the triangle making that "whump!" noise), and now even regular news outlets have taken up the cause of celebrity watching. Both trends expose the cynical attitude of GenMe. If we're not laughing about the news, we're laughing at the celebrities—a little schadenfreude directed toward the rich and famous people we'd all like to be.

SELF-ESTEEM VERSUS REALITY

Generation Me has also lost hope in our ability to make choices in our own lives. In some ways, these changed attitudes seem at odds with the focus on the self. If we see ourselves as independent individuals, why are we increasingly blaming others when things go wrong? It comes back again to the idea of self-esteem and feeling good about ourselves. Suppose that you're a student and you fail a test. If you acknowledge that you were lazy about studying—or just plain stupid—your self-esteem will suffer. If you can blame the teacher's unfair test, however, you can slide though the experience still feeling good about yourself. We say that bad things aren't our fault in an effort to preserve our self-confidence. "When there are few winners and many losers, it may be easier to protect one's sense of self-worth by not trying than to try and still not succeed," notes

an education book that argues against competition. What's the point in
trying something difficult? If we do, we might learn something—even if
it's just our own limitations. But the popular GenMe belief is to protect
the self at all costs. John, 23, says: "It makes more sense psychologically
to believe in fate. If you don't, your self-esteem will plummet each time
you fail."

A sterling example of the link between high self-esteem and making
excuses was the first episode of the British import game show *The Weakest Link*, the 2001 phenom with the cruelly singsong catchphrase, "You
are the weakest link. Goodbye." In an article titled "Amber Waves of
Self-Esteem," *Time* TV critic James Poniewozik noted that British contestants would look appropriately chastened when they lost. Americans,
in stark contrast, made excuses like "I was just getting warmed up" or
blamed their teammates' jealousy. As Poniewozik put it, "Being American means never having to say you're an idiot."

Our high self-esteem also doesn't lead us to believe we're in control
because, as one of the self-esteem programs puts it, we were taught to
value "who we are and not what we do." We're unique and special even
if we don't work hard, so why do it? Educational psychologist Maureen
Stout argues that the self-esteem movement disconnects reward from
achievement, producing cynical kids. She points out that 5- and 6-year-
olds start school eager to learn, but that "when they encounter teachers
who give them an A just for turning up in class . . . they have no choice
but to become cynical about the educative process."

And if they don't become cynical then, Stout says, they will once
they reach adulthood and discover that they have not been prepared for
the real world. This cynicism comes from the mismatch between self-
esteem and reality. GenMe is faced with an unusual set of circumstances.
From infancy, we are taught to express ourselves, to believe in ourselves,
to follow our dreams. Then we enter a world where getting into an Ivy
League university depends just as much on luck and circumstance as on
work and talent, and where even our local public university might not
admit us if we got B's in high school. The good job or the desirable pro-
motion might go to the person who works the hardest, or it might go to
the person who catches a lucky break. Our entire romantic life might
turn on the luck of meeting the right person at the right time. Even when
we decide to give it up for the day and relax, we read *People* and watch

Entertainment Tonight or ESPN to worship movie stars and athletes—our modern-day gods and goddesses who, for the most part, gained their ascendance through genes and circumstance. Our parents and teachers told us how special we were, but they skimped on the lesson that life isn't fair.

LIFE DETERMINATION BY LOTTERY

Generation Me's external beliefs are somewhat ironic considering the better health and safety we enjoy. Our generation has never been drafted to fight in a war. Life expectancy is at an all-time high, and advances in medical technology and pharmaceuticals make our lives better. Safety measures have radically improved in the last thirty years, on everything from cars to playground equipment. Can you believe that babies used to ride in cars without car seats, and that kids rode bikes without wearing helmets? Even considering the threat of terrorism, there are fewer negative, random events than in previous eras.

It's easy to take those things for granted, however, especially since this relatively safe world is the only one we have ever known. GenMe'ers focus on the things we've seen change, like the economy and the volatile job market. In an increasingly complex, competitive world, jobs and investments seem to depend more on luck than achievement. When only 5% of people are admitted to a graduate program—and most of the applicants are highly qualified—we quickly learn that luck plays a big role in our lives. The Yankelovich polling firm found that the first lesson this generation learned was "the marketplace is unpredictable. . . . you can't depend on any long-term plans." An article in *USA Today Magazine* noted that young people "seem to be less certain that hard work . . . will be rewarded with a better life and are increasingly skeptical, even cynical, about their prospects and the country in general." Or as Gaby, 20, puts it, "A typical saying in my generation is 'I was in the right/wrong place at the right/wrong time.'"

Recent college graduates find it difficult to summon up enthusiasm for the job market. "Putting in effort does not seem to be related to getting the appropriate reward," says Andrea, 22. "Getting a degree does not guarantee a stable job." Eric, 23, has the same beliefs even though he has been very successful. He described being "handed" a management job in a time-share company, making $45,000 a year when he was only 18. When the company was restructured and 75% of the employees lost their jobs, Eric says he "got lucky" and wasn't let go. Even though most of the breaks went his way, Eric says, "in truth I had nothing to do with it."

Though some of this attitude is based in realism, other members of GenMe have developed a skewed view of how success works. Perhaps because many role models on TV are actresses and athletes, becoming rich looks like a matter of luck. Apparently, some young people also believe that success in business usually happens overnight. *Generation X Goes to College* quotes Kelly, 18, who says: "Kids see people like Bill Gates who get rich out of nowhere. . . . It seems a lot of people get it that way, by not having to work. They just come into it real quick, like the lottery." Bill Gates is many things, but he's not a lottery winner; he founded a company and worked hard to make it grow. He may have been lucky, and he may have been opportunistic, but it's astonishing that anyone thinks he got rich without working.

We also realize that meeting the right person is often a matter of chance. The later age at marriage means that many of us meet our future spouses at bars or through random encounters at the gym, the park, or the grocery store. The most important relationship in our lives will probably happen because of luck. "I view the future union of myself and Mr. Right as a crapshoot over which I have no control," says Melissa, 24. Love, work, money—it's all out of our control, so why try?

THE VICTIM MENTALITY

Some GenMe'ers take things too far and make excuses when things don't go their way. Susan Peterson, who teaches at a community college in Arizona, has noticed this trend toward a lack of personal responsibility in her students. "Parents have always done [everything] for them, including choosing all their teachers in the public school system and arguing about every grade they received," she says. "As a society, we've created a new generation of young adults who blame everyone else for their failures."

In his book *A Nation of Victims*, social critic Charles Sykes argues that "the impulse to flee personal responsibility and blame others [is] deeply embedded within the American culture." It's gotten so bad, he says, that

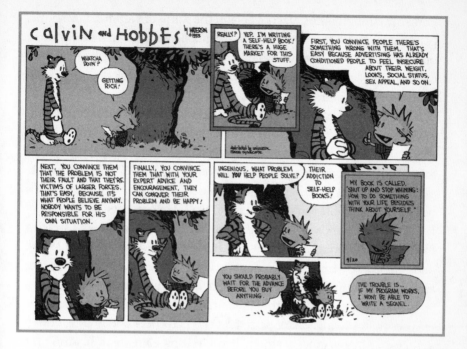

Watterson's satire of self-help books illustrates the growing popularity of blaming others for your problems, and codifies the somewhat paradoxical link between externalizing blame and focusing on yourself.

"The National Anthem has become the Whine." Other people blame a "disease" for their ineptitude—like the man who sued after getting fired for never showing up on time. It wasn't his fault, he said, because he had "chronic lateness syndrome." *The Myth of Laziness* author Mel Levine says there is no such thing as laziness—instead, people who can't get things done have "output failure." Defense attorneys will sometimes say that their clients were abused as children and thus not responsible for their actions. And of course there's always the famous Twinkie defense, that junk food and sugar are the real cause for murder. As Sykes puts it, "the plaintive cry is always the same: I am not at fault. [Fill in the Blank] made me do it."

Since the early 1990s, that blank has often been filled with "my parents," with books like *Toxic Parents* and *The Courage to Heal*. As Judith Warner points out in *Perfect Madness*, even parental insensitivity could be labeled as abuse, "which meant, essentially, that anyone with a humanly fallible parent . . . could claim the status of victim." Talk shows, psychoanalytic therapy, and books all encourage us to analyze just how our "dysfunctional family" has damaged us. *American Health* magazine commented, "Blaming parents for what they did or didn't do has become a national obsession—and big business."

Or just blame everyone. Leroy Wells, 22, a recent *American Idol* contestant, is a good example. When his audition aired on the show, he had to watch it from jail: he fired a gun into a car after getting into an argument and was promptly arrested. His brother explained, "A lot of people pick on him. He's had that problem since he was a kid." Turns out Wells had been arrested seven other times as well. He sure gets "picked on" a lot. The article ends by saying that he still wants to pursue a career in Hollywood. Although the crime rate has declined since the early 1990s, and thus fewer GenMe'ers are running afoul of the law, those who do are apparently coming up with more and more ridiculous excuses.

Corey Clark, 24, is another *American Idol* contestant more adept at excuses than singing. Clark passed several bad checks, including one to a Topeka, Kansas, grocery store. "It was during Christmas. It wasn't for me," he said. These charges and others got him kicked off the show, but he says the real reason he was dismissed is that he had an affair with Paula Abdul. Clark also made the link between self-esteem and excuses clear when he defended himself by saying, "The only person to look out for me is me. I've got to make sure Corey Clark is all right." He kept his promise: a few months later, he was arrested on a battery charge for throwing dishes at his manager.

The victim mentality is also prominently displayed in product liability lawsuits. In July 2002, for example, three New York City teenagers filed suit against McDonald's. Ranging in age from 13 to 19, all had eaten at the fast-food restaurant almost every day for years and were now severely overweight and in poor health. They blamed McDonald's for making them fat. A judge threw out the case.

Before the 1970s, lawyers considered product liability cases no-wins; they were matters of personal responsibility, and no jury would convict a corporation for the choices of an individual. In 1940, about 20,000 civil lawsuits were heard; by 1997, this had increased more than tenfold—or 1,000%—to around 210,000. In contrast, the number of criminal cases merely doubled over this same time period, suggesting that civil lawsuits increased five times faster than they should have. From 1993 to 1996 alone, product liability cases rose 82%. You don't even have to make a faulty product to get sued. One young man sued the Wake Forest University Law School because his professors used the Socratic method to question him and his classmates, which, he says, caused him fatigue and weight loss.

Many other lawsuits have become the butt of numerous jokes: the woman who sued because her coffee was too hot, or the obesity lawsuits mentioned before. It seems that when anything goes wrong, many people just want to sue whatever company is in reach. This is a foreign concept to the older generation. My uncle Charles, who owns an avocado farm, was using a trencher one weekend when he reached down too quickly and the machine cut off his thumb. Fortunately, doctors were able to reattach the digit. When he got back to work, one of his younger coworkers asked him if he was going to sue the company that made the trencher. "No!" exclaimed Charles. "It was my fault. Why would I sue them?" Although many people still share Charles's attitude, others think that it's natural to blame the product when things go wrong.

Of course, there are times when the excuses are real. "Personal responsibility," a favorite mantra of many conservatives, can't extend to cases where there is true racism, sexism, or lack of opportunity. There are true hardships and true explanations that deserve to be heard. Chris Colin was heartened when his politically conservative classmate John Doyle readily acknowledged that the playing field isn't always level. "Hard work is still the fundamental element of success, but some people, based on their situation, their circumstances, can work as hard as they want, but unless somebody steps in and gives them that boost . . . they're not gonna get to that level. And to say that they can . . . is foolish."

AN EDUCATION IN EXCUSES

The victim mentality arises full force in schools, where teachers often bear the brunt of these attitudes. Many public school teachers have told me that parents blame them when their children don't do well in school. Arguing over grades has become commonplace, perhaps because of the self-esteem curriculum and the "you can do anything" mentality. "Kids today have extremely high expectations," one student said. "And if they receive a D or an F, it always winds up being the teacher's fault somehow."

In *Generation X Goes to College*, Peter Sacks describes students who wouldn't show up for class or do the required assignments and then would complain when their grades suffered. One student who turned in abysmally written papers complained to the administration about Sacks's "tough grading." Another student asked if she still had to do a restaurant review assignment because "I've had a cold all week, and so I don't have any taste buds."

Sacks reports with irony that he had to throw out his "traditional approach to higher education whereby teachers assume students take responsibility for their decisions." He is not alone. "Students who receive a C, D, or F on a test or paper tend to hold the teacher personally responsible," said Daniel Kazez, a professor of music, in a letter to the editor in *Newsweek*. In his 2005 book *I'm the Teacher, You're the Student*, Emory University professor Patrick Allitt describes dealing with "those who didn't fulfill their assignments, or who plagiarized, and are now casting about angrily for someone to blame." Even "I meant to do that" has apparently become a worthwhile excuse. After Sacks pointed out some awkward passages in a student's writing, the student claimed, "Sometimes I like to write awkwardly. It livens up the material and doesn't make it boring."

Misbehavior is also explained away with excuses. In her 2003 book *Not Much Just Chillin': The Hidden Lives of Middle Schoolers*, Linda Perlstein reports that the most commonly uttered sentence at Wilde Lake Middle School is, "But I didn't do anything!" When students are asked why they were sent to the office, they say things like "Because Mrs. Wright blamed me for talking and I wasn't even talking." Youthful excuse making was probably common in other generations as well, but back then, parents took the teacher's side. Now, Perlstein reports, parents don't back up the teachers more than half the time. One veteran seventh-grade social studies teacher says, "I'm tired of the kids talking back, the parents talking back, the lack of interest in learning."

This is the new wrinkle: it's not just the kids who are defiant and argumentative—it's also the parents. *Time* magazine recently ran a cover story called "What Teachers Hate About Parents." Teachers described parents who specified that their children were not to be corrected or "emotionally upset," who argued incessantly about grades, and even one father who, after his daughter was reprimanded, challenged a teacher to a fist-fight. In a study conducted by Met Life, new teachers ranked handling parents as their most challenging task. Parents can also take the victim mentality to new heights. One set of parents sued a school that expelled their kids for cheating, saying that a teacher had left the exam on a desk, making it easy to steal it. (In other words, it's the teacher's fault that my kid cheated and was expelled.) Teachers will see this attitude more and more as GenMe has their own kids and believes that they couldn't possibly do anything wrong either.

Scott McLeod, the headmaster at a private school in New Orleans, has witnessed this trend firsthand. "The parents' willingness to intercede on the kids' behalf, to take the kids' side, to protect the kid, in a not healthy way—there's much more of that each year," he said in a *New York Times Magazine* article. Outside of school, some runaway parents apply these principles to sports as well; thus the increasingly common image of the soccer mom or dad yelling at the coach to let their kid play. And if the kid isn't any good? It's the coach's fault. McLeod sees it at his school; if parents "see their kid fail—if he's only on the J.V., or the coach is yelling at him—somehow the school is responsible for that." The rest of the article goes on to describe the parents' dissatisfaction with a coach who told it straight and didn't let kids get off by making excuses. Alums say that the coach made them men and want to name the gym after him; current parents think he's too hard on the kids because he "yelled" at them when they didn't do what they promised to do. With the older generation of gruff coaches rapidly retiring, parents will soon have less to complain about, but their kids will be cheated out of a character-building experience they would never have forgotten.

Some critics, like Sykes in a *Nation of Victims*, argue that the growing list of learning disabilities and behavioral disorders are another example of creating victimhood. Sykes and others maintain that these labels get parents off the hook—they can avoid admitting that their child is badly behaved or just not that smart. Between 7% and 15% of children are now categorized as "learning disabled," a term that did not exist thirty years ago (back then they may have been called "slow learners," a more pejorative and less diagnostic term). Although many psychologists and learning-disabled kids find the diagnoses helpful, definitions have been difficult to pin down and tests for learning disabilities have been hotly debated. Critics of learning disabilities argue that the diagnoses are a way to blame a child's poor academic performance on external factors. Some parents also abuse the labels, finding a doctor to say that their child is "exceptionally bright but with a learning difference" so they can have more time to take tests and thus do better.

Behavior problems are also labeled more often. By 1994, almost 5% of all children were diagnosed as having attention deficit/hyperactivity disorder (ADHD), and by 1996, 75% of these children were on Ritalin. And maybe these kids didn't need to blame a disease for their behavior—maybe they were just being kids. "What if Tom Sawyer or Huckleberry Finn were to walk into my office tomorrow?" asks Dr. Lawrence Diller, author of Running on Ritalin. "Tom's indifference to schooling and Huck's oppositional behavior would surely have been cause for concern."

No matter what your position on disorders like learning disabilities and ADHD, it's clear that these diagnoses were not as common just a few decades ago. Whether it's a good thing or a bad thing, assigning labels and explanations for kids' errant behaviors has become commonplace. We are now more likely to believe that behavior is determined by uncontrollable forces—although, sometimes, we can control them with Ritalin.

CONSEQUENCES OF EXTERNALITY AND CYNICISM

In many ways, these externalizing and cynical beliefs are adaptive; they help protect the self-esteem of GenMe in an increasingly difficult world. But too much cynicism and alienation can be self-defeating: why study for a test if it's going to be unfair? Why vote or learn about politics if it's not going to do any good? The startling growth of these attitudes goes a long way toward explaining the apathy and inaction so common today. With college and work getting more competitive, the trend toward externality (believing things are out of your control) is likely to continue. Teens who have been told their whole lives that they are special will desperately try to protect their self-esteem, and many will choose cynicism as their armor of choice.

Unfortunately, psychologists are virtually unanimous in their con-demnation of externality. This is somewhat stunning, as psychologists consider most traits and beliefs to be normal variations, with no "right" or "wrong" answers. But on externality, the research is definitive. People who believe that outside forces determine their fate are more likely to be depressed and anxious and cope poorly with stress. As we saw in the last chapter, GenMe displays record high levels of anxiety and depression. Believing that you don't have control might be part of the reason. If nothing you do matters, it's easy to give in to lethargy and despair. Psy-chologists call it learned helplessness.

Externality also doesn't bode well for keeping it together and staying out of trouble. Perhaps because they don't think their actions will have consequences, externals have weakened self-control and an inability to delay gratification. They are less likely to work hard today to get a reward tomorrow—an especially important skill these days, when many good jobs require graduate degrees. Externality and low self-control are also correlated with the impulsive actions that tend to get young people into trouble, like shoplifting, fighting, or having unprotected sex.

Another overwhelming stack of research finds that externals consis-tently achieve less in school, which makes sense, as externals believe that there's no point in studying. Having an internal feeling of control—believing that you can change your fate—is especially important for underprivileged children. A definitive report concluded that feelings of control were a better predictor of school achievement in minority chil-dren than *any other variable*.

The consequences for society as a whole are alarming. If everyone believes that nothing can be changed, that prophecy is likely to be self-fulfilling. And if we blame others for our problems, we might never make the changes we need to improve as people (sorry to sound like a Baby Boomer). As Robert Putnam argues in *Bowling Alone*, we are rapidly heading for a society low in the critical social capital it needs to grow. GenMe's concerns will be ignored if we do not get involved in politics and social change.

Julian Rotter, the author of the control scale I studied, began to real-ize in the 1970s that people were increasingly feeling that things were out of their control. The trend was in its infancy then, but Rotter knew what to look for, and he wasn't happy. "Our society has so many critical problems that it desperately needs as many active, participating, internal-minded members as possible," he wrote in *Psychology Today*. "If feelings of external control, alienation and powerlessness continue to grow, we may be heading for a society of dropouts—each person sitting back, watching the world go by." Dr. Rotter, welcome to my world. Whatever.

6

Sex: Generation Prude Meets
Generation Crude

I n Valerie Frankel's recent novel *The Not-So-Perfect Man*, 40-year-old
Peter asks out a 23-year-old woman. She replies,

> "I can't go out with you, Peter . . . you seem like the kind of guy
> who wants a relationship. I don't do that. I hook up."
> "Hooking up?" he asked. It sounded painful.
> "Going out in groups of girls, and picking up groups of guys, tak-
> ing them back to someone's apartment and having safe-yet-casual
> sex," she said. "I think I'm leaning toward lesbianism anyway. And
> even if I were attracted to you, I couldn't do much about it until my
> labial piercings heal."
> "Labial piercings," he said.
> "Four of them. Two on each side. Very tasteful. Refined," she said.
> Peter checked his watch, straightened his tie, cleared his throat.
> He said, "I'll be going now."

In case you haven't heard, "hooking up" has replaced dating among many
young people, even among those *without* tasteful labial piercings. A May
2004 *New York Times Magazine* article on teens hooking up got tongues
wagging about the practice, and the hookup scored its first book in *The
Happy Hook-Up: A Single Girl's Guide to Casual Sex*. It was soon followed
by *The Hookup Handbook*, which notes that hookups can range from
"making out to full-on sex" but are most distinguished by being "between
two people who don't necessarily have any foreseeable future or even a
hint of commitment."

Another new term is "friends with benefits," or a friend you do sexual things with—no romantic relationship or commitment implied. "I think you can compare friends with benefits to the driving range," says Sam, 16, interviewed for a 2005 NBC special on teens and sex. "There's no commitment to playing a round of golf—you just go there to work on your game, figure out what shots are working for you." (Casual golf, anyone?)

Or take Kristen, 21, who says, "I lost my virginity at the age of 13. But I would like to mention how mature I was about sex in general. I should be applauded, not shunned."

This is not your father's sex life—and it's *definitely* not your mother's. Hooking up is increasingly common, and even sex within boyfriend-girlfriend relationships begins at younger and younger ages. Waiting for marriage is, to put it mildly, quaint. The vast majority of Generation Me does not wait until they are married to have sex. Most do not even wait to graduate from high school. Emma, now 24, lost her virginity at 17 "to a boy I could just barely call my boyfriend." She explains, "No one I knew believed in waiting for marriage." Some of this is simple demographics: 62% of people in their 20s have never been married.

Even religious teenagers with strict parents soon find themselves sexually active. Patrick, 31, grew up in a strict Catholic family and attended a Catholic high school, but, he says, "I lost my virginity at the age of 17 to a girl I had known only a week." Things changed even more once he lived in a college dorm: "I found myself having more sexual partners and not feeling guilty about a one-night stand," he says. Or as a girl put it on the NBC special, "Our generation is supposed to be known as the wild one anyway. It's been the wildest one yet." Is this trend good or bad? Your opinion may depend on your generation. Many young people see these trends as the long-overdue shedding of arbitrary restrictions on sexuality, while some older people are often shocked by the sexual behavior of the young.

Whether you see the new sexuality as freeing or wanton, the tie to individualism is obvious: do what feels good for you, and ignore the rules of society. On the other hand, the changes in sexual behavior are so dramatic that it's not clear there are any universally agreed-upon rules about sex anymore. Why not do something pleasurable? It's your body—express yourself. Or as an ad for the birth control method Mirena puts it, "All you'll remember is the freedom" when you "put yourself in control." In a 1999 survey, college students' primary motivations for having casual sex were exploration or experimentation, satisfying their own feelings of sexual desire, and "spontaneous urge." Sonia, 21, believes that "different sexual behaviors bring more awareness and more confidence about yourself." Sometimes self-esteem comes in handy for reappraising things later. In their *Class of 2000* report, CBS interviewed one young woman who slept with three boys by the time she was 15. However, she says, "I don't regard myself as a slut because I have more self-respect than that."

Even deciding not to have sex is informed by the integrity of the self. In a 1999 episode of the college drama *Felicity*, the title character debates whether to have sex with her boyfriend. Her friend advises, "Our best decisions, the ones we never regret, come from listening to ourselves. And whatever you decide, you should be very proud." A *Glamour* magazine article advises, "Keep in mind that postponing sex until it's right for you—regardless of what anyone thinks—means you know your own mind." In her book *Her Way: Young Women Remake the Sexual Revolution*, Paula Kamen concludes, "In our individualistic American culture, that standard of being true to oneself is the driving force behind young women's sexual decisions." When Kamen asked young women about sexual choices (and life choices), their most common answer was "it depends on the person."

When I asked my students to write about differences among the generations, most chose changes in sexual behavior. It's one of the most noticeable changes in the lives of young people over the last few decades. Perhaps because of the trend toward openness, my students had no problem writing at length about when, where, and how they had sex and how comfortable they were with it. And how uncomfortable their parents were—even though most of their parents are Boomers.

GIVING IT UP

The 1960s might have been called the Sexual Revolution, but apparently they were just the beginning. For her master's thesis with me, Brooke Wells gathered data on sexual behavior and attitudes from research reports on 269,649 young people collected over four decades—

the most comprehensive study ever done of change over time in sexual behavior. Both men's and women's sexual behavior shifted with time, but the changes for women were the most striking. In the late 1960s, the average young woman lost her virginity at age 18; by the late 1990s, the average was 15. In other words, Boomers started having sex in college, while GenMe started having sex in high school. "Most people had the 'everybody's doing it' mentality in high school," says Miranda, 20. Other large studies of sexual behavior have found similar results. A 1990s study found that teenage girls lose their virginity at the same age that boys do, and today's young women were twice as likely as Boomers to have had multiple sex partners by age 18.

That's partially because Boomers had less time to rack up a long list of conquests: in 1970, the average woman was 20.8 years old when she married for the first time. So even at the height of the hippie years, almost half of Boomer women getting married for the first time were teenagers! In 1970, only 36% of women aged 20 to 24 had never been married; by 2000, that had more than doubled, to 73%. The average age at first marriage for men was 23.2 in 1970, which is now considered shockingly young for a man to marry. Clearly, even college-age "Free Love" was experienced by only a minority of Boomers, while for GenMe sex in high school is the majority experience. An Oregon high school sophomore interviewed by CBS puts it this way: "Sex is something that everyone does except for, like, the pope and Mother Teresa." Another sophomore added, "I don't think it's wrong to have sex when you're fourteen or so. Your body's ready, so why isn't it right?"

This has created a noticeable generation gap. Many students told me that sex was not even discussed in their household. "All of our parents would have heart attacks if we told them we had sex," says Bill, 19. "My mom won't even let a boy and girl share the same bed if they aren't married." Allissa, 22, agrees. "My parents found my diary a few years back and freaked out," she says. "It is hard to live in a generation where sexuality is acceptable, and have parents from a generation where it's not. All you can do is live life according to your generation, because it is all you know." Andy, 20, says, "From frat houses to the White House, there's no denying that sex is present everywhere. Everywhere but my parents' house, that is!"

All of my students who wrote about sex confessed to losing their virginity in high school—15 and 16 were the usual ages mentioned, though 12 and 14 also came up. And the same was true among their friends. Jose, 21, said his parents were very upset when he confessed that he'd had sex. "The majority of my friends had already lost their virginity after freshman year of high school," he says. "This was my sophomore year. I just assumed they knew."

Will this trend continue for GenMe'ers just now reaching adolescence? It's difficult to say. On the one hand, many high school students' lives are more structured now, and parents are more restrictive about teens' movements. The trend toward hooking up, however, seems well entrenched and suggests that more and more young people will dissociate sex from romance. This might not be entirely bad, given the devastating nature, and virtual inevitability, of the average high school breakup. If relationships are on the way out, fewer girls will feel pressure to have sex. It is difficult to see the average age of first sexual experience going any lower than 15, but it's possible.

WAITING UNTIL MARRIAGE? ARE YOU KIDDING?

Brooke's comprehensive study also showed a radical shift in attitudes. In the late 1950s, only 30% of young people approved of sex before marriage; now 75% approve. The change in attitudes was even more striking among young women: only 12% approved of premarital sex in the 1950s, compared with 80% now. Just as earlier generations found it somewhat shocking to hear about premarital sex, GenMe is shocked by the lack of it. Many ask how you'd know if you were sexually compatible with someone if you didn't have sex before you got married. "You wouldn't buy a car you haven't test driven, would you?" asks Emily, 25. Angela, 23, uses a similar analogy: "Not having sex with your future husband is like not trying on clothes before you buy them."

In a recent poll, 84% of single women with a college education agreed that "it is common these days for people my age to have sex just for fun and not expect any commitment beyond the encounter itself." Elaine, 24, certainly agrees. "Premarital sex is a must for me," she explains. "Sex is like anything else—it takes practice. The more practice, the more we feel at ease with the act and with ourselves." Felicita, 19, says, "I strongly disagree with people who say it is not morally correct to have sex before marriage. Marriage is a promise, but all promises can be broken. Marriage should not be the reason why someone chooses to have sex—love should be."

In its Summer 2004 issue, *Brides* magazine polled its readers with the question, "Are you planning to stop having sex before the wedding?" Only 6% of brides said they had not yet had sex with their fiancé at all; 24% were taking a break for a month before the wedding; another 24% were taking a few weeks off. The most common answer, at 46%, was "Are you kidding?"

Christina, 23, has been married for a year. "I don't see having premarital sex as a problem," she says. "As a married woman, I am actually happier knowing that I have experienced other people and I won't spend the rest of my life wondering what someone other than my husband might have been like." Christina's attitude is typical for GenMe women, who approach sex similarly to the way men do. Today's young women are not afraid to pursue sexual pleasure and are very assertive in going after what they want.

Author Paula Kamen studied magazines for young women (like *Cosmopolitan* and *Glamour*) and concluded that they were "unabashedly pro-sex for women. Their lack of shame in speaking candidly about a wide array of fears, experiences, and pleasures delivers a strong message to readers. The effect of such confident articles is ultimately to fight the age-old double standard for women." Many young women scour these magazines for sex advice, and the general message is it's your body, have fun, and do whatever you want to do.

What about those abstinence pledges you hear so much about? They don't work. A whopping 88% of teens who take abstinence pledges have sexual intercourse before marriage. These teens do tend to wait about a year and a half longer to have sex, and had fewer partners. However, participants in abstinence programs were less likely to use condoms and thus more likely to acquire sexually transmitted diseases like chlamydia or HIV.

High school students who make these pledges often forget them completely once they get to college and enter the world that Tom Wolfe portrays in his college sex romp *I Am Charlotte Simmons*. "My freshman year in college, only two of the fifteen girls I knew were still virgins. Now in our junior year neither of those girls is," says Lindsay, 20. Just about every aspect of college culture encourages sex: fraternity parties with abundant booze, the exhilaration of being free from prying parental eyes, the easy availability of partners in a coed dorm. At the University of Texas at Austin, there's a fountain with a stone sculpture of three leaping horses. Students joke that the horses will take off and fly when a virgin graduates. Let's just say that the horses are still there.

"My only friend who always claimed he was going to wait until marriage lost his virginity about a month ago," says Lisa, 21. "The guy had talked and talked about how special it was going to be, and then he just decided to do it! And not even with a girlfriend but with a friend." Afterward, he described it as "not that big a deal." Lisa concludes, "And that's what sex is today to so many teenagers, not that big a deal."

But sex is, of course, quite a bit of fun to talk about. Many Boomers are struck by how today's young people are so comfortable talking about sex. We know all the terms, and can say them with little embarrassment (except sometimes when talking to our parents). Perhaps because GenMe has grown up in a time of more relaxed gender roles, many of us have talked about sexual topics with friends of the other sex. Girls can ask boys what makes them get an erection, and boys can ask girls what turns them on. And, guys, you wouldn't believe what women talk about with each other. An amazon.com review of *Her Way* refers to the "enormous chasm" between generations of women in talking about sex. When Barbara Walters interviewed Monica Lewinsky in 1999, Walters asked, "And there were things that were done that made you as a woman happy and content?" As the review puts it, "It took women under 40 a few moments before they realized to what Walters was so coyly referring. The women of Generation (Se)X don't talk to each other like that. Even in public. They are a lot more explicit."

THE NEW THIRD BASE

Many other sexual behaviors are also now more common. Oral sex is now sometimes called "the new third base." Numerous newspaper stories have covered a supposed epidemic of oral sex among 12- and 13-year-olds in middle schools. Many kids say that oral sex is common by eighth or ninth grade. In the NBC special, 13-to-17-year-olds agreed that oral sex was "casual" and "not a big deal—it's not sex." If that phrase sounds familiar, recall that these kids were in elementary school when President Clinton was impeached: they learned a lot more in third grade than just their multiplication tables.

The results from our comprehensive study confirm that oral sex has become more popular, a trend that began long before anyone had ever heard of Monica Lewinsky. In the late 1960s, only 42% of high school and college-age women had engaged in oral sex. By the 1990s, 71% had. Another national survey found that this percentage increases even more once women leave college, with 83% engaging in oral sex.

Oral sex was commonplace when I was in college in the early 1990s. Sarah, who lived across the hall from my friend Beth, told us she gave her boyfriend oral sex five times a day. This was probably a record for its frequency, but the act itself raised no eyebrows. It was perhaps appropriate that the dorm we lived in was called Burton-Judson, usually referred to as BJ. If our parents had known about this, they would have fallen to the floor in a dead faint. When Beth went home for the summer, her mother had a somewhat belated "sex talk" with her. Her mother advised that it was best to wait until after college to have intercourse, and then said, "And oral sex—that's just disgusting," wrinkling up her nose in genuine revulsion. Beth stared at her, amazed, trying very hard not to laugh. She also hoped her mother never met Sarah.

One of the first—and perhaps the only—movies to deal honestly with oral sex was 1994's *Clerks*. College student Veronica confesses to her boyfriend, a store clerk named Dante, that she's had oral sex with thirty-seven guys, though she's only had sex (meaning intercourse) with three. It's clear that oral sex is not a big deal to her, but Dante is upset. "My girlfriend's sucked thirty-seven dicks!" he complains to a customer. "In a row?" the customer asks. When Veronica leaves, Dante shouts, "Try not to suck any dick on the way through the parking lot!"

Of course, oral sex in college seems quaint now that 12-year-olds are doing it in junior high school bathrooms. Actually, most kids aren't having oral sex; the NBC/*People* poll found that 27% of teens ages 13 to 16 have engaged in some type of intimate sexual activity—41% of 15- and 16-year olds, and 14% of 13- and 14-year-olds. But even 14% is a large number when you're talking about kids who are in seventh, eighth, and ninth grades. And kids who aren't doing it still know what it is. Linda Perlstein, the author of *Not Much Just Chillin'*, relates seeing a note passed in a seventh-grade class that said, "I want to give you oral sex. I really want to suck on your head." The recent novel *Rainbow Party* describes a gathering at which high school girls put on different shades of lipstick and provide oral sex to several guys, thus forming a rainbow at the base of the boy's penis. Because the book was aimed at the teenage market, there was an uproar from adults about whether this was appropriate for teens to read, and whether "rainbow parties" were actually common among teens or not. That's hard to say, but it is clear that oral sex is popular among teens because it can't get you pregnant and it's seen as less serious than sexual intercourse. That trend is likely to continue.

Yet you do have to wonder what's in it for the young women (as oral sex is almost always female-on-male instead of the other way around). When Katie Couric posed this question to the girls gathered for the NBC special, several answered "self-esteem." Giving oral sex to guys, they said, helped them become popular and feel good about themselves. So not only does sex satisfy the needs of the self, but oral sex performed on someone else does, too. I'm not sure I believe it, though—this sounds like self-esteem being used as an excuse. It's tough to see how something so one-sided could truly make you feel better about yourself.

However, more women are also receiving oral sex. Few women of earlier generations asked for this from men, and many didn't even know what it was. In Alfred Kinsey's studies in the 1950s, only 3% of the young women had received oral sex from a man. By the mid-1990s, however, 75% of women aged 18 to 24 had experienced cunnilingus. Music videos by female artists have contributed to the trend, with both Mary J. Blige and Janet Jackson heavily implying male-on-female oral sex in music videos by pushing down on a man's head until he's in exactly the right position.

HOOKING UP

The most striking shift in teenage and twentysomething sexual behavior in the last decade is the disconnect between sex and emotional involvement. A recent article in the *New York Times Magazine* by Benoit Denizet-Lewis detailed the new pastime of "hooking up," or casual, unattached sex or fooling around. Dating and boyfriend-girlfriend relationships, it noted, were out. "Most of the teenagers I spoke to could think of only a handful of serious couples at their school," Denizet-Lewis noted. One guy with a girlfriend said that his friends made him feel like a "loser" for being in a relationship. Teens believe that "high school is no place for romantic relationships. They're complicated, messy, and invariably painful. Hooking up, when done 'right,' is exciting, sexually validating and efficient." Heather, 24, neatly summarizes the generational change. "Once, sex was something you did with your husband, then it was what you did with the person you love, and now it is more for recreational purposes," she says.

Older adults may be surprised by the idea of sex as "recreation," as if it were tennis or jogging. But many young people see relationships as too emotionally fraught, a dangerous world of feelings and closeness. "Guys can get so annoying when you start dating them," says Caity, 14, in the NYTM article. Young people's behavior and beliefs reinforce the shift toward casual, or at least nonrelationship, sex. In the NBC/People poll, almost half of young teens said that their sexual contact was outside of a relationship. A 2001 study found that 60% of high school juniors who'd had sex had done it with someone who was no more than a friend. In 2004, almost half of college freshmen agreed that "if two people really like each other, it's all right for them to have sex even if they've known each other for only a very short time."

Boys seem especially thrilled with this state of affairs. "Being in a real relationship just complicates everything. You feel obligated to be all, like, couply. And that gets really boring after a while," says Brian, 16, in the NYTM article. "When you're friends with benefits, you go over, hook up, then play video games or something. It rocks." If the girl wants to date you, some guys say, you simply stop "hooking up." Says high school student Haris, "Now that it's easy to get sex outside of relationships, guys don't need relationships."

That often means more sex partners—a lot more sex partners. Jack, now 20, wrote that he was popular in high school and had sex with sixteen girls before he turned 18. Denizet-Lewis found that this was one of the reasons boys disdained steady relationships: it kept them from sleeping with many different girls. Boys would only date if they weren't hot enough to get lots of girls. Or, as a character on Law & Order: SVU put it, "Only ugly people date."

The Hookup Handbook provides a more lighthearted look at the sexual mores of the new millenium. Young authors Andrea Lavinthal and Jessica Rozler say that hooking up has definitely replaced dating, which, they say, "has gone the way of the dinosaurs, eight-track players, and stir-rup pants. Extinct. Vanished. Kaput." Features of the hookup, they say, often include "drunk dialing" (what used to be known as a "booty call") and "the walk of shame," which is what happens when you have to walk home from his place the next morning still wearing your attire from the night before: "a boobalicious top, a skintight pair of jeans (or an ass-cheek-exposing miniskirt), open-toed shoes, and a teeny-tiny purse that barely fits a tampon." Types of hookups include "The Fall-Down-Drunk Hookup," "Oops, I Did It Again (The Ex-boyfriend)," and "The Snuffle-upagus" ("The hookup you deny but everyone else knows really exists"). Occasionally, a series of hookups with the same guy leads to a relation-ship and skips the dating stage entirely. One woman says she knew she and her hookup were finally in a relationship when "they just hung out at his apartment and watched TV instead of going out, getting drunk, and hooking up."

Hooking up has been facilitated by technology like the Internet and cell phones. It's pretty simple—if you're a teenager, you can meet lots of people online, and then you ring them on their cells so you don't have to talk to their parents. Or if you're in your twenties, you can call your potential hookup even if he's blocks away at another bar. As *The Hookup Handbook* puts it, "if we didn't have these instant forms of communica-tion (like text messaging and IM), hooking up would be dating because you'd actually have to put more than just minimal effort into making something happen." The Internet helps too, with its myriad hookup sites. Thousands of options are at the click of a mouse, many with pictures and erotic banter in a quick little profile.

All of this means a whole lot of fun. Think about it: you can make out with that cute guy in the bar or the guy from your psych class, and nobody has to worry about who's going to call whom the next day. It's acceptable to hook up with someone you'd never actually date, so you can satisfy your urges with younger guys (what *The Hookup Handbook* calls "Pass the sippy cup"), cute but dumb guys, older guys, whatever. There's no turning down dates for Saturday if they're not made by Wednesday, no rules about how many dates you have to go on before you're "allowed" to kiss him or have sex with him. Just do what you want to do—how many other generations of women (or men) have had that privilege? As *The Hookup Handbook* notes in its very last line, "Your mother never had this much fun."

ART IMITATES LIFE, OR VICE VERSA?

Sex outside of marriage is, of course, very common on TV and in movies. Bed hopping fueled the plots of many episodes of *Friends* and *Seinfeld*, not to mention *Sex and the City*. "It was no big deal to me or my friends that we had sex before we were married," said David, 19. "We see it on TV and in the movies all the time." Monica, 16, said on the *Today* show, "If you just turn on MTV one day you're going to see sex everywhere."

Portrayals of teen sex have become more common and accepted in the two decades since the first wave of GenMe'ers were teens. Most 1980s movies showed teenagers talking about sex, but not actually doing it. In 1985's *The Breakfast Club*, one character claims she slept with her therapist, but then later admits she made that up. Another says that he slept with a girl, but "you don't know her—she lives in Canada." But this is just a lame lie—he's actually a virgin.

By the late 1990s, the high school students on *Dawson's Creek* were actually having sex—one of them with his 36-year-old English teacher. Most of the kids on *Beverly Hills, 90210* had sex, too. Donna said she wanted to wait for marriage, but, as 21-year-old Kathy put it, "everyone else thought she was crazy." Of course, Donna gave it up eventually, and before marriage. The 1999 movie *American Pie* is about four high school seniors who aim to get laid before they graduate, and all of them do (after, of course, the famous sex-with-a-pie scene).

Postmillennial shows like the current teen soap *The O.C.* portray teen sex as commonplace and relatively casual. Ryan talks about hookups at parties. Seth and Summer, both 16, have sex even though they have never been on a date together. Summer confesses to Seth afterward that she was a virgin, explaining that she didn't tell him before because "I had this reputation to uphold, and I figured you'd think less of me or something." Not so long ago, a high school girl with a "reputation" was a bad thing—now it's a good thing. This is art imitating life; according to Tunesia, 16, interviewed on the *Today* show, "any publicity is good publicity when it comes to girls and sex."

But life also imitates art quite a bit. A 2004 study of almost 2,000 teens found that those who watch TV with a lot of sexual content are twice as likely to engage in intercourse as those who watch less. "The impact of television viewing is so large that even a moderate shift in the sexual content of adolescent TV watching could have a substantial effect on their sexual behavior," said Rebecca Collins, the study's lead author. Watching sexually explicit TV led to teens having sex two to three years earlier, with media-savvy 13-year-olds acting the same as more sheltered 15- or 16-year-olds. Another study found that young black women who watch many rap music videos are more likely to have multiple sex partners and to acquire a sexually transmitted disease.

Fashion reflects the shift toward freer sexuality. Although it makes me feel old to say it, girls did not wear belly-exposing shirts when I was in high school in the late 1980s. Well into the mid-1990s, the fashion was to wear big, blousy shirts (gather round, children, and let me tell you about the wonderful days of stirrup pants). This look covered your body pretty well, which is perhaps why it's now so out of fashion. Now the style is the more skin, the better, and bonus if your T-shirt says something provocative. Thirteen-year-old Maya, interviewed for a 2005 *People* magazine story, said she's going to "wait until I'm 20" to have sex. In the picture accompanying the article, however, she's wearing a T-shirt ripped into a V-neckline that declares in large letters, "Hot n' Naughty."

Some of the worst offenders are in advertising and music. Sex sells, and "barely legal" is a theme. Pediatrician Meg Meeker calls it the "very aggressive marketing of sex to our kids. Everywhere they go they are saturated with visual and auditory messages about sex." Linda Perlstein, the author of the book on middle schoolers, says that at teen dance clubs many kids imitated "freaking," something they'd seen in music videos, where a boy rubs himself against a girl's butt. "Children as young as eleven simulate sex on the dance floor as rappers bleat about oral gratification," Perlstein reports. The lyrics, she notes wryly, "made great use of the fact that 'motherfucker' and 'dick sucker' rhyme."

In *The Disappearance of Childhood*, Neil Postman argues that television and movies have removed the usual barriers to young people learning about sex. Any casual flip through the channels confirms this argument. Every time I do this, I wonder if I'll even be able to have a TV in the house once I have children; most of what I see isn't appropriate for a 12-year-old to watch, much less a 6-year-old. Perlstein saw the effects of this in middle school, where sexual terms and talk are "part of their vocabulary and psyche in a way that it didn't used to be."

It is next to impossible to protect children from these influences. The television I watched in the early 1980s taught me lots of things my parents would have preferred I not know, even though it pales in comparison to TV these days. The commercials were often the most "educational"; mostly, we learned that looking sexy was the most important thing in the world. When I was 10 and my brother was 8, one of our favorite pastimes was recording cassette tapes of ourselves parodying the TV we watched. (My favorite of our creations: a fake commercial for a toilet store in which we recorded a flush and then said, à la Cronkite, "And that's the way it is . . . in Toiletland.") Most of our spoofs, though, were for the stuff we often saw advertised on TV: shampoo, deodorant, and shaving cream. "That makes you look sooo sexy," I would croon like the women in the commercials. When we wanted to play the tape for our grandparents, though, we realized they might not like this part. So we rewound and I said "handsome" over "sexy" in about ten places (due to our bad dubbing skills, it usually came out "sexhandsome"). Looking back, I am struck by the idea that two elementary school kids thought it necessary to protect their sixtysomething grandparents from hearing the word "sexy." That's because fifty years ago, 10-year-olds did not talk about how "sexy" shaving cream was. Of course, 10-year-olds these days say a lot worse than that, especially now that at least one shampoo commercial features simulated orgasms. I can't imagine parodying that for my grandparents.

Nor can I imagine what my brother and I could have learned if we'd had the Internet. There's so much porn out there that the hit musical *Avenue Q* claims, in its funniest song, that "The Internet Is for Porn." When 12-year-olds are looking at it, though, it's not funny anymore. In the *New York Times Magazine* article on hooking up, many boys said they'd begun looking at porn on the Internet pretty regularly by 12 or 13. "Who needs the hassle of dating when I've got online porn?" asked one Boston teenager. A Kaiser Family Foundation study found that 70% of 15-to-17-year-old teens have seen Internet porn. And just in case you're behind on your Web surfing, this is not just ordinary erotica we're talking about; a lot of it involves hardcore bondage and lots of other stuff I don't even want to think about. And if that weren't scary enough, young girls who post to Internet message boards sometimes find themselves pursued by older men. It's no wonder that parents are concerned about these issues—sex just seems so much more available, and so much more dangerous, than it was when they were young. And they might be right.

THE DOWNSIDES: STDS AND
UNWANTED PREGNANCY

One reason for the danger is sexually transmitted diseases. Cases of chlamydia in young women increased by six times between 1987 and 2003. Among entrants to the National Job Training program, 10% of women and 8% of men tested positive for chlamydia. However, gonorrhea cases were down over the same time period, as were syphilis cases. Nevertheless, about 25% of people diagnosed with STDs are teens. Colleges are also a common place to acquire an STD, as a 2000 study found that between 1 in 3 and 1 in 4 college students had had unprotected sex at least once in the past year. In an interview in *Emerging Adulthood*, one young man said he found out that a woman he slept with had been with a male stripper. After "doing the math," he says he thought, " 'Holy cow! I had sex with California just now!' And that made me nervous."

A recent study examined the sexual geography of a small-town high school in the Midwest over the course of eighteen months. About half of the students were sexually active, and these teens began having sex, on average, at age 15. Of the 832 students surveyed, 288 were linked in an elaborate chain of sexual contacts that, the authors say, is "the worst-case scenario" for the spread of STDs. This occurred because many students had several partners, who themselves had several partners, thus creating an elaborate web of connections. This map differed quite a bit from previous studies on adult sex, which usually find that only a few people provide most of the links in the chain; the chain ends with less promiscuous people. Not so here, where 61% of the sexually active adolescents had had more than one sexual partner in the eighteen-month time span. The recent prevalence of "hooking up" suggests that STD transmission may accelerate in the coming years.

The spread of STDs may be exacerbated by young people seeing sex portrayed on television without any reference to safe sex practices. A recent Kaiser Family Foundation study found that 75% of TV shows con-

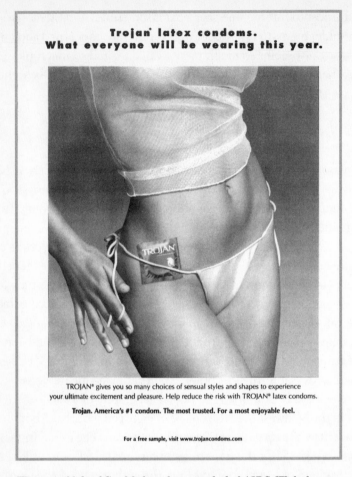

**Trojan° latex condoms.
What everyone will be wearing this year.**

TROJAN® gives you so many choices of sensual styles and shapes to experience
your ultimate excitement and pleasure. Help reduce the risk with TROJAN® latex condoms.

Trojan. America's #1 condom. The most trusted. For a most enjoyable feel.

For a free sample, visit www.trojancondoms.com

The sexual life of GenMe has always included AIDS. With the new
prevalence of hookups, condoms are pretty close to becoming
the fashion statement this Trojan ad suggests they are.

tain sexual content, but only 15% of those mention safe sex. Movies are
similar—sexual encounters rarely feature condoms. Presumably, this is
because sex sells but protection doesn't. When watching TV, says college
freshman Joyce Bryn, "No one wants to see anyone say, 'Hold on, let me
put on a condom.'"

But maybe they should, because sex can now kill you. Just as the early
wave of GenMe was heading into our teenage years in the mid-1980s, the
threat of AIDS broke onto the national media scene after Rock Hudson's

death from the disease. We were welcomed into sexuality by the scary equation that sex = death. Younger GenMe'ers have never known a world without AIDS. If you want to capture the purest form of terror and anxiety in a bottle, talk to someone who has just taken an HIV blood test. and is waiting for the results. Like most people in my generation, I went through this particular rite of passage over the longest two weeks of my life. For everything else, I realized, you could think, "It could be worse." Not in this case—it was difficult to think of anything worse than dying of AIDS in your twenties. "HIV test results will determine not what your future is going to be like, but whether or not you will have a future at all," I wrote in a *Michigan Daily* column in 1995. "The imagination runs wild about a positive test, no matter how you try to stop yourself. How will you tell your parents? What would you do if you only had 10 more years to live? Quit school? Watch less television? Convince your partner to stay with you even though you can't have sex?"

In the 1995 movie *Kids*, a 16-year-old named Jenny unexpectedly tests positive for HIV. When she takes a cab several hours later, the driver asks her why such a young person could look so sad. He rattles off all of the reasons he can think of—boy troubles, fights with parents, and so on—and reassures her that whatever it is, it will go away and she'll be fine. Jenny sits in the back of the cab, unable to tell him that he's wrong—her problem is not going to go away.

The threat of AIDS has become somewhat less terrifying in the years since the drug cocktail was invented and being HIV-positive is not such an immediate death sentence. But even though AIDS doesn't get the press it used to, it's still out there. It is the fifth leading cause of death for people aged 35 to 44, killing 5,867 people in that age group in 2001 alone. More than 2,000 people between the ages of 25 and 34 still die of AIDS every year. And not only might it kill you, but you might give it to someone you love—your partner, your child. Screaming and yelling in anger, walking out, getting someone pregnant—all pale in comparison to giving someone a fatal disease.

On the other hand, the second wave of GenMe has turned around the statistics on teen pregnancy. Births to teens aged 15 to 17 were down 42% between 1991 and 2003. Births to very young teens, those between 10 and 14 years old, fell by 57% in the same time period. The abortion rate for teens aged 15 to 19 also fell by 16% between 1990 and 2000.

Though more teens are having sex, their lowered pregnancy rate shows that more are using birth control. These two might even go together; teenagers who assume they will have sex soon might be more likely to carry condoms or go on the Pill.

At the same time, attitudes toward abortion are growing more conservative. In 1992, when the first wave of GenMe was in college, 67% of college freshmen agreed that abortion should be legal. This higher level of support might have been caused by media attention to the topic, as the Supreme Court considered several abortion cases in the early 1990s. By 2004, support for legal abortion had dropped to 54%, bringing the figure back down to where it was in the late 1970s and early 1980s. This might be tied to the decreasing teen birth and abortion rate; fewer teens know someone who got pregnant. It is somewhat ironic that among college students there is apparently more sex but less support for legal abortion. If abortion is again challenged in the Supreme Court and can no longer be taken for granted, attitudes might shift rather quickly back toward support as they did in the early 1990s.

I'M SINGLE

In 2002 and 2003, my boyfriend and I attended seven weddings (an occupational hazard of being in your early thirties). Six of these couples had lived together, many for more than a year. That tally increased to seven out of eight when we got married ourselves in 2004, after living together for a year and a half and buying a rather expensive though small house together. I had been skeptical about living together, but Craig said that all of his friends who married had lived together first. He saw it as the next logical step in our relationship. Apparently, he's not alone. In a 2001 poll, 62% of young people said that living together is the best way to predict if a relationship will last, and 43% say they wouldn't marry someone unless they had lived with him or her first. A 1990s study found that 64% of people in their twenties had lived together without benefit of marriage, a number that is likely higher now.

Being single is not what it used to be. Someone who is technically "single" (as in not married) may have been in a relationship for ten years. Although most middle-class couples still get married eventually, it is seen as a later step in a process that begins with dating (or hooking up), moves on to seeing each other almost every night, and makes an intermediate stop at living together. Many people, especially the younger half of GenMe, have begun to use "single" to mean "not dating anyone." Author Linda Perlstein saw a girl's website that said, "Hi I'm Adrienne. I am 11 and single."

Living together, in particular, has radically changed the landscape of "single" people. Previous generations would have been shocked if couples lived together before marriage—and they are shocked when young people do so today. Tyler, 20, moved in with his girlfriend after they had dated for about six months. When his grandmother found out, she yelled at him, saying that she was "so disappointed." Tyler's sister Michelle, 22, also lives with her boyfriend; she describes her grandmother's comments as "rude." The authors of *Midlife Crisis at 30* relate one of their mother's comments about living together in her day: "My mother would have absolutely killed me. Actually, scratch that. I wouldn't have ever *thought* about doing something so unrespectable. . . . it would have been like saying 'Hmmm, should I take that express shuttle to the moon?'"

Today in the United States, more than 11 million unmarried people live together. The rate of living together outside of marriage increased 500% from 1970 to 1990, and another 72% between 1990 and 2000. Couples who wait to live together until after the wedding are now the minority, and this trend is likely to continue.

Brian, 23, said that living with his girlfriend happened naturally. They had been spending a lot of time together, and he cleared some space for her things at his apartment. "Oh my gosh, I have a shelf!" she said. Before long, they were living together. Brian understands just how different his situation is from previous generations. "My girlfriend's grandmother would say, 'If you give out the milk for free, nobody will buy the cow.' Now, living together is a normal step in a relationship."

There are also large financial incentives to live together. Sharing the rent with someone—even if you need a bigger place—is a huge savings these days with rents and mortgages so high. And if you're making a middle-class income, you'll pay less tax to Uncle Sam if you stay single. This "marriage tax penalty," once several thousand dollars on average, has been rolled back considerably in the last few years. However, people with taxable incomes of $58,650 or more in 2004 still paid more tax when married—thousands of dollars more if they were high-income.

Then there's the cost of a wedding—the latest estimate puts the average at a whopping $20,000. In major cities like New York, it's over $40,000. Living together sounds pretty good when you think about it this way.

Marriage is also increasingly optional even with parenthood. In 2003, 34.6% of babies were born to unmarried women, the highest rate ever recorded. That's more than 1 out of 3. (Even though the teen birthrate is down, so many more unmarried women in their twenties and thirties are having children that this figure continues to rise.) If the United States follows trends in Europe, the number of children born outside of marriage may rise to half of all births. As with sex, art has imitated life, with single mothers portrayed more often on TV. But reactions to it have changed quite a bit in just ten years. When the unwed Murphy Brown had a baby on her eponymous sitcom in 1992, then vice president Dan Quayle chastised the show's writers for setting a bad moral example, and many people agreed with him. But when Rachel on *Friends* gave birth without benefit of marriage in a 2002 episode, the collective reaction (according to *Time*'s TV critic James Poniewozik) was "Awwww." "None of the Friends has had a baby the 'normal' way," Poniewozik points out. "Chandler and Monica adopt. Ross has kids by his lesbian ex-wife and his unwed ex-girlfriend. Phoebe carries her half brother and his wife's triplets. . . . The message of *Friends*, in other words, is that there is no normal anymore and that Americans—at least the plurality needed to make a sitcom No. 1—accept that." And it's not just on TV, of course. When 1 out of 3 babies is born to a single mother, who has time to criticize them all?

ARE THESE CHANGES GOOD OR BAD?

Well, that depends on whom you ask. Some young women believe their greater sexual freedom is an unmitigated good. This fits the trends discussed earlier in the book—if we're going to have more freedoms, why not sexual freedom? "I definitely think our generation is lucky because we didn't have the same constraints our parents did," says Priya, 18. The authors of *The Hookup Handbook* dedicate the book to "every girl who lives life by her own rules—not *The Rules*."

When one of my students, then 23, wrote a paper on changes in sexuality, she did not describe younger people as more sexually active;

instead, she wrote that they were "less sexually repressed." Older people may think that the younger generation is disturbingly promiscuous, but the younger generation flings it right back—sure, we're a little loose, but you're just uptight. Sometimes neither characterization is complimentary. Lynda, 25, suggested the title for this chapter, and although it's a great title, neither "Prude" nor "Crude" is very flattering.

In other words, how you perceive the generational trend depends on your generation. No matter what your opinion, though, it's clear that individual freedom has once again won out against restrictive social rules. Don't forget the condoms.

7

The Equality Revolution: Minorities, Women, and Gays and Lesbians

On March 7, 1965, five hundred people began to walk in Selma, Alabama. The crowd of protestors, black and white, planned to march to the state capital, Montgomery, to demand equal voting rights. They made it only to a bridge on the outskirts of Selma. There, state troopers pelted them with tear gas and beat them with billy clubs so brutally that many were left bleeding or unconscious. Some of the troopers' horses stepped on protesters and broke their ribs. There was so much violence that the incident came to be known as "Bloody Sunday."

Reflecting on the events forty years later, Congressman John Lewis noted that in 1965 all of the troopers were white men. When they re-created the march in 2000, however, "The group of troopers were men and women, White, Black and Hispanic," he said. "And when we reached the bridge, they cheered."

Lewis's comment is striking for a number of reasons. First, the principles of the civil rights movement have been fully accepted by most Americans—they are ideas to be cheered and celebrated rather than beaten out of people. Not only that, but state troopers are now every race and both male and female. So are engineers, lawyers, doctors, and many other professions that were once almost exclusively white and male.

In just four decades, the United States has undergone a transformation of attitudes about women, minorities, and gays and lesbians. The revolution of equality was, without question, the largest social change in

America in the last half of the twentieth century. No other trend has had such a colossal impact on every aspect of our lives. We might debate the particulars of affirmative action, gay marriage, and sex differences in intellectual ability, but even conservatives now accept the general principle that race and sex should not preclude people from pursuing the profession they desire.

It is difficult to underestimate the enormity of this change, and the relatively short amount of time it took. Segregation was still rampant in the 1960s, and Hispanics were still referred to as "Spanish." In 1970, when the first Generation Me babies were born, just 5% of graduating law students were women. Now it's 47%, an almost tenfold increase. In the 1970s, police still raided gay bars and arrested people, and no one on TV was gay—not even Liberace, and especially not the dad on *The Brady Bunch*.

This is one of the last chapters in the book precisely because these changes are so pervasive and strong. These are not the trends that surprise people. Yet you may not realize just how much things have changed until you consider the details. We take so many things for granted now that it is easy to forget what things used to be like, especially if you are a member of GenMe and never saw it with your own eyes. We have been taught equality since we were babies, if not by our parents, then by TV. Notes Chris Colin in *What Really Happened to the Class of '93*, " 'Tolerance' and 'acceptance' might have become buzzwords in the '90s, but my generation had dealt in those concepts since *Sesame Street*." This tolerance goes hand in hand with the decline in social rules I discussed in Chapter 1; GenMe may have left behind some of the good social rules about politeness, but, following in the footsteps of the Boomers, we have also left behind some of the bad social rules about everyone living life in the same way, and minorities and women staying in their "place." We are less likely to believe in moral absolutes, so we are tolerant and accept diversity in all its forms.

This is the good-news portion of the book: Most people would agree that equality is the unmitigated upside of the focus on the self. In valuing the individual, our society looks beyond race, sex, and sexual orientation to the talents of each person. In practice, it doesn't always happen—the most powerful among us are still white men—but a staggering amount of progress has been made. Whether it reflects reality or not, the American ideal in the twenty-first century is for each person to realize his or her potential. We no longer believe, as many people once did, that people of color should limit themselves to menial jobs or that a college education is wasted on a woman (because she will "just" have children and stay home).

These changes in beliefs have been accompanied by large changes in behavior, life paths, and personalities. GenMe lives these differences every day. And that goes for white men, too. Compared to your father or grandfather, you're much more likely to have a female boss, a friend of another race, or a wife who works outside the home. And even if you don't, you will see those things all around you.

Perhaps because I am a heterosexual white woman, much of my research on the equality revolution is about changes for women. There have also been huge changes for racial minorities and gays and lesbians, and I will cover those as well, though not as extensively, given my less thorough expertise about these equally important trends.

CHANGES FOR MINORITIES

As the example of the Selma march illustrates, race relations in the United States have undergone a sea change in forty years. Racism and even segregation still exist, but they are not the systematic, institutionalized practice they once were. Monique, 21 and African-American, notes that her grandmother went to segregated schools and wasn't even allowed to play with white children. Although Monique says she has seen racism in her life, her grandmother's experiences "seem like another world. I cannot even imagine having to deal with the issues she dealt with."

Being a minority in the United States today is much different from forty or fifty years ago. There is a growing minority middle class. In 1970, most blacks did not even have a high school diploma; now 80% do, and almost four times as many blacks are college-educated. The percentage of college degrees awarded to Hispanics has almost tripled since 1980. These trends are likely to continue as college-educated minorities have their own children and pass on their ambitions and success.

These changes are all around us in popular media, from the black newscaster to the Mexican-American actress. Like other trends, these changes were mostly in place by the time GenMe came along. From *The Jeffersons* ("Baby movin' on up . . .") to *The Cosby Show* to *George Lopez*, we're accustomed to seeing diversity on TV. Lawyers, judges, and doctors on TV now are just about every ethnicity. We do not find this unusual; most of us fail to notice it or comment on it. It's generally the Boomers who say, "Wow, isn't it great that Condi Rice is the first black woman to be secretary of state?" "Sure," GenMe thinks, "it's great, but what did you expect? She's smart and capable, so where's the news story?"

Of course, racism still exists. Charles, 27, interviewed in *Emerging Adulthood*, recalls being called the n-word while at sports camp as a kid, and as a teenager, he got pulled over for "Driving While Black." Black and Hispanic job applicants still face an uphill battle against stereotyping and discrimination, and there is still an enormous racial discrepancy in income and education. Sixty-one percent of black and 36% of Hispanic young adults say that it has been difficult for them to get the financial support they needed to get a college education; in contrast, only 4% of whites and zero Asian-Americans say it has been difficult. This is simple math, as black and Hispanic young people are more likely to come from lower-income families. As the aftermath of Hurricane Katrina demonstrated all too vividly, there is still an enormous racial gap in poverty. There may be a burgeoning black middle class, but there are also untold masses of minorities who live on next to nothing.

And most people admit to engaging in at least some racial stereotyping. The musical *Avenue Q* even has a matter-of-fact song about it: "Everyone's a Little Bit Racist." ("Ethnic jokes might be uncouth/But you laugh because they're based on truth.") Black comedian Dave Chappelle was equally straightforward—and hilarious—about race on his sketch show, which was wildly popular among college students. In one sketch in 2004, he hosted a mock game show called *I Know Black People*, with questions about the meaning of the term "badonkadonk" (hint: the same as "junk in her trunk") and why black people like menthol cigarettes (to which a white contestant admits, "I don't know," and Dave replies, "That is correct. Nobody knows"). There's social commentary amid the goofiness as well. When Dave asks how black people can "rise up and overcome," a white contestant says, "By getting out there and voting." Dave deadpans, "That is incorrect."

The 2004 movie *Crash* coaxes laughs during its wrenching stories about race by having its characters say the racist things that most of us only think: a black man muses that someone must have gathered all the Hispanics together and "taught them all to park their cars on their lawns"; a white man accuses a black woman of getting her job through affirmative action; a Hispanic woman makes fun of an Asian woman's inability to pronounce her *l*'s. The rest of the movie brings together many of the beliefs and actions that still characterize race in America: the profound distrust between blacks and the police; the overt prejudice and discrimination against Arabs; the grinding poverty still endured by most people of color. And in the end, the characters' beliefs don't line up with their actions: all is not what it seems. It's a pretty good metaphor for race relations in general.

Nevertheless, much has changed. Most white people no longer work and live in places where they could expect not to interact with those of other races. Now workplaces, neighborhoods, and even many marriages are integrated. In a 2000 poll, 70% of high school seniors said that race relations at their school were good, and 72% said they have a close friend of another race. Though we are a long way from complete racial integration, all-white neighborhoods are almost completely gone. In 1960, almost 80% of whites answered yes when asked, "Would you move if black people came to live in great numbers in your neighborhood?" By 1990, only 25% of whites agreed. Overtly reported racial prejudice has become so rare that researchers now use indirect methods to measure it.

Some of this is simple demographics: among Americans born between 1977 and 1994, only 62% are white (compared to 75% of Baby Boomers and 85% of the World War II generation). GenMe is just more comfortable with racial crossovers, in everything from dating to music. One of my students was a Filipino young man who lived, breathed, and ate hip-hop music; he proudly pointed out that one of the best hip-hop DJs is also Filipino. But, he says, "I am proud of my culture but not ethnocentric." He's not alone. More and more young whites and Asians enjoy rap music and watch *Chappelle's Show*. It's pretty much taken for granted that black people, their culture, and their music are cool. And so is Hispanic and Asian culture—it's a small sign of progress, surely, but who can get through the week without eating tacos, sushi, or Chinese takeout?

So have the changes in race relations over the last four decades had psychological effects? Back in the 1940s, psychologists Kenneth and Mamie Clark performed a famous experiment in which they gave black children the choice of playing with white dolls or black dolls. Most of the black children chose to play with the white dolls, leading the authors to conclude that the black children had very low self-esteem. In its *Brown v. Board of Education* ruling against segregation, the Supreme Court mentioned these results as an example of the inferiority felt by black children.

I wanted to see if this was still true: Do blacks and other minorities have lower self-esteem than whites, and has this difference changed over the generations? In the largest, most comprehensive study ever done on racial differences in self-esteem, Jennifer Crocker and I gathered data from 712 samples of 375,254 people of all races and ethnicities who filled out self-esteem questionnaires between the 1950s and the 1990s.

In the 1960s and early 1970s, black and white Americans scored about the same on measures of self-esteem. During the 1980s, however, black Americans' self-esteem increased until it was noticeably higher than whites'. By the 1990s, 58% of blacks, and 61% of black college students, displayed above-average self-esteem. This is surprising given the usual belief that ethnic minorities will have lower self-esteem; clearly, young black Americans feel good about themselves. In fact, blacks' self-esteem is higher than that of any other racial or ethnic group.

The change over the decades also tells an intriguing historical story: the Civil Rights movement and the general shift toward racial equality has had a striking effect on the self-esteem of minority youth. Black GenMe kids grew up hearing that Black Is Beautiful, seeing people who looked like them play doctors and lawyers on TV, and (particularly if they were middle-class) expecting to go to college—why shouldn't they feel good about themselves?

Some of the increase in blacks' self-esteem in recent years might be traced to school programs. Similar to the general self-esteem programs mentioned in Chapter 2, many school districts have specific programs aimed at minority youth. Sondra, 20, participated in one of these programs when she was in the fifth grade. The school's small number of black children were brought together in a group, where they learned about their culture and were taught to take pride in their background. "We were really proud of who we were and where we came from," says Sondra.

"The pride I received by being a part of this group has allowed me to know exactly who I am today and what I want to become in the future." These groups have become even more common in recent years.

A glance at any recent high school history textbook shows that this ethnic pride is fostered even in schools without specific programs. When the Boomers were growing up, history textbooks were basically the history of white men, and discussed slavery for its political implications rather than for its effect on African-Americans. Native Americans were portrayed as enemies. Now history texts are careful to emphasize the victimization of Africans and Native Americans, and vividly describe their cultures. Ethnic minority youth see their history taught in school and come to understand more about their cultures and their origins.

This trend is not limited to black youth. In our comprehensive study, we found that Hispanic and Asian young people's self-esteem has also increased relative to whites'. Though both groups still score lower than whites on measures of self-esteem, this gap has narrowed over the last three decades. It will most likely continue to narrow as younger generations are increasingly indoctrinated into the American ideal of high self-esteem.

Many Asian and Hispanic children of immigrants walk a delicate line between their parents' communal culture and the individualistic ethos of the United States. On a 2005 segment of MTV's *My Life (Translated)*, Korean-American reporter SuChin Pak talked about immigrant children's college experiences. When SuChin went off to Berkeley, her parents moved in next door to her dorm! "Like every good Korean daughter, I always did exactly what my parents told me to do," she says. SuChin then interviewed Sonia, a 19-year-old Mexican-American struggling to study for her college classes because her parents expect her to cook, clean, and take care of her younger siblings. ("What have you ironed for me?" her father asks her.) Sonia thinks about dropping out of college, but decides to stay in school when her parents say they will support her and that they want her to "become somebody."

Many young Hispanics take pride in their ethnic identity and fully recognize that their generation has opportunities that their parents never dreamed of. Twenty-four-year-old Jose says that his mother attended school in Mexico only until the third grade. She worked as a maid and as a seamstress at a sweatshop after arriving in the United States when she was 13. When Jose finished high school, he says, he was "indifferent" about college, since he had already completed more schooling than anyone in his family. Yet when his college acceptance letter came, "I read the first sentence and started to cry. I wanted to thank God for giving me so much. I told my mother this was just a start and that I would do everything possible to be the best man I could be." Laura, 22, grew up in a poor Hispanic family in Miami and got a scholarship to a prestigious private college in the Northeast. Though fitting in at the college was difficult, she was empowered by the experience. "Being from a different generation has given me the opportunity to be educated, to take opportunities and make great things out of them," she says. "I have come to see myself as a role model for future generations."

Some young people find that even experiences with ignorance or prejudice can heighten their ethnic pride. Rosa, 21, is Cuban-American and grew up in Miami. When she moved to northern Florida for college, she was shocked when people came up to her and said things like "What are you? Are you Mexican?" She finally realized that many of these students, as she put it, "came from places where the closest thing to Spanish heritage was the Taco Bell on the corner." She says this helped her focus more on her identity. "I had never felt so Cuban in my whole life!" she said. "It really became a huge part of how I saw myself, and I started to appreciate every part of my culture—the food, the music, and even the language."

These stories clearly show one of the upsides of individualism: young people who appreciate their culture and can take advantage of opportunities their parents never had. Although economic pressures still limit the goals of many minority youth, their race or ethnicity is no longer an automatic disqualification.

But is the upswing in minority kids' self-esteem an unmitigated good? As I argued in Chapter 2, maybe not. It's certainly good for young people to take pride in their ethnic identity, no matter what their background; feeling comfortable in your own skin is obviously important. But like the general self-esteem programs, ethnic self-esteem programs often take things too far and focus on the wrong causes. Raising children's self-esteem is not going to solve the problems of poverty and crime. It doesn't do much good for a child to have high self-esteem if his grades are poor, he gets in trouble in class, and he has no concrete plan for the future. Ethnic differences are a prime example of the disconnect between self-esteem and achievement. For example, Asian-American kids usually report the lowest self-esteem of all ethnic groups, but they often achieve the most academically. Black youngsters have the highest self-esteem, yet lag behind in academic achievement. And because self-esteem does not cause school achievement, self-esteem programs are once again putting the cart before the horse. The time spent on self-esteem programs—for children of any background—is probably better spent on teaching academics and self-control.

CHANGES FOR WOMEN

One of the biggest sporting events of 1973 was the tennis match between Billie Jean King, 29, and Bobby Riggs, 54. Hyped as the "Battle of the Sexes," the match inspired countless water-cooler bets. While today few would bet on the aging player, at that time many people believed that a woman could never beat a man in sports, no matter what his age or her skill. When King arrived on the court, Howard Cosell commented on her hairstyle, saying she could be a Hollywood actress if only her hair were longer. Not surprisingly, Cosell was virtually speechless when King won—and won easily.

Sexist attitudes and discrimination against women went far beyond sports, of course. Before the late 1960s, medical schools systematically capped the enrollment of women at 5% of each class, regardless of how many talented women applied. When former Supreme Court Justice Sandra Day O'Connor graduated near the top of her Stanford Law School class in 1952, no law firm would hire her (although one firm offered her a position as a secretary). As late as the 1970s, there were no female news anchors, few female lawyers, and even fewer women scientists. The *New York Times* and other newspapers ran want ads under "Help Wanted: Male" and "Help Wanted: Female." In 1964, Virginia congressman Howard Smith, a staunch opponent of civil rights for blacks, added sex discrimination to the Civil Rights Act as a joke, in hopes of defeating the bill. In his speech, he quoted a sarcastic letter from a woman complaining about "sex discrimination" in the shortage of husbands, as the House of Representatives roared with laughter. The bill passed anyway, sex discrimination clause intact. I have always imagined Congressman Smith kicking himself well into the next decade.

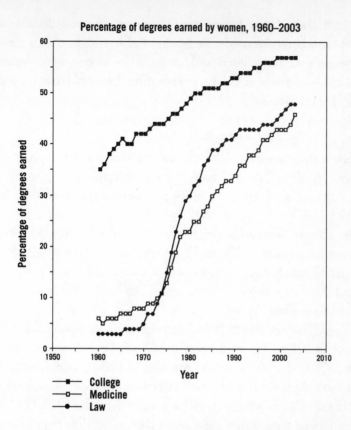

Percentage of degrees earned by women, 1960–2003

College
Medicine
Law

Women now earn the majority of college degrees, and almost half of all medical and law degrees.

If Smith were alive today, he would be flabbergasted by what he saw. Girls play soccer alongside boys. Women earn 57% of college degrees and almost half of degrees in law and medicine. Television news is filled with female reporters and anchors, sometimes reporting on the actions of the many women now in government leadership positions (including eighty-three in Congress, an all-time high). Most women in their twenties have never been married, and four times as many women in their early thirties are unmarried now compared to 1970. More than four times as many women had their first child after the age of 30 in 2000 compared to 1975. Couples in which only the husband works account for only 28% of married couples aged 25 to 39. Women are now the majority of accountants, financial managers, medical scientists, and pharmacists. All of this seems normal to us, but it would have been shocking just a few decades ago. When my mother graduated valedictorian of her high school class in 1962, she was told that women could be nurses, teachers, or secretaries— that was it. Like most women of my generation, I was told that I could be whatever I wanted to be.

Changes in Attitudes

Think about these questions for a minute: Should men and women share housework equally? Should women participate in the professions and in business? Should boys be given more encouragement to go to college than girls? These are some of the items on a questionnaire called the Attitudes Toward Women Scale. As you can probably tell right away, it was written in the early 1970s, and I was convinced that it would show a large generational change, partly because my answers to those three questions, and those of everyone I knew, were "Definitely," "Definitely," and "No! Are you kidding?"

So I spent the summer of 1995, when I was 23, gathering data on 71 samples of 19,101 college students who had filled out this questionnaire between 1970 and 1995. Though I was sure I'd find change in this scale, I wasn't entirely certain what the pattern would look like—after all, weren't the 1980s a more conservative decade than the 1970s? In 1991, Susan Faludi had argued that there was a *Backlash* against feminism during the decade of Reagan and the Moral Majority. So would attitudes toward women slide backward during the 1980s?

Nope. Attitudes about women's roles continued to become more egalitarian throughout the 1980s and into the early 1990s. Although Faludi was right that the media in the 1980s was not profeminist, young people seemed to ignore this. The change over the three decades was also substantial. The average 1990s college woman had more feminist attitudes than 87% of her counterparts in the early 1970s, and the average 1990s college man had more feminist attitudes than 82% of early 1970s college men. What was once the province of hippies and radicals had become mainstream. At least the attitudes had, even if the labels hadn't. As Paula Kamen found in her 1991 book *Feminist Fatale*, young women believed in feminist values but rejected the label "feminist" (prompting the frequent statement, "I'm not a feminist, but . . . ," after which the young woman makes a strong statement about equality between the sexes).

Surveys done by other researchers show a very similar pattern. Among people under age 29 polled in 1993, twice as many preferred a female boss to a male boss; in contrast, those over 65 preferred a male boss by almost 9 to 1. While 70% of people 65 and older in 2000 agreed that "it is much better for everyone involved if the man is the achiever outside the home and the woman takes care of the home and family," only 21% of people aged 18 to 22 agreed.

So why was there a media obsession with tearing down feminism and unearthing day care abuse scandals (almost all later proved to be untrue) during the 1980s? Probably because the country was reeling from the breakneck pace of cultural change. In 1984, for the first time, the majority of married women with children under 6 were in the workplace. At college graduation ceremonies in 1982, American women earned more undergraduate degrees than men for the first time in history. In 1987, 40% of law degrees went to women, eight times more than in 1970.

Many GenMe babies weren't even born when these changes happened in the 1980s, and the older ones (like me) were just entering adolescence. So, as always, we entered a world where things had already changed, and we soaked it up like little sponges. Even in my conservative Texas town, a favorite school film in the early 1980s was *Free to Be You and Me*, an anthology of songs and stories designed to fight sexism (my personal favorites: "William Has a Doll" and the one where the prissy girl who always says "Ladies First" gets her way—she gets eaten by the tiger first!). We would sit entranced in the dark room as the puppet babies discussed which of them was a girl or a boy and the cheerful theme song began, about a place where the children are free and "every boy grows to be his own man . . . every girl grows to be her own woman."

Those born in the 1980s and later didn't even need a film to tell them this stuff. Equality between the sexes is such a given that Anne, 16, says that in her neighborhood "being a feminist is considered almost nitpicky and trivial." Heather, 19, agrees. "Girls of my generation take everything for granted. We grew up with the understanding that girls were equal to guys. I think of it as something that should come naturally, not as a privilege." Other young women recognize those who fought for women's rights before them—including their mothers. Erin, 20, says: "My mother was a housewife. She urged me to break the tradition of women sacrificing their identities and their opportunities to be a mother. Women are finally starting to emerge from their domestic quarantine, and I am proud to be a part of a new generation of women who won't stand for it any longer, and grateful to my forerunners who made it possible." Erin is not the only one unwilling to enter the "domestic quarantine." In 2004, only 1 out of 1,000 incoming college students chose "homemaker (full-time)" as their expected career. For the future, this means that either fewer and fewer women will stay home with their children, or more and more women will end up with a role they never expected to have.

These trends, like so many, have their roots in the movement toward individualism and the self. Many young women said their mothers explicitly told them to act as individuals. "My mother has always encouraged me to be independent and never depend on anyone but myself," wrote Melinda, 22. "She wants me to be able to stand on my own two feet and not depend on a man when I'm married." Elizabeth, 20, says that her mother "continually told me never to surrender my power as she did, to find a way to do right by my children, but to do right by myself also." Tiffany, 18, says that her mother was married and had a child by 19, a life she has no desire to replicate. "I want to be able to live my life and become a pediatrician," she says. "I don't want to depend on my husband or anyone else. I want to be able to show people, and myself, that I can achieve the goals I have set for myself."

The feminist message for women is inextricably linked to the individualist message, and whether girls heard the call of independence from their family or only from the outside culture, they listened. Gender equality is so taken for granted now that these trends are unlikely to reverse; girls growing up right now will become the most liberated generation of women in history—until their own daughters outstrip them.

Changes in Personality

Obviously, our beliefs about women and their roles are very different than they used to be. But does this mean that women actually *are* different now, with different personalities and different behaviors? Specifically, are GenMe women more likely to have personality traits that were once associated more with men? Could expectations have changed, while women remained just as unassertive and passive as they were before?

As you might remember from the introduction, this was the question that drove my very first study of generational differences. After noticing that college women in the early 1990s were scoring very differently than 1970s women, I decided to do a systematic study of the question. I gathered 103 samples of 28,920 college students on two questionnaires that measured stereotypically masculine and feminine traits. The "masculine" scale items included words like competitive, independent, never give up easily, self-reliant, forceful, and ambitious. Sure enough, college women endorsed these traits at a higher rate with every passing year. More than 50% of 1990s women scored as "masculine" on the scale, compared to only 20% of early 1970s women. The average 1990s college woman reported more "masculine" traits than 80% of Boomer college women in the early 1970s. The change was so large that by the early 1990s men's and women's scores on the scale of so-called masculine traits were indistinguishable. The generational change in personality had turned the very definition of the scale on its head: clearly these traits were no longer masculine, but simply human.

Much of this is probably due to upbringing. For one thing, more than eight times as many girls participate in interscholastic sports now than in 1972. Before the passage of Title IX, girls' athletics was almost a joke, with little funding and even less enthusiasm. Many girls today don't even realize that it was once unusual for females to play sports, since girls and boys now participate in sports at a nearly equal rate. It's likely that sports participation has affected girls' personalities, as research shows that girls who participate in sports are more likely to develop traits like independence and competitiveness.

Many young women told me that their fathers encouraged them to play sports and didn't treat them differently than their brothers. "My father never drew a line between what girls should do and what boys should do," said Amanda, 25. "My sister and I played soccer, and got filthy playing outside tending to goats and chickens and catching snakes." I also had a father who made few distinctions between the sexes. To this day I can throw a softball from third to first because my dad showed me how—no "throwing like a girl" for me. And when my mother and I watched beauty pageants, it was my dad who would walk through the room and mutter disapprovingly, "Meat market." It was always clear to me that my dad cared a lot more about my ability to throw a ball than my ability to look good doing it—quite a change from the dads in the 1950s, many of whom would never have allowed a girl to play softball.

It's now cool for girls to play sports . . . although this ad suggests
you still need to worry about how you smell while doing it.

Although girls actively played sports in the 1960s and 1970s as well, girls'
and women's athletics are much more widespread and accepted now.

GenMe girls have also seen their mothers work outside the home
more than any other previous generation. In a 2000 survey, 82% of 18-to-
22-year-olds said their mothers worked outside the home at least some of
the time when they were growing up, compared to 65% of the mothers of
Boomers and only 34% of the mothers of the World War II generation.
Studies have found that girls with working mothers are more likely to
embrace traditionally masculine traits like ambition and independence.
Seeing Mom go off to work provides a daily role model for girls, showing

them that women have roles outside the home. Many GenMe women—and men—take it for granted that mothers will work at least part of the time.

As I continued my research, I wondered if women had also grown more assertive. Assertiveness—standing up for one's individual opinions and rights—is an important trait for succeeding in the business and professional world. Assertiveness is also inherently associated with status, suggesting that women should display more assertive personalities during times when they have more status.

I gathered 168 studies of 52,464 college and high school students conducted between 1931 and 1995. The data lined up perfectly with the theory: women's status in the larger society, measured by levels of education and later age at first marriage, correlated very highly with young women's self-reported assertiveness. At times in history when more women earned college and graduate degrees and waited to marry until their mid-twenties, women were more likely to agree with statements like "I am quick to express an opinion" and less likely to agree that "I have avoided asking questions for fear of sounding stupid." Women are also now less likely to say that they are overapologetic or that they find it difficult to express anger. The average 1990s college woman was more assertive than 67% of Boomer college women in the late 1960s.

The changes in assertiveness were so strong that by the early 1990s there was no longer a sex difference in the trait; college women were just as assertive as college men. This did not surprise Natalie, 19. "Throughout school, I was taught to be assertive and view myself and my peers as equals, male or female," she says. "My mom always believed I could be a doctor or a lawyer, or even president." Maria, 20, describes herself as very assertive and says she becomes frustrated when her mother acts passively. "You can only get things done if you are aggressive," she says.

Perhaps because of these assertive attitudes, women are increasingly invested in work and education as integral parts of their identities. I looked at this as part of a larger study on the link between self-esteem and socioeconomic status, which includes job status, income, and education. My colleague Keith Campbell and I examined 446 studies of 312,940 individuals. For men, the correlation between self-esteem and socioeconomic status has decreased; men now show a weaker link between their self-esteem and their job status or education than previous generations did. For women, the opposite is true; the correlation between women's socioeconomic status and self-esteem has grown stronger with each generation. In fact, women's self-esteem is now more strongly linked to their work and education than men's is. Work, income, and education, once relatively unimportant to a woman's identity, are now even more important to women than to men.

Yet when women get home, we often face a sink full of dirty dishes. How does that make young women feel? The title of the recent edited volume *The Bitch in the House* pretty much sums it up. In one of the essays, E. S. Maduro, 24, describes her feelings of anger at her live-in boyfriend when she comes home to a messy apartment. "Does it just not occur to him that I worked all day and might like to come home to a place where I don't immediately have to start cleaning in order to feel some sense of peace with where I am?" she writes. "I will cook and clean, and all the while think about how I am falling into the same trap of housework that my own mother feel into."

Her mother, however, saw things differently. "The fact that I did all the shopping and cooking and cleaning at home was just part of the territory; all the women I knew did this, and I never thought to question or resent it," she writes. "You seem to feel in your essay that I have some anger about all I did, particularly the domestic roles that fell to me. But I do not now, and don't believe I ever did, feel angry about these roles and tasks."

But GenMe women do. I find the peacefulness in the mother's letter very typical of her generation, and very atypical of my own—we just have no tolerance for such blatant inequality. (To put it more succinctly, we don't put up with that shit.) GenMe women spend less time on housework than our mothers did; but we expect to split things 50-50 with our male partners, and when this doesn't happen we often explode. Or we do the work to avoid the fight, since we've fought about it so many times before, but are still steaming inside.

The Generation Me Man

And where are the men in all of this? On the scale that measures attitudes toward women, their opinions have shifted right along with women's, though they still espouse more conservative views than women (which might explain why conflict between the sexes has persisted). Men have also increased in assertiveness and stereotypically masculine traits just as women have, suggesting that both men and women have caught the train toward greater individualism. But have men taken on more stereotypically feminine traits, as women have embraced masculine traits? Maybe, but maybe not. College men's scores on measures of nurturance and caring from the 1970s to the 1990s show mixed results; men's scores on nurturance increased on one scale but not on another. Even on the scale that showed change, the trend was not nearly as strong as the shift toward more assertive and independent traits for women. So women have become more stereotypically "masculine," but men show only a weak trend toward more stereotypically "feminine" nurturance. It does seem that young men are now more comfortable with the more appearance-based "feminine" things—witness the recent emergence of the manicure-loving, fashionable-shoe-wearing metrosexual. Suddenly, just because you know how to dress well doesn't necessarily mean you're gay. But a man who has primary responsibility for his children is still very rare.

However, today's fathers are clearly more involved than those of previous generations. It's no longer considered wrong for men to change diapers, but does that mean that men are actually changing the diapers? Well, sometimes—and definitely a lot more than the men of previous generations. Married fathers spent three times as much time interacting with their kids in 1998 as they did in 1975.

Nevertheless, the emphasis on individualism means that work remains on its exalted throne. It's still uncommon for the man to be the one to stay home with the kids, even if he makes less money than his wife. A lot of men say they would find it isolating to be at home; others say they would lose prestige in their careers if they took too much time off. There's still a stigma against stay-at-home dads, though this is fading some with time. With more women earning college and graduate degrees, there will be more and more couples in the future in which the woman earns more than the man. GenMe might very well make stay-at-home dads cool.

Especially in the time before parenthood, young men are a fairly liberated bunch. Even those who are conservative in their politics don't usually expect their wives to always stay home or to do all of the housework. Although men usually don't think much about women's earning power, this may change as housing gets even more expensive. One friend of mine, an investment banker, told me that he thought New York men were looking for successful women who made a lot of money—having two good incomes was the only way to afford a decent apartment! A 2004 poll found that 79% of young men say they'd feel comfortable dating a woman who earned significantly more than they did. Men are also now more likely to value spending time with their kids: 72% of fathers say they would "sacrifice exciting opportunities and higher pay at my job for more time with my family." Young men are helping out around the house—dads are spending 50% more time on housework than they did a generation ago. It's still not what it should be—but it's progress.

But Aren't the Changes for Women Reversing?

Every once in a while, the media grabs hold of some set of statistics designed to show that women are retreating back into the home. In 1994, the cover of the business magazine Barron's featured black-and-white pictures of 1950s housewives under the headline "Workin' Women: Goin' Home!" The story reported that fewer women in their early twenties were working, reversing a decades-long trend. It turned out that if you looked at the statistics more closely, fewer men in their early twenties were working during this time, too—partly because of the recession and partly because more young people (men *and* women) were enrolled in college and graduate school. Labor force participation among mothers continued to go up. Not exactly a return to 1950s domesticity.

More recently, several news outlets have declared that more women are staying home with their children (thus first-wave GenMe women, as women ages 25 to 35 are the most likely to have young children at home). *Time* magazine ran a cover story in 2004 titled "The Case for Staying Home." Newspapers breathlessly announced in 2002 that Census figures showed a decline in the number of working women with children under a year old. This figure was 58% in 1998 and 55% in 2000. More recent data suggest that this trend has not been very consistent: the number of working women with infants was back *up* in 2002, to 57%, and then back down to 55% in 2003. A change of 2 to 3 percentage points that doesn't stay still for more than a year is hardly a reason to declare a return to the 1950s, especially considering that virtually *no* women with employed husbands worked when their children were infants during the 1950s.

But let's say we take this seriously; maybe this small change is the first step in a coming trend. But I don't think so. Why? Because the economy entered a recession—and then a "jobless recovery"—during the early 2000s. The labor force participation of *men* aged 25 to 34 dipped 1.6 percentage points during the same time period. So some women—and some men—who got laid off and had small children decided not to aggressively look for a new job right away, or just plain couldn't find another job. This exact scenario happened to my friend Janet, whose tech company in the Bay Area laid her off in 2003 when she was pregnant with her second child. She decided it would be too difficult to find another job while pregnant and is now home with her two children. She will be back in the workforce before long to pay the substantial mortgage on their small house. So will most women.

That's the other truth that this coverage tends to gloss over: fewer and fewer families can survive on one income. As I discussed in Chapter 4, you need two incomes to buy a house in many areas of the country. Women also earn a substantial portion of family income, a percentage that is likely to grow ever larger over time because a sizable majority (57%) of college degrees now go to women. The number of women enrolled in graduate and professional schools has also steadily increased. For example, the entering class of medical students in 2004 was 50% female, up from 42% just ten years before in 1994.

These realities suggest that we will never go back to stay-at-home moms as the majority of mothers. These stories continue to get press simply because they make media companies lots of money. They might be based on flimsy statistics and nonexistent "trends," but women will pick up a magazine, like the March 2004 *Time*, with an adorable child, dressed in white, who looks longingly up at his mother. Guilt sells magazines, but it won't pay the mortgage, so women's prominence in the workplace is here to stay.

But Weren't Things More Liberal Back in the 1970s?

Some in the media also buy in full-scale to the mythology that the Baby Boom generation was filled with feminists who married late and concentrated on their careers, in contrast to the current generation that now wants to turn back the clock. For example, a 1997 article in *Time* magazine proclaimed that twentysomethings were now marrying at earlier ages, "reacting in part to what they perceive as miscues by their older siblings, not to mention their parents, who attacked life with a single-minded career focus and a no-ties-to-hold-you-back attitude—and ended up with no ties at all."

This is unmitigated crap. Boomers—the older siblings and parents the article refers to—married at ages that would now be considered shockingly young. The median age at first marriage for women in 1970 was 20.8 (in other words, almost half of the women marrying for the first time in that year were teenagers). In 1980, the median age was still only 22. So Boomers were not a generation that postponed marriage. Steve Martin and Diane Keaton's characters in *Father of the Bride*, who married at 21, exemplify typical Boomer behavior. (See the figure on p. 99.)

The article went on to say that "pollsters, trend watchers and merchants are convinced that couples are getting married earlier than a few years ago," citing several wedding registry managers, one of whom claimed that among brides "their average age in 1990 was 27; today it's 24." A pollster goes on to say, "It'll take years for the numbers to catch up, but attitudinally, this generation is marrying younger." But data from the Census Bureau, readily available on the Internet and in government publications, soundly refutes this. The median age at first marriage for women in 1990 was 23.9, and in 1995 (the latest data available when the article was published) was 24.5. So it went *up*, not down. And what about the prediction that the age would go down after 1997? Not true either. The median age of marriage for women in 2002 was 25.3, up by more than half a year since 1995. The median age for men went up from 26.1 in 1990 to 26.9 in 1995; it remained at 26.9 in 2002.

Why did this article get things so wrong? Contrasting generations makes for good copy, whereas "the trend toward later marriage is continuing" does not. The reporter also didn't seem to consider that the economic boom of the late 1990s might have sent young brides to wedding registries previously out of their reach. Economics drove the trend, not an actual lowering of the age of brides.

The 2004 *Time* article about women choosing to stay home with their children made a similar generational contrast—also one that's dead wrong. It noted that older women "who came of age listening to Helen Reddy roar" were dismayed that many younger women were leaving the workforce. Yet when these same Boomer women were raising children, more of them—*not* fewer—stayed home. In 1980, only 45% of married women with children under 6 were in the workforce. In 2003, it was 60%. The article goes on to say that "in the highest household-income bracket ($120,000 and up), Reach Advisors found that 51% of Gen X moms were home full time, compared with 33% of boomer moms." This fails, however, to take into account the obvious fact that the GenXers' children are younger on average. This difference is probably based on age rather than generation, and thus is extremely misleading. When the GenX women have older children, they will most likely return to the workforce at even higher rates than Boomer women. Once again, the fever for the "Next Generation Turns Back the Clock to the 1950s!" story triumphed over the facts.

These articles blithely ignore the fact that social change doesn't happen overnight: it takes decades for momentum to build and for the once-radical edge to become mainstream. Boomers did not reinvent the world in one fell swoop. Change happened slowly, and as it did, GenMe was growing up. GenMe has never known a culture where almost half of the women getting married were teenagers, and where women were expected to stop working for good after the birth of their first child. The younger the woman, the more likely it is that she earned an advanced degree, that she married (or will marry) after the age of 25, and that she will work after she has children. GenMe women are the most liberated generation in history. Boomer women may have blazed the trail, but GenMe has walked that newly cleared path since we were young.

Well, But: The Big Caveat

So it seems clear that the "young women are going back to the kitchen" story of the last few years is just not true. Yet the arrival of a child can rock the most deeply held notions of sexual equality. As Susan Douglas and Meredith Michaels point out in *The Mommy Myth*, "a dad who knows the name of his kids' pediatrician and reads them stories at night is still regarded as a saint; a mother who doesn't is a sinner." GenMe dads are more involved than ever, which is fantastic; it's just that "more than ever" often still means "not much." In spite of the tremendous progress in diaper changing, bath giving, and baby cuddling among men, in the vast majority of cases it's still Mom who knows where Madison's shoes are and when Jacob takes his nap.

GenMe women are expected to lead a schizophrenic existence. We are told (and believe) that we can do anything, but once we become mothers "anything" becomes "that you can do from home" or "that is strictly 9 to 5" (ha!). Even "anything that pays enough so you can afford a British nanny" isn't good enough—do you really want "someone else raising your children?" Writer Peggy Orenstein said that after going around the country lecturing on self-esteem, she realized that, "there was this big gap in messages between what we were telling teenage girls and what we were telling women when they came to be around 30. For girls and teens, we say, 'You Can Do Anything,' and then for women, we turn around and say, 'You Can't Have it All.'" As a culture, we still carry an incredible amount of ambivalence toward working mothers that working fathers are still able to neatly sidestep.

Obviously, there is much more acceptance of working mothers now than in previous decades. But there is still an incredible amount of resistance to day care and nannies, which are—like it or not—the logical outcome of women fully participating in the working world. Many people still strongly believe that day care is harmful. At a recent party, I met a charming, incredibly bright 3-year-old who could rattle off the names of dinosaurs whose pronunciation stumped most of the adults in attendance. After the child left with her mother, one woman asked if the mother stayed home. She was surprised to learn that the child was in full-time day care—the implication being, of course, that a child who went to day care couldn't possibly be that smart.

In fact, children who attend day care centers are actually *smarter*; a comprehensive study shows that they score higher on measures of cognitive development and academic achievement than children exclusively in their mother's care. This study, published in 2003, was conducted by a government agency (the National Institute of Child Health and Human Development, part of the National Institutes of Health) and involved more than 1,000 children at ten locations around the country who were followed since 1991. The results are particularly strong for children who went to day care between the ages of 2 and 5, but even children who went to day care when they were younger than 2 showed a trend toward improved intellectual development. The results were the strongest for kids whose mothers had less education, but there was still a trend toward day care improving cognitive development even when mothers' education was controlled. *None* of the results showed lowered cognitive development from day care.

But you would never know this from watching the news; this study was not covered in any major media outlet that I could find. Instead, newspapers and television endlessly cover all of the bad stuff that can happen when mommies work. Movies like 1992's *The Hand That Rocks the Cradle* promoted the terrifying message that nannies are evil, which was seemingly verified in real life by the 1997 Louise Woodward shaken-baby case. During the course of that trial, the majority of the vitriol was directed not at the manslaughter-bound nanny but at the child's physician mother (how dare she leave her child with a nanny?) even though the mother worked only three days a week.

At the same time, standards for mothering have reached unrealistic heights. The popularity of attachment parenting—cosleeping, baby wearing, and breastfeeding for at least a year—comes, ironically, at a time when more and more women are working and thus less able to do these things. In 2005's *Perfect Madness*, Judith Warner criticizes the American standard of übermothering in which women's lives are completely consumed by their children's activities, leaving no time for anything else. Perhaps, she muses, this is what happens when women quit corporate jobs to stay home—they become just as competitive at home as they were in the boardroom. Douglas and Michaels label this new standard of intensive mothering "The New Momism." "It is no longer okay," they point out, "to let (or make) your kids walk to school, tell them to stop bugging you and go outside and play, or God forbid, serve them something like Tang . . . for breakfast." In a recent poll, 4 out of 5 parents said it is harder to be a parent today than it used to be.

It's enough to make one long for the days of yesteryear, when the goal of most mothers was to get the kids out of their hair so they could go play cards. Although these women were unquestionably good mothers as a group, that generation did not adhere to the belief that kids should be monitored—and preferably taught something—every minute, as society now believes. A sociological study found that despite more mothers being in the workforce, mothers in 1998 actually spent *more* time one-on-one with their kids than mothers did in 1965 and 1975, and they spent *twice* as much time teaching and playing with them. Given modern work schedules, this seems like an impossible time equation until you realize the differences in standards for motherhood between the two eras. Favorite phrase of Cold War–era mothers: "They're around here somewhere." These days, mothers are supposed to know exactly where their kids are every second—and be a teacher, a doctor, a chauffeur, and a developmental psychologist. Mothers are expected to be interacting with their kids every minute that the kids aren't watching *Baby Einstein* tapes.

Of course, if you have enough money and enough fame, all of this is easy, and the societal message is that it should be easy for you, too. As Douglas and Michaels hilariously document in their chapter "Attack of the Celebrity Moms," women's magazines now devote endless pages to profiling the mothering of the rich and famous. We learn that Kirstie Alley pays for all of her houses with cash; that celebrity moms all say that having a baby is much more important than being famous; and that it's hard to be a working mother even when you have two nannies and a housekeeper. (Boo-hoo.) One *People* magazine cover story titled "The Sexy New Moms" flatly stated, "Postpartum depression isn't an option for such celebrity moms as Whitney Houston, Madonna, and supermodel Niki Taylor." The authors wryly comment, "Unlike you, being subjected to sleep deprivation and raging hormones was a choice for these women, and they just said no."

Even if we realize the ludicrous nature of these media portrayals, we are still left with a world in which women prepare for careers but find little support once they have children. Peggy Orenstein describes the modern world as "half-changed," where "old patterns and expectations have broken down, but new ideas seem fragmentary, unrealistic, and often contradictory." In *Midlife Crisis at 30*, Lia Macko and Kerry Rubin express "the echoing, pervasive anxiety" of young women living with "the persistent gap between What Has Changed in terms of women's progress and What Has Stayed the Same in terms of old-school corporate structures and rigid social conventions." GenMe mothers, many of whom work outside the home, can lay out every one of these contradictions. Men and women are equal; no, wait, kids are your responsibility as the woman. You need two incomes to survive; no, wait, learn to live on one income. You should retain the status and satisfaction of working; no, wait, it's more important to stay home. There's a reason I discussed many of these problems in the chapter on depression and anxiety. As Douglas and Michaels put it, "Both working mothers *and* stay-at-home mothers get to be failures."

Even if the work-versus-stay-home decision is crystal clear to you, the realities of both situations aren't always manageable. You might have always wanted to stay home, but then find that you can't make ends meet if you're not a two-income family. Even if finances aren't an issue, you might find yourself unprepared for life cooped up with young children every day (and let's face it—who really *is* prepared for that?). If you're fine with going back to work, you might find it difficult to construct a manageable work schedule, and even harder to find good child care (and perhaps impossible to find good child care that's affordable). As Orenstein puts it, young women have "a sneaking suspicion that the rhetoric of 'choices' is in part a con job, disguising impossible dilemmas as matters of personal preference."

Almost everyone I know has a difficult time with these issues. Amy, 32, is a high-ranking corporate executive. After her son was born, she asked her boss if she could take a few more months of unpaid leave after her twelve-week maternity leave was up, and if she could work part-time after she returned to work. Her boss said no on both counts; Amy would have to come back to work, and full-time. Amy decided to resign; for one thing, the day care near her office only takes children older than a year (which is surprisingly common). Fortunately, Amy is a very valued employee, so her boss called back the next day and offered her six more weeks of unpaid maternity leave and a three-day-a-week schedule, but only until the end of the summer. Also fortunately, Amy's mother, a teacher, can watch the baby during that time. After that, Amy will have to find other child care arrangements and go back to working the twelve-hour-days that are standard in her profession. She has no idea what she will do. And this is someone with two advantages most people don't have—a high-ranking job and child care provided by a relative. Yet it's still a mess.

In *Perfect Madness*, Warner documents the new "problem that has no name": young families struggling to pay the mortgage and take care of their kids in a country with little support for parents. Warner was living in France when her children were born, a place featuring the mandatory paid maternity leave and low-cost preschools common in Europe (yes,

Virginia, there are places where these things exist). French culture also saw nothing wrong in leaving kids with babysitters every once in a while so the adults could enjoy a night out. Warner was shocked to return to the United States, where so many parents felt cast adrift and worn down by doing everything themselves. It is no coincidence that Warner subtitled her book *Motherhood in the Age of Anxiety*. The contradictions and lack of good choices for women with children lie at the center of her attack. When you've always been taught that you have choices and then something goes wrong, she writes, "you tend . . . to assume you made the wrong choices—not to see that the 'choices' given you were wrong in the first place."

Warner argues that many of these problems can be traced to individualism and inertia: young women's belief that we should handle everything on our own, and our cynicism that trying to change government policies would just be "knocking their heads against the wall." These are, of course, two central aspects of the GenMe personality. Our inherent self-focus and lack of confidence in political action lead us to assume that there are no other solutions to either (a) staying home and giving up income and a career, or (b) working and scrambling to find and pay for expensive day care. Young authors Macko and Rubin found the same thing: "Our peers were all wrestling with the same issues, yet responding to them by turning their anxiety inward and focusing on their own lives instead of seeing the bigger picture—let alone lobbying for universal changes." Douglas and Michaels sum up the "prevailing common sense" of the last two decades as "only you, the individual mother, are responsible for your child's welfare: The buck stops with you, period, and you'd better be a superstar." So we're supposed to raise our kids without help from anyone, an unrealistic expectation in the best of times. But it's what we believe, so we soldier on. This is one of the more solvable problems faced by our generation; more about that in the next chapter. Sometime in the next decade, the system will begin to break down: either more and more women will forgo having children, or government policies will change. Before that happens, there will be more and more tired, frustrated, and angry parents—particularly moms, but a growing number of dads, too (because if momma ain't happy, nobody's happy).

But would we go back? Hell, no. "I think women having more opportunities than previous generations is a good thing—a very good thing. I cannot think of a single reason why it could be bad," says Natalie, 21. Certainly, some GenMe women might desire to return to a simpler time when families could get by on one income and staying at home with one's child was the only accepted course. But more of us would rather not. We cannot begin to imagine what it was like to be told that only some professions were open to us. We cannot imagine making an absolute choice between having children and continuing to pursue a career. And we cannot imagine being told girls can't do something.

ATTITUDES TOWARD GAYS AND LESBIANS

On a 2005 episode of the teen soap *The O.C.*, 16-year-old Marissa, usually heterosexual, starts dating a lesbian. She's reluctant to tell her friend Summer about it, because she's worried that Summer will think it's strange. But when Marissa finally confesses, Summer says, "Huh," considers it for a moment, and then concedes, "She *is* pretty hot."

Describing the revolution in equality would not be complete without mentioning the enormous change in attitudes toward gays and lesbians. There is little question that American society has grown more accepting of homosexuality recently, and nowhere is that more evident than among young people. When I requested stories on my website about "being open to differences among other people," everyone who responded wrote about tolerance for gays and lesbians. Even young Republicans often don't understand what all of the fuss is about; a recent article in *Time* magazine found that otherwise conservative college Republicans are remarkably uninterested in gay marriage as an issue. While only 30% of the overall American population supports gay marriage, 59%—nearly twice as many—of 18-year-olds do.

Elizabeth, 27, went to a conservative Catholic school growing up, but often babysat a lesbian couple's son. "I always thought this was so cool," she says. "I thought, 'Wow, I don't care if they are lesbians or not.'" When Megan, 15, was in middle school, her gay teacher brought his partner along on a school trip to Washington, D.C. Her schoolmates' parents thought this was inappropriate and called the school. "But my friends and I never really understood what the problem was. I really don't see how bringing his partner along was any different than if he had brought his wife—which our parents would have had no trouble with, of course," Megan says. "People make homosexuality into such a big deal, but I just don't understand why anyone would care if two people want to be together. It's like race or gender—you can't control it, so why would anyone try to force someone to change?"

Despite the parents' protests, Megan's story illustrates change because she can tell it. Apparently, everyone knew the teacher was gay; it was just his partner coming on the trip that they didn't like. Not that long ago, a gay teacher who was out of the closet would have been fired outright—no trip to Washington, D.C., and no job at all. In fact, this happened to my favorite high school English teacher in 1989 in suburban Dallas. Despite being one of the best teachers in the school, the rumors caught up with him after two years and that was it; the school used some flimsy excuse not to renew his contract.

Don't forget—in 1989 there had never been a major TV character who was gay. *Ellen* didn't come out of the closet until 1997, and even then several major advertisers yanked their support after the episode aired and Ellen appeared on the cover of *Time* under the headline "Yep, I'm Gay." (As if people hadn't figured this out yet about a woman who regularly did her stand-up routine wearing men's shirts, suspenders, and tennis shoes.)

It's pretty amazing to realize that a gay television character was controversial as recently as 1997; when I went to look up this date, I was sure it was 1992 or 1993 instead. (Although the Seinfeld line "Not that there's anything wrong with that" beat the curve, premiering in 1993.) After 1997, things changed remarkably quickly. *Will and Grace* was an instant hit after its premiere in 1998, and a year later the teen show *Dawson's Creek* had a 16-year-old gay character. In 2000, *All My Children* introduced the first lesbian teen on daytime television, especially interesting since daytime TV skews toward an older demographic. And now Ellen Degeneres has a successful daytime talk show, where her sexual orientation is accepted but rarely acknowledged. It just is.

And we can't ever forget the stunning though now faded glory of *Queer Eye for the Straight Guy*, which premiered in 2003. An entire generation of kids is growing up seeing straight men freely hug gay men, and gay men having all of the answers while the poor slobby straight dude shaves wrong and breaks things in the kitchen. And let's not even talk about moisturizer. Main point: gay people are not only queer, and here, but they are very, very cool.

Young people often comment to me that they have a casual attitude about homosexuality that their parents don't understand at all. Lauren, a 21-year-old from North Carolina, was describing to her parents how a male friend of hers liked interior decorating, but, she added, "He's not gay—he has a girlfriend." Her father was shocked that Lauren was so nonchalant about sexual orientation. Jake, 28, has a gay uncle, but Jake's father and his family refused to acknowledge his homosexuality. When Jake and his fiancée invited Jake's uncle and his partner to their wedding, his parents were angry. "I quickly seized the opportunity to finally address the issue," said Jake. "I explained to them that I have no problem with whatever sexuality a person chooses. I also told them it made me feel good that my 48-year-old uncle would take his first step toward coming out to the family at my wedding."

Some teens find their experiences at odds with their religious upbringing. For many, this means that they see gays as sinners, and/or believe that gays can change to be straight. Others find themselves questioning their beliefs. Abby, 25, grew up in a conservative Christian town in rural Virginia. When she was 16, a boy she knew named Daniel told her his story: he was gay and had made out with a friend. When his parents found out, they kicked him out; other students tormented him at school. Daniel said, "If this is a choice, why would I have made it? It cost me everything." Abby had been wondering whether homosexuality really was a choice, as she had been taught at church, and something clicked inside her at that moment. "My sixteen-year-old world shifted on its axis," she wrote later. "I lost my faith that day, but I found the heart of humanity."

Daniel's experience is not unique; gay teens still face widespread harassment and ostracism. Sam Hanser, 16, told CBS's *Class of 2000* that at his high school in Massachusetts "groups of people would just come up to me and shout all sorts of stupid epithets. A lot of people called me 'faggot' and spat at me." In a CBS poll of high school students, 33% said gays and lesbians are the butts of jokes and abuse at their school. Among those who knew a gay person, 44% said that abuse occurred. Perhaps because of this type of treatment, gay teens are significantly more likely to commit suicide than straight teens. GenMe also confronts these issues at much younger ages than previous generations did. "Kids are coming out a lot earlier than they would have ten or twenty years ago," says Virginia Merritt, a psychiatrist who works with gay teenagers. Among high school seniors in the CBS poll, 2 out of 3 said they knew someone in their grade who is gay.

So if Americans are more tolerant of homosexuality than they were ten years ago, why are so many states passing laws against gay marriage, and why are so many people so opposed to it? Remember first that it's mostly older people who are adamantly against gay marriage; young people are much more accepting. As more of GenMe ages into adulthood, the number of people strongly against gay marriage will drop considerably. In addition, many people are opposed to gay marriage now simply because no one even thought to ask the question until about fifteen years ago—back then gays and lesbians were still fighting for even more basic rights, such as antidiscrimination laws. As recently as 2003, homosexual intercourse was illegal in the state of Texas. Now that more gays are "out of the closet," some people are scared of what that means. Angela, 22, says, "The backlash against gay marriage and gay and lesbian couples adopting children has happened because these issues are more visible. Panic is setting in where there should be adjustments to make the process smoother for everyone involved."

Angela is right—there is still panic out there. In 2002, my graduate school friend Carla Grayson and her partner, Adrianne Neff, petitioned the University of Montana, where Carla was an assistant professor, to provide health care benefits for Adrianne, who was staying home to care for the couple's 22-month-old son. Four days after a newspaper story reported on the lawsuit, Carla and Adrianne awoke in the early morning to the sound of the smoke detector going off. They ran to the front door to escape but were met by a wall of fire. Carla climbed out the window and Adrianne handed her the baby, finally escaping herself. The fire was ruled an arson, and police investigated it as a hate crime.

Although what happened next in no way made up for the crime, it was still notable. More than 700 townspeople turned out for a rally in support of the couple. A sign on the door of the Missoula First United Methodist Church read: "Open Hearts. Open Minds. Open Doors." Carla and Adrianne were touched by the support. "I know now that I don't have to watch over Carla and our son alone," Adrianne said to the crowd. "I feel like I am putting my family in the hands of this community—and it's a good place to be."

This story also illustrates how the change for gays has been slow in coming, and that although some straight people's attitudes are now much more tolerant, it's still very difficult to be gay or lesbian in the United States. Coming out of the closet to parents is terrifying; though certainly many parents are more tolerant now, there are few other bits of news that carry such a high risk of your parents never speaking to you again. There is still overt discrimination against gays, and of course your romantic relationship is not recognized under the law the way straight marriage is. And whether your partner gets health care benefits depends on the capricious circumstance of what state you live in and what job you have. Fight for them in the wrong place, and someone might burn down your house.

So although there's been a huge amount of change in attitudes recently, this change is more incomplete than those for minorities and women. GenMe gays and lesbians still face many challenges that their straight peers never will. But it wouldn't surprise me to see us all working together as the years pass to create even more tolerance and opportunity. No matter what your opinion on these issues, it's hard to deny that the tide of history flows toward equality.

8

Applying Our Knowledge:
The Future of Business and
the Future of the Young

S o here's how it looks: Generation Me has the highest self-esteem of
any generation, but also the most depression. We are more free and
equal, but also more cynical. We expect to follow our dreams, but are
anxious about making that happen. In a recent poll, 53% of high school
seniors said that growing up is harder now than it was for their parents.

The first wave of GenMe faces a very different world from what we
were led to expect as children. The messages of our youth were unflag-
gingly optimistic: You can be anything. Just be yourself. Always follow
your dreams. To borrow Alan Greenspan's phrase, our upbringing was
irrationally exuberant. Irrational, because when we reach adulthood we
often find ourselves lonely, rejected by graduate schools, stuck in a boring job, and/or unable to afford a house. ("Your job's a joke, you're broke,
your love life's DOA," goes the theme song of *Friends*, though many of us
find no one is "there for" us either). Like the dot-com economy of the late
1990s, the bubble of high expectations bursts once GenMe hits adulthood. Older generations have also faced these struggles, but GenMe has
been led to expect bounty in a time of famine. In a 1980s Talking Heads
song, a rich man wonders, "How did I get here?" and says, "This is not my
beautiful house! This is not my beautiful wife!" as if he is unsure how he
obtained the riches around him. GenMe feels the opposite—we wonder
instead, "Where is my beautiful house? Where is my beautiful wife?"
(And "Where is my fulfilling job and my shot at fame?") The gap

between expectations and reality has widened to a yawning gulf of disappointment.

There has been some good news in the last decade, particularly in teen behavior. Although 17% of teens said they seriously considered suicide in 2003, this was down from a staggering 29% in 1991. Teen pregnancy decreased markedly: births to teens aged 15 to 17 were down 42% between 1991 and 2003, and the abortion rate for this age group also fell. The violent crime rate, which is driven by the behavior of young men, fell 35% between 1992 and 2002. Fewer teens said they carried a weapon to school, and although 33% of high school students were in a physical fight in the last year, this was down from 43% in 1991. Even alcohol use is down among teenagers.

However, these encouraging trends may be due to the kids themselves rather than any systematic change in our culture. As the book *Freakonomics* shows, much of the crime drop of the 1990s can be traced to a surprising source: the nationwide legalization of abortion in 1973. After this time, millions of unwanted children were simply not born. Those children—all of them unwelcome, and many of them poor—might have been the most likely to commit crimes as teenagers and young adults. They might also have been the most likely to get into fights, carry weapons, and drink alcohol. The teen girls among them might have been the most likely to become pregnant. But they didn't, because they didn't exist. So American culture probably can't take credit for the improvements that began in the early 1990s, when more teenagers than usual grew from babies who were planned and wanted.

THE DELICATE ART OF PREDICTING THE FUTURE

What can we expect from Generation Me in the future? With the youngest of this generation (those born in the late 1990s) still in elementary school, there's a lot of future to predict. As more GenMe'ers reach adulthood over the next few years, there will be a full-scale collision between their high expectations and the unfortunate realities of modern life. More and more young people in their twenties will be disappointed that they cannot pursue their chosen profession, that their job performance is criticized, and that they cannot afford to buy a house. This will lead to a lot of anxiety, depression, and complaining. Older generations will perceive this as whining, but they should realize they created this monster by telling kids they could do anything they wanted. More and more employers will notice that their young employees seek fulfillment in their jobs and expect to be quickly promoted. A recent Associated Press article labeled the current generation of young people "The Entitlement Generation" and described how young workers want everything "right now." Most of the employers described the behavior of their teenage service employees, suggesting that this trend will appear in other businesses once the second wave of GenMe'ers graduates from college and begins adult careers.

GenMe will continue the shift toward equality across races, men and women, and gays and lesbians. The country will become progressively more color-blind, which might reduce racism, but is also likely to reduce support for affirmative action programs. Race will become increasingly complex as it moves beyond the old issue of white versus black. Hispanics are already the largest minority group in the United States, and Asians, though a small percentage of the overall population, are a large presence at universities and in the professions. More and more young people are multiracial, with parents from different racial groups, making race issues even more difficult to define. Race will become less important as a defining characteristic as more children with multiple racial identities are born. In a century or two Tiger Woods might be the rule rather than the exception.

Because young people are much more tolerant of homosexuality than older people, gay marriage and other reforms might well become a reality in the next few decades. Gays will continue to move toward the mainstream of American life, and more will come out of the closet as this identity becomes more accepted. Young people's tolerant attitudes toward homosexuality will stay with them as they age, so that in a few decades the majority of people in their fifties and sixties will be accepting of gays and lesbians.

Women will continue their pursuit of college degrees and their moves into the professions. This will be especially true in fields that deal with people rather than things (a preference that has a large sex difference). Because doctors, lawyers, and politicians all work with people, women will be the majority of young people in these professions within the next ten to twenty years. Engineering and physics, on the other hand, are likely to always remain majority male.

GenMe has a strong desire to have children: 75% of 2003 college freshmen named "raising a family" as an important life goal, compared to only 59% of Boomer college students in 1977. Whether young people will reach this goal is uncertain, given their career ambitions, the paucity of affordable child care, and the growing expense of child-related costs like housing and health care. This is yet another area where GenMe's ideals will conflict with reality, leading to anger and dissatisfaction. More and more young people want to become parents, but more and more will find that they cannot have children and maintain a middle-class standard of living. Many who do have children will find themselves unprepared to be full-time caregivers (a role often necessitated by the high cost of child care). Given that only 1 in 1,000 incoming college students chose "full-time homemaker" as their probable career, many GenMe'ers, mostly women, will find themselves staying at home when they never expected to do so.

If the United States does not develop a better system of child care (something I discuss more later), more women will choose not to have children. If that is the case, the United States will experience the underpopulation problems already prevalent in Europe and Japan. The Social Security system will fall apart, and the economy will falter. The ideology of the population may also change, perhaps negating some of the equalizing trends I just predicted. If women in conservative religious groups have significantly more children than other women, the political leanings of the country will begin to shift. This may be happening already, although it does appear that young people as a group are liberal on many social issues such as gay rights and race relations.

And what will GenMe's children be like? This is not as futuristic a question as it sounds—first-wave GenMe'ers are already in the prime child-rearing years of 25 to 35. It is difficult to tell right now if GenMe is adopting the same child-rearing approach as their parents, but it appears that they are. As a result, the next generation may be even more self-focused. Over time, more and more parents might draw the line at children's bad behavior and begin using more discipline. Another trend that will shape today's and tomorrow's children is the decreasing standard of living for young families. As the economic squeeze of housing prices and child care expenses intensifies, fewer children will get good quality day care or have their own yard to play in. The next generation will have fewer siblings, as fewer families will be able to afford large houses, day care for multiple children, and several college tuition bills. Only children will become more common. There will be a growing gulf between rich children and poor children as economic pressures sort people more definitively into the haves and the have-nots.

In the following sections, I'll discuss what these trends mean at a practical level. I'll start with the implications for employers and marketers, who are managing and selling to this generation right now and will be for years to come. I'll then move on to what comes next—things that all of us together, and parents and young people in particular, can do to change things for the better in the future, for this generation and the next.

FOR EMPLOYERS

What do these generational changes mean for managers who work with younger people? The first step is to try to understand Generation Me—realize that younger employees may have a very different outlook on life. The times that shaped GenMe'ers as children are very different from those experienced by older generations. You can't blame someone for absorbing the culture around him. Realize that GenMe's attitudes are not wrong, just different. Just trying to see things from their perspective will help a lot. At minimum, think about how old your employees were during certain events; avoid the mistake of one man I worked with who asked where I was when JFK was shot. (Answer: Not born for eight more years.) People born in the 1980s will soon dominate the young workforce; many of them do not remember Ronald Reagan's presidency, the USSR, or Michael Jackson with dark skin.

Some young people will arrive with a feeling of entitlement, believing they deserve everything right away. This generation has "shockingly high expectations for salary, job flexibility and duties," notes the AP "Entitlement Generation" article. Mike Amos, a franchise consultant for Perkins Restaurants, says, "It seems they want and expect everything that the 20- or 30-year veteran has the first week they're there." This is the natural outcome of the self-esteem movement, but as an employer it's too late to change your young employee's upbringing. Be prepared to explain to young people that success and privileges will not happen overnight; add that you know this is frustrating, but it's the way business works. Your patience and understanding will pay off. "The manager who says I don't have time for that is going to be stuck on the endless turnover treadmill," says Eric Chester, a consultant on young people in the workplace. Not surprisingly, 60% of employers say that their workplaces suffer from tension among the generations.

The best thing you can do is realize that this generation is not "spoiled" and does not "have it easy." GenMe has been raised thinking we were special and getting lots from Mom and Dad, but when we hit young adulthood we face an enormous mismatch between what we expect and what we actually get. Before you say "Poor babies," realize that the inflated cost of housing and the ultracompetitive market for college and good jobs would be difficult even without our high expectations. A boss who understands this will have a much easier time connecting with young employees. Young people are unlikely to change overnight, and berating them isn't going to do any good.

So what, specifically, can you expect from your young employees? They will work hard, but even harder if they are praised and appreciated. This is true of any generation, of course, but it is especially true of GenMe'ers, who were raised on extensive praise and almost expect it. This generation is not motivated by feelings of duty—working hard is not virtuous in itself, but it is worth it if they are singled out and recognized. They will be frank and might have few qualms about sharing information you might consider sensitive or private. They appreciate directness rather than abstraction. They do not have automatic respect for authority and will feel free to make suggestions if they think it will improve things. You may have to earn their respect rather than receiving it simply by your position in the company. "If you just expect them to stand behind a register and smile, they're not going to do that unless you tell them why that's important and then recognize them for it," says John Spano, a human resources director for a movie theater company, interviewed in the AP article. Of course, this applies even more to college-educated employees, who will have an even greater desire to understand what they're doing and be praised for it.

Your young employees will learn best by doing. Raised with the Internet and in collaborative learning classrooms, they are not used to sitting through long, boring lectures. Training seminars will put them to sleep if they are not interactive. A generation raised not just on television but on cable, they will perk up during a presentation with video clips and moving graphics. They'll perk up even more if you can get them involved through a demonstration or role-playing. One-on-one training should be Socratic and task-oriented—don't just show them something, but have them do it themselves.

You will find that your young employees are very flexible and used to dealing with diversity. If you need someone to meet clients who are from a different culture or background, a young person—even if he or she is not from the same background—will adapt to this situation well. Young people today often have friends or schoolmates from different backgrounds, listen to diverse forms of music, and eat ethnic food the way earlier generations ate bacon and eggs. On the other hand, young employees may need some guidance on how to deal with older people. They may come off as disrespectful when they are merely being friendly and informal. Some young employees might need to be taught to "clean up" when talking to older folks, using "Mr." and "Mrs." and speaking more formally.

Today's young employees also appreciate flexible schedules and independence. They don't respond well to micromanagement, and will find rigid schedules stifling. Consistent with this theme, they will also respond to a casual dress code. GenMe loves doing their own thing and will like working at a place that values this. The book *Generations at Work* advises that you "include the phrase 'we want you to have a life' at least three times during the [job] interview." Work for work's sake is not a big hit with this generation, though in a "fun" workplace they might be more willing.

One downside to this generation is that they do not take criticism well. The self-esteem ethos in schools and parenting has valued protecting young people's positive self-feelings over all else. Some GenMe'ers attended schools where teachers did not correct their mistakes, and others had parents who let them do whatever they wanted. They are used to feeling important and having their work praised. When you need to criticize their work, begin with something positive and explain the reason behind your criticism. Do not be surprised if you encounter defensiveness. Things will go better if you can take that in stride and not get defensive in return; just explain exactly why it's wrong and move on. Over time, young employees will grow more accustomed to criticism; it might just take longer since they are not as familiar with it.

Expect this generation to be ambitious, sometimes wildly so. The optimism of youth, combined with the instant gratification that technology has provided, often leads to impatience. Some young people will expect that they will be a senior manager within five years. It might be best if another young person—perhaps someone with just a few more years' experience—explains the usual length of career paths. This is especially true of the most qualified young people; even more than others, they have been encouraged to have lofty ideas about their future. Other young employees may have the idea that their job is only temporary, and before long, they'll break into acting, sell their screenplay, or get on *American Idol*. Don't worry—they'll find out soon enough that they shouldn't quit their day job. Others will want to explore many different career paths before settling down. Much of this comes from the Twixter phenomenon, in which young people spend their twenties uncommitted to careers and relationships, free to pursue many different possibilities. But young people will stay at a job if they feel they are valued for their unique abilities.

Realize how important salary is to this generation. Every generation has valued compensation, of course, but young people today face an uphill battle to buy houses in a real estate market that has far outpaced inflation. Even dual-income couples have a difficult time finding affordable houses in many cities now. Add in escalating costs for health care and child care, plus a staggering amount of college debt, and young people are often in very precarious economic positions. Nothing raises the ire of a young person more than an older person who doesn't understand current economic realities and assumes that we're out spending our money on luxuries. I'll never forget a faculty meeting at which an older professor said he thought the $50,000 salary for a new position sounded too high. Perhaps because he bought his own house forty years ago, he seemed oblivious to the fact that a $50,000 annual salary won't even buy a two-bedroom condo in San Diego anymore. Though it's true that GenMe is more materialistic, we are also finding it difficult just to pay for the necessities of life.

One of the best recruiting tools you have for this generation is good benefits. Jobs with decent health care plans are difficult to find these days, and there is nothing more demoralizing for a young employee than to find out they are paying $500 a month for health care and still have to wait four months to see a doctor. A job with an excellent health care plan is extremely difficult to leave. Retirement plans are also a surprisingly good recruiting tool considering the youth of this generation. GenMe assumes Social Security is not going to be there to support them, so they will have to stand on their own. With so many more dual-income families, perks like on-site day care, flexible schedules, work-at-home options, and generous parental leave policies will also significantly improve retention. Hewlett-Packard instituted many of these reforms during the late 1990s and now has one of the lowest turnover rates in the business. These types of programs are already growing in popularity and will continue to do so as women constitute a larger and larger percentage of the college-educated workforce (women now earn an incredible 57% of college degrees). Even for young people without children, flexible scheduling is a big hit. They're willing to get the work done, so who cares if they take a long lunch to see a friend who's in town?

You probably already realize that your young female employees are a very different breed from the women of previous generations. They will be just as confident and assertive as the men you employ. They're still different from men in other ways, however. Cultural expectations for feminine appearance have grown even more demanding in recent years, for example. And women don't take to trash talking and blunt teasing the way men do; this sex difference still persists. (Women do not call their friends "Dumbass" like men do in that odd masculine cross between affection and insult.) On the flip side, realize that young men no longer find it odd for guys to be interested in cooking or interior decorating; the metrosexuals among them will also be interested in fashion. Gender is a fluid concept to this generation.

For economic reasons, two incomes will continue to be the norm for this generation. Most women with children return to the workplace soon after their maternity leave is up. However, many women would rather work part-time after having children, so don't be surprised by this request should you hear it. Over the next few years, you should also not be surprised to hear such requests from new fathers. Men are getting more and more involved in child rearing, and many young men are not willing to miss out on their children because they have to work twelve hours a day. With more women getting a college education, an increasing number of men will make less than their wives. Most day care centers close at 5:30 or 6:00 P.M.; that's often a nanny's quitting time as well. Thus late meetings will lead to frantic calls to spouses and lots of stress. Managers might still have to call late meetings, sometimes, but they need to realize the impact they will have.

FOR MARKETERS AND ENTREPRENEURS

Marketers and salespeople already know about—and use—the self-focus of Generation Me. This generation is, by definition, interested in products that satisfy their personal wants and help them express themselves as individuals. At the same time, this generation feels a tremendous amount of anxiety about succeeding in life. The market for products that help young people get into college or graduate school, do well in interviews, and look good for those interviews will continue to grow. Young women in particular will respond to an advertising campaign that shows them how to dress professionally in a way that is still attractive. This balance is still difficult to strike, and more and more young women are anxious about their job or graduate school interviews. They've gotten mixed messages from TV and movies about how to dress on such occasions, since these sources often show professional women showing lots of leg and cleavage (anything for ratings). Sisterly advice in this department will be welcomed.

Young people are also starving for good advice on career paths. Ten years ago, who had ever heard of a "life coach?" Companies like My Guidewire (myguidewire.com) ask if you are "unhappy with your job" or "wanting to shift from surviving to succeeding," and promise to help you "gain a competitive advantage" (for a monthly fee, of course). Expect this market to expand as more and more young people find it difficult to navigate the transition from college to first job, or find themselves dissatisfied with their first job (or second, or third). With more college graduates emerging with business and psychology degrees, many young people will gladly pay someone to help them find a job that uses their skills.

The continuing rise in the age at first marriage and young people's long working hours both suggest that Internet dating services and "speed dating" will continue their rise in popularity. Services that attempt to match people on certain characteristics will do particularly well, as they save time by sifting through the pool of candidates. Products aimed at single people will also be good bets. Grocery items in smaller packages might do particularly well; people who live alone are sick of watching half a loaf of bread turn to mold and half the cheese learn to walk inside the fridge. The popularity of the 2-serving bag of salad is a good illustration of a product whose time has come: it saves the busy person from taking apart heads of lettuce and provides the product in the right amount. It also makes a nice profit. Other products that can corner this market will do well.

With the move away from dating and toward hookups, the already huge market for appearance-enhancing products will continue to expand. As Paris Hilton taught us, being "hot" is the ultimate good. Women—and, increasingly, men—will flock to the clothes and products that convey sex. The plastic surgery trend will continue as standards for appearance require unreachable perfection.

One sobering fact is that young people today have less money left over for luxuries, decreasing the market for some items and increasing it for others. Spiraling costs for housing, health care, and day care mean less discretionary income. Even if housing prices dip somewhat (a debatable point), that might just bring more young people into mortgages that tie up 40% of their pretax income. As the squeeze sets in, even fewer people will be able to afford large down payments, increasing the market for second mortgages and home equity lines of credit. The continued demand for child care and the increasing cost of day care centers both suggest that home day cares will continue to be profitable, as will nanny services. There will also be an increasing demand for affordable preschools, as more and more research proves its benefits. The trend toward educational products for children will continue as parents realize that the competition for the best schools will only increase in the coming decades.

Marketers looking to target a specific age group during the next decade will find that those born between 1988 and 1991 are a good bet. This is the largest four-year cohort of people in twenty years, since the birth rate spiked at this time (reaching its peak in 1990) and decreased after that. It's the closest thing to a baby boom we have. As this group enters college and the workplace over the next few years, they'll exert a larger-than-normal influence on the culture. It won't be anything like the dominance of their Boomer parents, but it should still register.

WHERE DO WE GO FROM HERE?

Like most of my generation, I am skeptical that simply calling for change will actually change anything. But there are three changes that would make an enormous difference in the lives of Generation Me and the generations who follow us. One will cost no money and might even save money; another may cost universities a small amount but will greatly benefit their students; and the last will vary in cost, but even the most expensive changes may end up paying for themselves.

Ditch the Self-Esteem Movement and the Unrealistic Aphorisms

It is not who you are underneath, but what you do that defines you.
—*Batman Begins*, 2005

The first change we must make is to abandon our obsession with self-esteem. Instead of creating well-adjusted, happy children, the self-esteem movement has created an army of little narcissists. Schools should eliminate self-esteem programs. It does not do any good for a child to hear that he or she is "special" or to "win" a trophy just for participating. Decades of research have shown that high self-esteem does *not* cause good grades or good behavior. So the programs are not doing any good. What's more, they may actually be harming some kids by making them too self-centered. Praise based on nothing teaches only an inflated ego. The purpose of school is for children to learn, not for them to feel good about themselves all the time.

Another facet of this movement says that teachers should not correct children's mistakes, lest this hurt their self-esteem. This is extremely misguided: children learn by having their mistakes corrected, and their self-esteem is hurt when they later find out that they've been doing something wrong for years and aren't prepared. "We are in danger of producing individuals who are expert at knowing how they feel rather than educated individuals who know how to think," writes education professor Maureen Stout. Children will feel good about themselves—and rightly so—when they develop real skills and learn something. Children also need to learn how to deal with criticism, in preparation for the inevitable day when it is not delivered as gently as you—or they—would like. We are doing young people an enormous disservice by sending them into an increasingly competitive world thinking they will be praised for substandard work. It is too late to change this for adult GenMe'ers, who are now struggling to succeed in college and the working world after having their self-esteem boosted throughout their childhoods. But schools can still make these changes for the younger members of GenMe and for future generations.

Fortunately, many schools do still correct children's mistakes. However, the majority of schools consider it their mission to cultivate children's self-esteem, even though decades of research make clear that this is a waste of time. Some schools say instead that they aim to help each child cultivate his or her unique skills and abilities. This is fine as long as that still means that all kids learn math, and that kids still learn that people differ in their talents. There is nothing wrong with being good at some things and not others—that's life.

Many schools have stopped publishing the honor roll, since kids who don't make the list might "feel bad." But feeling bad can be good; it can motivate hard work. The Japanese have known this for ages, which is why Japanese kids often say they're no good at something, work really hard, and then blow American kids out of the water in international tests. We have to get away from the notion that negative self-feelings are to be avoided at all costs. There is no need to shelter kids from differences in abilities among people; they're going to encounter this in college or the workplace soon enough anyway. Publish the damn honor roll. In a culture obsessed with sports, it's the very small bit of high school glory enjoyed by the kids who will someday be our doctors and lawyers.

Parenting magazines should stop insisting that a parent's most important duty is to raise a child who "likes herself." As any parent of a two-year-old can tell you, most kids like themselves just fine—and make the demands to prove it. Even as children grow older, most are confident and self-assured. It's true that a small percentage of kids might need extra encouragement, but a much larger percentage will believe you if you say they are the best kids in the world. Children do not need to be sheltered from failure. "We do not need to completely shield our children from pain, discomfort, and unhappiness," advises the sane book *The Over-Scheduled Child*. "When life undoes all that hard work, as real life invariably must, our carefully 'shielded' children may not have developed the tools they need to cope with adversity." If children are always praised and always get what they want, they may find it difficult to overcome challenges as adults. "The risk of over indulgence is self-centeredness and self-absorption, and that's a mental health risk," says psychologist William Damon.

Much of the "self-esteem movement" actually encourages narcissism, or the belief that one is better and more important than anyone else. Narcissism is a very negative personality trait linked to aggression and poor relationships with others. Somehow we've developed the notion that it's not OK to have a few insecurities, but it is OK to think you're the greatest and everyone else should get out of your way. Instead, children should learn to have empathy and respect for others. Eventually, children will learn that the world does not revolve around them. As an added bonus, children who are sensitive to others' needs get along better with their peers and thus enjoy all of the benefits that come with good friendships. Children are naturally self-centered; growing up is the process of learning how to empathize with other people.

Instead of children doing "All About Me" projects, or writing "commercials" advertising themselves, perhaps they could learn about another child in the class. What is her life like? What are her beliefs, and why does she have them? What has she learned from her experiences? Children would learn a lot more from this type of project, and might also develop empathy in the process.

Psychologist Roy Baumeister argues that parents and teachers should focus on teaching self-control instead of self-esteem. Children who learn how to persevere at a difficult task and delay rewards until a later time grow up to accomplish much more than children who do not have these skills. Children should be rewarded for good behavior, not indulged when they whine or get upset. Kids who learn to control their emotions and actions will reap the benefits for years to come. Their actions are more important than their feelings about themselves.

We also need to stop talking in unrealistic platitudes, and this goes for teachers, parents, and Hollywood screenwriters alike. We must stop telling children "You can be anything you want to be" or "You should never give up on your dreams." Why? Because both of these statements are patently untrue. Not everyone is good at what he would like to do, and even if he is, the profession might be very competitive and full of talented people. Adults cannot follow their dreams all the time, but must deal with the practical matters of getting a job that pays the bills. It's fine to tell kids to try to find a profession that they enjoy, but talk of "dreams" and being "anything you want" creates unrealistic expectations that are bound to disappoint. We're raising idealistic children who expect the world and can't even buy a condo, who believe that every job will be fulfilling and then can't even find a boring one. It's especially tempting to utter these aphorisms to smart and talented kids, but they especially need to realize that it will still take a lot of hard work and luck to make it—lots and lots of smart people don't get in to the law school of their choice or get their dream job. Yes, your talent will open up more possibilities, but it doesn't actually mean that you will be able to do *anything* you want to do. I have never met someone who was truly, objectively, good at *everything*.

Not only do these phrases create unrealistic expectations, but they can also give kids the idea that the world is an ever-expanding, scarily large universe of possibilities. Author Chris Colin quotes his classmate Lesley Kato, who says: "I was told, growing up, that I could do whatever I wanted, and I fully believed I could. And therefore I had no idea what to do."

Instead, children should learn that growing up is a gradual process of learning what you're good at and what you're not. Then they have to figure out how to apply that to a career. There are some talents that aren't going to lead to a paying job, and others that might. It's also useful to consider their skills in relation to other people—what do you do better than most people? (Again, ignore the empty self-esteem proposition that you shouldn't "compare yourself to others"—everyone else will, so you might as well start now.)

These skills also need to be viewed through a realistic lens. Even the extremely skilled baseball player is unlikely to make it to the major leagues. The extremely talented actor probably won't become a movie star. Few people realize how difficult it is to get into med school or land a university teaching job. This doesn't mean that young people should be discouraged from pursuing these professions, but that they should be prepared for how difficult it might be.

Another aphorism that should be chucked is "You must love yourself before you love others." A mountain of research shows that people who have good relationships with other people are happier and less depressed—and have higher self-esteem. The idea that self-esteem rises fully formed and perfect from inside the individual is a complete myth. We develop our sense of ourselves primarily from interacting with others. There is nothing wrong with this. Not only that, but narcissists—people who *really* love themselves—are horrible relationship partners. Self-centered people are rarely fun to be around, and we all know this. So why do we keep telling people to love themselves first before others? Beats me. An aphorism that makes a lot more sense, to modernize John Donne, is "No one is an island."

Provide Better Career Counseling for Young People

A few years ago, *The Ambitious Generation* reported that young people overwhelmingly expect to attend college, go on to graduate school, and pursue professional careers. The subtitle of the book was *America's Teenagers, Motivated but Directionless*. That's because young people are usually not told how to achieve those goals. As the book documents, many parents focus on their kids getting into the "best" college, not the college that is best for the young person and his or her career goals. In some fields, doing internships and developing contacts are key; in others, college grades count. Many teens are very focused on a goal but have no idea how to achieve it; parents and counselors can help them take the practical steps toward reaching their goals. Many books and websites detail some of this "insider" knowledge.

Not every teen should be encouraged to go to college. A whopping 97% of parents believe that college is necessary or at least helpful for succeeding in life. For most teens, this is probably true. But there are many high-paying and rewarding occupations that do not require a college degree. Just to offer a few examples: plumbers, auto mechanics, carpenters, and electricians make excellent money. Young people who enjoy mechanical things and have little interest in college should not be browbeaten into going. If they learn a skilled trade, they'll often be making more money than a college graduate of the same age. A cultural value shift is also in order. College-educated people should consciously reconsider their attitudes toward skilled trades and give them the respect they deserve. It should not be an embarrassment to be without a college degree if you're in a job that requires skills not taught in college.

Students who do go to college need more career direction. Most college students are ill equipped to choose a future profession and receive little guidance during their four years at school. As noted in the marketing section above, many companies have stepped in to fill the gap with job search services. Placement offices at universities have a tough job, and students often need more help than they can provide.

One way to solve this is to start early by teaching students about the career paths in their field. A few years ago, our psychology department at San Diego State began requiring a one-credit class for psychology majors called Academic and Career Opportunities in Psychology. Many older faculty members were against requiring this course, as it does not teach psychology per se. My younger peers on the faculty thought it was a great idea, and so do I. I would go further: every college student should take a class like this in their major, preferably during their sophomore year. It's true that college should primarily be about learning, but universities should realize that students need more guidance if they are going to apply what they learn to a desirable job. Job placement offices at colleges can only spend so much time with any one student, and often students arrive without any clear idea of what kind of job they would like. Career path classes organized by major can give students the information they need to help decide on a profession. In the SDSU course, students learn about career opportunities and graduate schools and get a primer on job search skills. Students also get help developing an educational plan that will help them reach their goals.

Ideally, these classes should feature guest appearances by alumni who can give students a view of what it's like to work in a specific profession, and perhaps provide a useful networking contact. In general, there should be more opportunities for alumni to visit campus and give advice and mentoring to young people. Like most of my faculty colleagues, I don't know much about nonacademic career paths, and I wish there were more resources for students to hear from people who do.

Create More Support for Working Parents

In the coming years, two of the greatest problems for young people will be getting health care and child care. Both eat up increasingly large chunks of young families' incomes. As much as I'd like to delve into it, the debate over nationalized health care is beyond the scope of this book. With premiums heading skyward, the system might well be broken within ten years. Clearly something needs to be done about it, but what, when, and how is incredibly complicated.

Child care, on the other hand, is relatively simple: most mothers work, and their kids need care. Yet there is no nationalized system, and young families often have few choices; good care is very expensive, and even mediocre care is hard to find and still costly. Millions of people deal with this every day. Solutions would be expensive, but nowhere near the cost of nationalized health care. Working families already have huge costs. As the book *The Two-Income Trap* documents, the best predictor of whether a woman will file for bankruptcy is motherhood. Compared to a childless couple, a family with children is more likely to be late on credit card payments and more likely to have their home foreclosed. American parents are going broke trying to pay the mortgage and the child care bill.

So why isn't anything being done about this? Why is the United States one of the few industrialized nations without mandatory paid maternity leave or state-sponsored day care? Why aren't the problems of young families—the expense of day care, the cost of housing, the lack of good choices—at the forefront of politicians' agendas, instead of Social Security and prescription drugs?

It's at least partially because young people have not put them there. Two of GenMe's most prominent characteristics are our individualism and our lack of political engagement. These two trends are related: we firmly believe that no one is going to help us, so we have to stand on our own. Many of us don't vote. We don't think political action will do any good. We think everything is up to the individual, even though millions of us are experiencing the same problems at the same time. We're so uncomfortable with group action that we have seemingly thrown in the towel for getting back any of our tax dollars. If older Americans faced a problem that made their checkbooks impossible to balance, they'd take political action and get results. We do basically nothing. In *Perfect Madness*, Judith Warner writes, "There is right now no widespread feeling of social responsibility—for children, for families, for anyone, really—and so [young parents] must take everything onto themselves. And because they *can't*, humanly, take everything onto themselves, they simply go nuts."

Ever since large numbers of mothers went to work in the 1970s, we Americans have had our collective heads in the sand about day care. Our workplaces and much of the rest of our lives are still structured as if we all had wives at home. Yet couples in which the husband works and the wife doesn't are only 28% of young marrieds, not even a third. Even that minority would benefit from many of the changes suggested to improve things for working parents, such as paid maternity leave and state-sponsored preschool. It is as close to bulletproof as a political issue gets: in a 2002 poll, 82% of women and 75% of men said they would support a system of paid parental leave. A 1999 poll found that 74% of women and 70% of men believed that government should do more to help working families.

Imagine getting into your time machine and seeing this: kids playing together at a day care completely free of cost to their parents, with children learning about colors and shapes and letters while their parents work. And when mom or dad swings by to pick up the kids, there is a hot meal waiting to take home. Unrealistic? No, because that time machine didn't zip you into the future; it transported you to the past. From 1943 to 1945, the United States government ran child care centers for women who worked in war-related industries, hot meal and all. Imagine what we could do now in the time of such newfangled devices like the copy machine, the ballpoint pen, and the microwave oven.

Actually we don't even need to imagine it; the U.S. government already subsidizes day care for hundreds of thousands of children right now: the children of military personnel. The government pays an average of $3,400 a year per child to offset the cost of child care, with families paying between $37 and $98 a week on a sliding scale dependent on income. (Just for the sake of comparison, $98 a week is less than half the cost of unsubsidized day care in the average center). Far from being sterile institutions, these day cares are, author Ann Crittenden reports, extremely well run and stimulating for children. Government child care sounds scary on the face of it, but the day care enjoyed by these military kids sounds more like heaven. If only we didn't have to join the Army to get it.

Here are some specific suggestions for how governments (local and national) can help working families.

1. *Create a nationwide system of paid parental leave.* When the Family and Medical Leave Act passed in 1993, conservatives predicted that it would hurt business. That didn't happen, and in fact the next seven years were some of the best the economy ever had. The law, however, mandates only *unpaid* leave, a difficult proposition when many mortgages these days require two hefty incomes. Canada and many European countries provide paid parental leave for a *year*. The United States has nothing. Of 168 industrialized nations around the world, 163 guarantee paid leave for new mothers. Not only is the United States one of the 5 countries without paid parental leave, but we are also one of the few that does not mandate paid vacation for workers. As a result, a third of women workers in the United States get no paid vacation at all. For someone living paycheck to paycheck (i.e., most people), no paid leave often means going into considerable credit card debt to have a baby.

The tide may be turning, however. California recently introduced a paid leave system that pays 55% of your income for six weeks. It is not paid through taxes but through a small payroll deduction. It's a small step, but it's a step. A system of mandated paid parental leave nationwide would be an even better step.

2. *Create a system of public preschools for 3- and 4-year-olds.* This will benefit both GenMe parents and their children. Children who attend preschool are smarter and more academically prepared for school. The benefits are especially large for lower-income kids, but middle-class kids show significant gains as well. Children at this age are eager to learn; it is a unique opportunity to capture kids at their best and create children who will become confident readers and great math problem solvers. Yet when not publicly funded, preschool is out of the reach of most lower-income families and a big strain on the already taxed budgets of the middle class. Florida recently introduced a program of part-time preschool for all 4-year-olds in the state, and Oklahoma has a similar program. States that wish to keep current workers productive and create better workers for the future should follow suit. And the money that middle-class families save on preschool will probably go right back into the economy—most families with young children are so strapped for cash that they will probably have the money spent the minute their state funds the program. In addition, as Crittenden argues, the tax revenue generated by more women working might also offset a good portion of the cost of these types of programs, particularly if they are full-time. Even if preschools aren't funded, a national system for accrediting them would be extremely helpful to parents.

3. *Make child care expenses tax-deductible.* If you haven't used the day care tax credit yourself, you might think that the tax code already allows this deduction. But the amount of expenses allowed are pitifully small, barely enough to put a kid in day care for two months, not an entire year. The amount is capped at such a low figure that the average family gets back only a few hundred dollars. Another program available through some businesses allows parents to have an account to pay for child care that draws from pretax funds, but the limit on this account is also only a fraction of the amount needed to pay for full-time care (about $5,000 a year, when full-time care often costs over $12,000 a year, and sometimes more). This account can also only be used for day care centers, and not for more informal arrangements like many nannies or babysitters. It is also only available for some jobs.

Compare this with the incentive to buy a house: *all* mortgage interest is tax-deductible (even if your house is worth several million—and this is *still* deductible even under the Alternative Minimum Tax). Yet few child-related expenses are tax-deductible. It is in the government's best interest for people to have children and for both parents to keep working, since working creates more income tax, as do child care centers, as will the children themselves eventually (not to mention that their paychecks will be sorely needed to fund the Social Security system, assuming it doesn't collapse before then). Crittenden also details other changes to the tax code that would benefit working families, such as taxing the second earner's income at a lower rate. The authors of *The Two-Income Trap* write, "Any program that helps families save money is a program that helps keep the middle class secure."

What will happen if these changes aren't made? More and more people will find that they cannot afford to have children. Others will find that they cannot combine children and the career they love or need to get by, creating the loss of many talented workers from the labor force and ghettos of families with working dads and stay-at-home moms living in apartments. If things continue as they are, the United States will experience a declining population and all that that entails for Social Security and the future economy. This is happening already: in 2002, the U.S. birth rate hit an all-time low. The total fertility rate was 2.0, below the so-called "replacement" rate of 2.1. This is very likely to continue, as everything associated with children is skyrocketing in price: houses with enough bedrooms and in good school districts, health care, child care, a college education.

4. *Change school hours.* At virtually no cost to themselves, local schools could save working parents thousands of dollars a year, improve student performance and behavior, cut the crime rate, and reduce the teenage pregnancy rate. How? By bringing school hours more in line with business hours. I'm not talking about after-school programs—just shifting the hours when kids are in school.

The vast majority of school-age children have mothers who work: in 2003, 77% of married women and 85% of divorced and widowed women with children aged 6 to 17 worked. At the moment, parents of younger kids have little choice but to pay for day care in the afternoon, since their children are released from school around 2 or 3 P.M. and parents don't get off work until 5 or 6. After-school day care is expensive, often costing $500 a month or more. Once kids are older, they are usually left at home to fend for themselves in the afternoon. Teenagers and an empty house: great combination, right? Yet the early school day is the norm around the country, with many high schools starting at 7:30 A.M. and releasing at 2:30 P.M. Some even start at 7 A.M.!

If schools instead started at 9 A.M. and released at 4:30 or 5, a number of benefits would accrue. Day care costs for the parents of young children would go down, often to zero, and teenagers would not have the entire afternoon to get into trouble. And they do get into trouble—a large percentage of teenage pregnancies occur between 3 and 5 P.M., as do a large percentage of teenage crimes. Other teens sit in front of the television, surf the Web unsupervised, or play video games for hours.

The early start time of many high schools also runs exactly counter to the ingrained tendencies of the average teenager. A biologically driven shift in circadian rhythms makes it next to impossible for adolescents to fall asleep and wake early. This is *not* laziness; it is a well-documented biological tendency. (For a great description of this research, see *The Promise of Sleep* by renowned Stanford sleep expert William Dement.) In addition, teens are more impaired by sleep loss than adults are and need at least an hour more sleep than adults. For a school that starts at 7:30, this means getting up, at the latest, at 6:30 and thus going to bed at 9:30 (to get the nine hours of sleep teens need). What teenager goes to bed at 9:30? Very few, so most are simply tired all the time. Teens who begin school at 7:30 A.M. are simply not awake. School start times ask teenagers to come to school an hour earlier than most adult jobs begin, at a time when they need more sleep and have a difficult time falling asleep before 11 P.M. or midnight, if not later. Research shows that lack of sleep can lead to anxiety, depression, drug use, car accidents, and aggression. As teenagers are already vulnerable to these dangers, it is important to do everything we can to help them get enough sleep.

Changing school start times can have amazing effects. When the Edina, Minnesota, school system shifted their start time to 8:30 A.M., academic performance improved and misbehavior went down. Teens were more awake and alert in classes and learned more, and everyone's mood improved.

Some parents might protest that they need to be at work early, and then what will they do with their kids? First, this is a minority of people—most businesses start at 8 or 9 (whereas very, very few adults end work at 2:30 or 3 in the afternoon). Also, most elementary schools already have a system of supervising kids in the cafeteria if they need to be dropped off early; many serve breakfast. Older teenagers can sleep later and get ready on their own in the morning. Even teens who wake earlier are much less likely to get into trouble in the morning than during the long stretch of parentless afternoons. Parents and coaches might also protest that a later day leaves less time for sports. But isn't it more important that kids are awake to learn and not spending entire

afternoons unsupervised? Why compromise the education of everyone, and the dollars of many hardworking parents, for the conve-
nience of sports programs? Sports practice can be held in the morning
just as well, or after 4:30 P.M. if need be. It makes a lot more sense for
a few athletes to get up early so that everyone can learn more, instead
of the current system where everyone gets up early and many fall
asleep in class. A later schedule might also require some older teens
with jobs to adjust their hours, though these adjustments would probably be more positive than negative. Teens would be able to "close" at
their retail or fast-food jobs at 9 or 10 P.M. and still get enough sleep
before the next school day.

Later school start times make sense for so many reasons, and the
research on teen sleep has been around for more than ten years now.
School boards and administrators should take action on this issue as soon
as possible. It would cost so little, and benefit so many.

FOR PARENTS

There are also many personal solutions to the dilemmas faced by Generation Me. If you are a parent, you might be wondering how you can help
your children avoid some of the pitfalls of being young today. First, recognize that you will not be able to isolate children completely from the
influences of their generation. Your children will be heavily influenced
by their peers, the media, and the broader social environment. You can,
however, counteract some of the more negative influences by reinforcing
positive traits.

• *Junk the self-esteem emphasis and teach self-control and good behavior.*
Self-esteem has limited benefit, whereas self-control is linked to success
in life. You can teach your children self-control early on by realizing that
even toddlers notice the consequences of their actions. If a child cries and
cries for a piece of candy at the grocery store and you give it to her, you
have just taught her that crying is an effective way to get what she wants.
The next time she wants something, she will cry and whine, because that
worked last time. Instead, give the child treats for good behavior. Many
parents cave in to a crying child because it feels easier, or because they
can't stand to deprive a child of something she wants. However, you're

depriving her of a lot more if you give in. Rewarding the child who asks nicely teaches social skills as well as self-control. Resist the urge to give children everything they want, and teach them the importance of working toward important goals. There are many excellent books on gentle, firm discipline that teach self-control (Ruth Peters's book *It's Never Too Soon to Discipline* comes to mind). Discipline doesn't always mean punishment; it usually means not rewarding bad behavior, and praising good behavior.

• *Do not automatically side with your child.* Imagine that your neighbor knocks on your door one day to tell you that your child has been skateboarding outside her house, an activity that is not allowed in your neighborhood. How would you respond? Some parents would immediately defend their child, saying it could not have been their son or that he was just trying to have some fun. While it's instinctual to protect your children, this reaction teaches your child that he is not responsible for his actions. It would be a better lesson to ask your child not to skateboard because it is against the rules and disturbed your neighbor. There are some social rules that are worth following, and this is not a war of "us" against "them."

The same principle applies when a child says she flunked a test because the teacher was unfair. Defending your child by going after the teacher lets your child know that she can blame others for her problems. Children who believe that grades are just up to the teacher usually underperform in school, because they don't see the point in studying. A child may also learn that Mom and Dad will always solve her problems, a lesson that will backfire later in life.

If fewer parents complained to teachers, teachers would also have more time and energy left over for what they do best: teaching, not arguing with parents. Choose your battles very carefully when dealing with your child's teacher.

• *Limit exposure to violence.* As Joanne Cantor explains in her book *Mommy, I'm Scared,* many children become extremely frightened after watching violent or scary television programs or movies. Most parents limit young children's exposure to these programs, but school-age children can also be seriously affected by them. Even the evening news can make many children anxious. Cantor found that many college students still feel afraid when remembering scary movies or TV shows they watched as children or adolescents. As TV and the movies become more violent, children need to be protected from these harmful influences more and more.

Violent TV, movies, music, and video games can also cause aggressive behavior. A huge amount of research finds that kids exposed to violent media go on to act aggressively in real life. This is one area where the scientific research is definitive. Many people I mention this research to (including my own husband) say things like, "But I played violent video games and I'm not aggressive." Maybe, but that's not the way science works—it relies on average effects across hundreds of people, not individual stories. If you heard that eating apples made kids more aggressive on average, you would never let your child eat apples. We defend violent movies, TV, and video games because we enjoy them ourselves, but that doesn't make them any less harmful.

• *Don't use words like "spoiled."* Yes, young people often focus on their own needs. But guess who taught them to do this? You. Even if you didn't, the entire culture has fed GenMe this message since they were born. Many older people dismiss the concerns of young people, particularly those in their twenties, as "whining." But it is the natural result of high expectations meeting reality. Many older people also forget just how confusing and overwhelming it can be to "have your whole life ahead of you"—that sounds good, but it's also scary. The anxiety and depression that result from this confusing time need to be taken seriously. When young people are told that there's no reason for them to be depressed, this just makes them feel more depressed and alone. Calling a depressed person spoiled just makes the problem worse.

FOR YOUNG PEOPLE

If you're young yourself, you might be wondering how you can sidestep some of the more negative trends of GenMe. Having just navigated my twenties myself, I'll try to give you a road map to avoid some of the bumps that I—and many of us—encountered. Some of my suggestions may seem intuitive, but others might surprise you.

• *Limit your exposure to certain kinds of TV.* Shows like MTV's *Cribs* and VH1's *The Fabulous Life of . . .* detail the extravagant homes and cars of wealthy celebrities. They're tremendously entertaining, but they can also be depressing. You see all of the things that you'll probably never have (and maybe didn't even know you wanted!). Avoid overexposing yourself to the lifestyles of the lucky few and look around you in real life—there are probably plenty of people with less money than you.

• *Avoid overthinking.* Research in the book *Women Who Think Too Much* by Susan Nolen-Hoeksema finds that young people—particularly young women—are more likely to brood over their problems than older people. It's a common cycle: You begin by mulling over a particular problem and before long you've spent half an hour turning it over and over in your head. Nolen-Hoeksema calls this overthinking, and research has linked it to an elevated risk of depression. Talking it over with a friend is a far better solution. You're still considering your problems, but sharing them with someone else unburdens you enough to stop overthinking. People who seek support from others are consistently more mentally healthy than those who don't.

• *Value social relationships.* Keeping up a friendship takes work—often work and time we feel we don't have in our busy lives. But one day you'll look up and wonder where all of your friends went. You will be much happier if you make the extra effort needed to see friends and family. E-mail and the phone are great, but person-to-person contact is better. It goes against our instincts, but we should also try to make those little social gestures that came so naturally to previous generations: welcoming a new neighbor, having friends over for dinner, joining a club. And if you're single, don't neglect dating. Yeah, it sucks sometimes, but all it takes is one. And like George Burns said about getting old, dating is better than the alternative.

You are going to hear a lot of people tell you that being alone is great, because of the old self-esteem mantra. This is just plain wrong. In *Conquering Your Quarterlife Crisis*, there's a section called "Why Is It So Hard to Live Alone?" One of the "mentors" in the book, Raquel Aviva, 32, offers as her lesson, "You don't always have to count on others. Work on counting on yourself." When she felt lonely after her boyfriend moved out, she turned her apartment into a shrine of eighties memorabilia. (After all, things = happiness. Not.) Now she says she is comfortable in her solitude. Later in the book, Michael Coviello, 25, says, "I wish I had known at 21 that true happiness and strength come from inside our hearts and not through others." Although both of these young people are well meaning in their advice, I believe they are misguided. People who have good relationships with others—partners, family, friends—are happier and less depressed than other people. Very, very few people are happy living an isolated life. If you hate living alone, you are one among many. Instead of telling yourself that you ought to be happy with this arrangement, spend your time dating, seeing family, and laughing with friends. Not only will this help you feel better, but eventually these social activities will help you find someone to live your life with, and you won't live alone anymore. And if not, you'll still have a great group of friends.

• *Combat depression naturally.* There are some simple, natural things you can do to fight depression. I have already mentioned the first two: socializing and avoiding overthinking. You are also less likely to feel depressed if you: (1) get enough sleep, (2) expose yourself to sunlight for at least an hour a day, (3) exercise regularly, and (4) eat a diet rich in omega-3 fatty acids (found primarily in fish, especially salmon, halibut, herring, white tuna, and trout; flaxseed oil supplements are another source). University of Kansas professor Steve Ilardi has shown that these steps improve mood as much as prescription medication; he calls the therapy Therapeutic Lifestyle Change. He theorizes that the more we re-create the life of our hunting and gathering ancestors, the happier we will be. Although Ilardi's program is in its beginning stages, research has already shown that the individual elements (e.g., light exposure, omega-3 acids) can reduce depression. Ilardi's therapy often works for people whose depression has not responded to medication. "I'm not anti-medication," he says. "It's just that for a lot of people [drugs] don't work—and if they do work, it's short term. Relapse is a huge issue. So, if you can achieve superior results long-term without medication, the advantage seems pretty clear."

• *Cultivate realistic expectations.* Have realistic goals rather than believing that you should "follow your dreams" no matter what. It's fine to aim high, but talk to your parents and teachers about your goals and the time line you have in mind. You will not be CEO of your company in five years. It might be difficult to get into graduate school. If you move to L.A. to become an actor, you will be lucky to make enough money so you don't have to wait tables, much less become a movie star. Only a few people become rich or famous with little effort. For most people, it takes hard work just to get a halfway decent job and keep it.

If you really want to get realistic, listen to the advice of John Pozniak, 27, interviewed in *Conquering Your Quarterlife Crisis*. "Will you always hate going to work? Yes. It is a way of life," John says. "There is a support group for it called Everyone, and they meet at the bars on Friday." There is hope, though, in a way. "The key is to find a job that doesn't suck 'as bad,'" he says. "The good thing is since your job sucks, everything else you do seems that much better and more rewarding."

• *Get involved in your neighborhood and community.* The fulfillment that GenMe seeks might be found in helping other people. It's one of the best ways to find deeper meaning in life and build those true relationships that are otherwise so hard to find.

There are already many young people who are taking this advice. A few chapters ago I mentioned Drew Lichtenberger, 28, who says that many people his age experience what he calls "The Twenties BeatDown." Like many young people, Drew had a great job in business but then realized it wasn't fulfilling. He now works at his alma mater Virginia Tech, helping prepare college students for their transition into the professional world. He says he is "passionate about developing people." One of his main messages is that volunteering and helping others is one of the best ways to be fulfilled and gain meaning. He leads a high school youth group and encourages other young people to get involved in volunteer work as well. A man he respected once told him, "The only way that you'll ever feel good about yourself is by helping other people," and he passes this advice on to young people who are looking for meaning and fulfillment. "Individualism and serving yourself are dead ends," Drew says. "Service to others and leaving a lasting legacy is really at the core of the deepest human needs. Strong relationships and community keep us true to who we are and help us see what our lives are meant to be."

Drew's friend Eric Latham, 24, partnered with the American Cancer Society and spent the summer of 2005 walking across America to raise money for cancer research. Matt Caccavale, also 24, biked across the country to raise money for housing for the poor (see www.bikeandbuild. org for journals of many riders). The Bike & Build website is filled with interesting stories and messages from proud parents and friends encouraging the riders.

As these young people demonstrate, GenMe is far from selfish. And these are not isolated examples; on average, GenMe volunteers significantly more than previous generations. While only 64% of high school seniors volunteered in 1990, more than 76% did in 2001. Among college freshmen, 66% volunteered in 1990, compared to 83% in 2003. People in their early twenties in 1998 volunteered their time 39% more frequently than people that age in 1975. More detailed survey questions suggest that for most young people, volunteering is a short-term activity rather than a long-term commitment. Nevertheless, there are young people who are willing to commit themselves to good causes for long periods.

This is the upside of the Twixter phenomenon of young people taking time during their twenties to find out what they want to do. Many young people volunteer and end up finding a career from their experience. For instance, my cousin Sarah Kilibarda volunteered for Catholic Charities for two years after she graduated from college, helping immigrants with their legal paperwork. She then went to law school and now works as an immigration lawyer. Even if you don't find a career from volunteering, you will more than likely develop valuable skills and make some great friends. Just as important, many people discover that feeling of meaning that they found missing—the emptiness that often comes from pure self-focus.

Generation Me has come of age at a unique time in American history. We were raised to believe in ourselves, and to have a wildly optimistic outlook. Yet we are entering adulthood at a time when just getting by is increasingly difficult. Many of us will weather this collision of youthful expectation and harsh adult reality by becoming anxious or depressed. If you are a young person, I hope you have come to realize that you are not alone. If you are older, I hope you have gained the understanding that young people today were raised differently than you were, and that growing up today is not easy. In the coming years, I hope that we will all realize that we can't make it solely on our own. Generation Me needs realistic expectations, careful career guidance, and assistance when we become parents. In return, we will gladly lend our energy and ambition toward our work and toward helping others.

Appendix

Further Details About the Scientific Studies in This Book

I f you've turned here, you're probably curious about the psychological terms and search methods I've used. A few topics that often raise questions:

Personality traits and attitudes. What exactly are traits? Basically, they are the internal attributes of people that cause their behavior. Traits summarize the way someone behaves across most situations. For example, someone who expresses her opinions and speaks up when she feels wronged would be high in the trait of assertiveness. Most questionnaires ask fairly specific questions; one measure of assertiveness asks, "If a friend unfairly criticizes you, do you express your resentment there and then?"

So if a questionnaire wanted to measure the trait of "silliness," it might ask about a number of different silly behaviors, like making funny faces, asserting amusingly absurd statements, and playacting unconsciousness. We learn to group behaviors this way very early. If you do all of the things I just listed, for example, you will eventually hear from your child, "Mommy, you're silly!" So when you read that a trait (like anxiety or assertiveness) has changed, remember that this seemingly abstract concept is based on these more specific questions about actions in real life. Traits are really about behavior.

I also mention attitudes, mostly in Chapter 7. In the psychological sense, an attitude is a favorable or unfavorable opinion of a group or a group's actions. If you have a strong attitude and express it, you have "attitude" in the more colloquial sense. Here, though, I will focus mostly on attitudes toward the roles of certain groups. For example, attitudes toward the roles of women have changed quite a bit. Like the questionnaires on traits, attitude questionnaires also ask specific questions (e.g., Do you agree or disagree that "Sons in a family should be given more encouragement to go to college than daughters"?). Attitudes are about beliefs, often deeply held beliefs.

The content of the questionnaires used in the studies. As you've seen, I get my data from people's responses to questionnaires. These questionnaires usually consist of a number of statements that people are asked to agree or disagree with. Sometimes they can answer only yes or no, and other times they give their response on a scale, say from 1 to 5. A few questionnaires use what's called "forced choice," meaning you have to choose which statement out of two you agree with the most. The statements tend to ask about specific behaviors, feelings, or opinions. It's fairly difficult to know what these specifics are, though, if you just hear the name of a scale. To give you a better idea of what the questionnaires are actually measuring, I quote at least a few items from the questionnaires I studied when I describe the results. It helps, for example, to know that one of the items on a scale measuring narcissism is "If I ruled the world, it would be a better place." This shows that the questionnaire isn't just talking about physical vanity. When my students fill out the narcissism questionnaire in class, someone will inevitably raise his hand right away, announce that he scored high on narcissism, say "I think that . . . ," and proceed to go on and on about himself and his ideas. It increases my confidence in personality questionnaires every time.

Changes in college populations. You might wonder how I can draw conclusions about generations on the basis of college student samples. Haven't those samples changed a lot recently? Surprisingly, the answer is no. A large yearly study found that the median income of college students' parents, when adjusted for inflation, did not change between 1965 and 2000. College students come from middle-class and upper-middle-class families, and this has not changed much over time. There has not been a large influx of working-class students, partially because yearly tuition increases have kept four-year colleges out of reach for many. Changes in racial composition are also small, with minority student enrollment increasing only a few percentage points in the last forty years. College enrollment for black students actually declined during the 1980s. Most college student samples remain mostly white just as they were in earlier eras. There have, however, been large changes in gender composition; 36% of college students were women in 1958, compared to 58% in 2002. To correct for this, I analyzed the data within gender; for example, I looked at the changes in women's anxiety scores over time, and men's anxiety scores over time. In most cases, the results were very similar.

In many of these studies, I also looked at samples of schoolchildren. Children of elementary school and middle school age are almost always enrolled in school, and their samples have not changed much in composition (compared to the small changes in college populations). These samples are also more diverse and thus better represent the country as a whole. When I compared the results for children and college students, they usually showed exactly the same pattern. This gave me further confidence that the changes were not an artifact of shifts in college student samples. It also showed that children were not immune to these larger social changes—the generational shifts appeared in samples of children as young as 9. Kids are absorbing the ways of their society, and they are doing it at an early age.

Willingness to admit to problems. Perhaps the changes in the questionnaires happen because people now have fewer qualms admitting to problems. There are several reasons why I think this doesn't account for much of the change. First, I collected data on a scale measuring socially desirable responding—how much people change their questionnaire answers in order to look good in the eyes of others. When I matched that to data on other questionnaires, they weren't correlated over time. So changes in traits happened independent of people's comfort with admitting to things. Also, the questionnaires across all of these studies were given on paper and not in interviews, and they're anonymous—respondents don't put their names on them. The questionnaires also ask about specific symptoms ("Some unimportant thought runs through my mind and bothers me") rather than asking point-blank something like "Are you anxious and depressed?" The responses to all of the symptoms are added up to form the score, so the respondent only admits to small parts of a problem at a time. Finally, the changes described in this book are diverse. Some of them are in "good" traits (like self-esteem), but others are in "bad" traits (like anxiety), and some (like who controls your fate) have questions worded so there is no obvious "good" or "bad" answer. If people were more comfortable admitting to bad things, we'd expect to see change only in traits that are considered undesirable, but the changes show up in all kinds of characteristics.

The effects of specific events (like 9/11/01). It's difficult to tell. I have to estimate the year data were collected based on the date of publication, since most researchers don't report the exact year in their articles. Statistically speaking, this means, if anything, that changes are stronger than I've found (as the imprecise year introduces more uncertainty). Even if I could pinpoint the exact year, though, I'm guessing that the change would still be slow and steady. Specific events don't have as much influence as the social climate they create over a period of years. Social change does not happen overnight, particularly in traits and attitudes— characteristics of people that tend to be fairly stable. In fact, I've found in several studies that the change in traits lags about ten years behind statistics such as divorce rate, age at marriage, or crime rate. Because these are college students who are about 20 years old, this suggests that we absorb the environment that surrounds us when we are about 10 years old. Morris Massey, who traveled the country lecturing about generational differences in the 1970s and '80s, calls this "Where were you when you were 10?" and my data support this idea. The environment we experience as children stays with us our whole lives.

Age differences versus generation differences. You might also wonder why all of the library work I did was necessary. Why not give these personality questionnaires right now to a big sample of people of different ages? Shouldn't that tell us how generations differ? If we did that, though, we wouldn't know if age or generation was causing the difference. First, I'll show you some examples of differences that are clearly one or the other. Let's say we find that people in their twenties have more energy than people in their forties. Does this mean that the generation of people in their twenties is more energetic than those in their forties and always will be?

Probably not; every generation finds that their energy level decreases as they age. This is clearly a difference due to age and not to generation. In contrast, consider your skill with Internet message boards, ATM machines, and programming your VCR. If you're a little older, these might not be your strong suit. (My parents, for example, still don't use ATMs—they *go to the bank*. I just don't get it.) This is clearly a difference based on generation and not age, because people who are young now will not suddenly forget their current technology skills when they are older.

But in a one-time sample of people of different ages (called a cross-sectional study), it's impossible to tell if differences are due to age or generation. If a study finds, for example, that people in their twenties are more anxious than people in their forties, this could be due to aging (maybe people become less anxious as they get older) or to generation (maybe the younger generation will always be more anxious than the older generation). The method I use gets around this problem by looking at samples of people of the same age collected at different points in time. Each of these data sources is a snapshot in time of what each generation was like when they were young, either when they were children or were young adults in college. Because age is held constant, it's clear that generation and time are the forces at work. Of course, it's possible that people of all ages showed these same changes; if so, that would be a time-period effect rather than a generational effect, and I can't rule that out. I can tell you that things changed over time, just not if older people changed as well. But anyone who has observed people knows that young people are more susceptible to change. For example, older people don't use computers as proficiently because they didn't learn how when they were young. Social change hits the young first, and I wanted to see how that happened from the 1950s to the present.

Without a time machine, I couldn't get these data myself. Since so many psychological scales have been used over and over, though, the library became my time machine. Those old journals and dissertations were my looking glass to the past, showing me how things used to be and how they are now.

Notes

Introduction

2 *Reflecting on her role:* Ryan, Joan. "The Millennial Generation." *San Francisco Chronicle,* December 13, 1998.

2 *head of the Roper Youth Report:* Tapscott, Don. 1998. *Growing Up Digital.* New York: McGraw-Hill; p. 94.

5 *One advertising executive called the early 1990s:* Hornblower, Margot. "Great Xpectations." *Time,* June 9, 1997.

8 *As early as June 2000, Time:* Okrent, Daniel. "Twilight of the Boomers." *Time,* June 12, 2000.

8 *Morris Massey, for years a popular speaker:* Massey, Morris. 1979. *The People Puzzle.* Reston, VA: Prentice-Hall; p. 21.

9 *Marketing studies, for example, find:* Smith, J. Walker, and Clurman, Ann. 1997. *Rocking the Ages: The Yankelovich Report on Generational Marketing.* New York: HarperCollins.

10 *Ellen Degeneres said that the most important: Ellen.* CBS, January 27, 2005.

10 *Dan Atkins, 17, says:* Tapscott, Don. 1998. *Growing Up Digital.* New York: McGraw-Hill; p. 94.

10 *Here's Mario, a recent college graduate:* Robbins, Alexandra, and Wilner, Abby. 2001. *Quarterlife Crisis.* New York: Tarcher/Putnam; p. 42.

12 *In his popular syndicated column:* Adams, Cecil. 1984. *The Straight Dope.* Chicago: Chicago Review Press; p. 14.

12 *I begin by searching computer databases:* For example, see Twenge, J. M. 2000. The Age of Anxiety? Birth Cohort Change in Anxiety and Neuroticism, 1952–1993. *Journal of Personality and Social Psychology,* 79: 1007–1021; or Twenge, J. M. 1997. Changes in Masculine and Feminine Traits over Time: A Meta-Analysis. *Sex Roles,* 36: 305–325.

1 You Don't Need Their Approval: The Decline of Social Rules

PAGE

19 *Compared to Boomers in 1973:* Smith, J. Walker, and Clurman, Ann. 1997. *Rocking the Ages: The Yankelovich Report on Generational Marketing.* New York: HarperCollins; p. 87.

19 *Young people say:* Mitchell, Susan. 2003. *American Generations.* Ithaca, NY: New Strategist Publications; p. 47. From the 2000 General Social Survey, National Opinion Research Center, University of Chicago.

20 *Filmmaker Kevin Smith:* Hornblower, Margot. "Great Xpectations." *Time,* June 9, 1997.

23 *But when researchers tried:* Perrin, S., and Spencer, C. 1980. The Asch Effect—a Child of Its Time. *Bulletin of the British Psychological Society,* 33: 405–406.

Notes

Notes 249

24 *In 1924, a group of sociologists:* Remley, Anne. "From Obedience to Independence." *Psychology Today,* October 1988.
24 *In Growing Up Digital, an 11-year-old girl says:* Tapscott, Don. 1998. *Growing Up Digital.* New York: McGraw-Hill; p. 195.
25 *A 1977 manual for teachers:* Hedges, William D., and Martinello, Marian L. 1977. "What the Schools Might Do: Some Alternatives for the Here and Now," in *Feeling, Valuing, and the Art of Growing: Insights into the Affective,* Alexandria, VA: Association of Supervision and Curriculum Development yearbook.
25 *A book on generations in the workplace notes:* Zemke, Ron; Raines, Claire; and Filipczak, Bob. 2000. *Generations at Work.* New York: AMACOM.
25 *"I was excited to see Britney:* Nichols, Kristy. Letter to the editor. *People,* September 13, 2004.
26 *"Society has gotten increasingly callous":* Steptoe, Sonja. "Minding Their Manners." *Time,* June 7, 2004.
26 *A company founder visited:* Raines, Claire. 1997. *Beyond Generation X: A Practical Guide for Managers.* Menlo Park, CA: Crisp Publications; p. 40.
26 *Business professor John Trinkaus finds:* Trinkaus, J. 1998. Compliance with a School Zone Speed Limit: Another Look. *Perceptual and Motor Skills,* 87: 673–674.
26 *fewer observe the item limit:* Trinkaus, J. 2002. Compliance with the Item Limit of the Food Supermarket Express Checkout Lane: Another Look. *Psychological Reports,* 91: 1057–1058.
26 *More people cut across parking lots:* Trinkaus, J. 1994. Cutting Corners: An Informal Look. *Perceptual and Motor Skills,* 79: 1089–1090.
26 *In 1979, 29% of people failed:* Trinkaus, J. 1997. Stop Sign Compliance: A Final Look. *Perceptual and Motor Skills,* 85: 217–218.
26 *number of people who paid the suggested fee:* Trinkaus, J. 2004. Honesty When Lighting Votive Candles in Church: An Informal Look. *Psychological Reports,* 94: 1435–1436.
27 *In 2002, 74% of high school students:* www.josephsoninstitute.org/Survey2002/survey2002-pressrelease.htm.
27 *In 1969, only 34%:* Bronfenbrenner, U., et al. 1996. *The State of Americans: This Generation and the Next.* New York: Free Press; p. 4.
27 *a 2002 survey found that 80%:* Heyman, J. D. "Psssst . . . What's the Answer?" *People,* January 24, 2005.
27 *one of the heirs to the Wal-Mart fortune:* Ibid.
27 *In a 1997 survey, 88% of high school students:* www.school-for-champions.com/character/newberger_cheating2.htm.
27 *Three times as many high school students in 1969:* Bronfenbrenner, U., et al. 1996. *The State of Americans: This Generation and the Next.* New York: Free Press; p. 4.
27 *in 2000, 26% of high school boys:* CBS News. 2001. *The Class of 2000.* Simon & Schuster eBook, available for download; p. 67.
28 *Education professor Maureen Stout tells:* Stout, Maureen. 2000. *The Feel-Good Curriculum.* Cambridge, MA: Perseus Books; p. 93.
28 *Students seemed uncomfortable:* Sacks, Peter. 1996. *Generation X Goes to College.* Chicago: Open Court Press; p. 84.
29 *Sacks interviewed a veteran teacher:* Ibid., p. 29.
29 *In her first class, she always announced:* Ibid. p. 89.
29 *In Growing Up Digital, Don Tapscott describes:* Tapscott, Don. 1998. *Growing Up Digital.* New York: McGraw-Hill; pp. 155–157.
30 *Tapscott argues that the current generation:* Ibid., p. 88.
30 *As a famous New Yorker cartoon:* Steiner, Peter. *New Yorker,* June 5, 1993, p. 61.
30 *"Parents are no longer eager:* Pickett, Debra, and Fuller, Janet Rausa. "Teens Shifting Balance of Power." *Chicago Sun-Times,* April 27, 2003.

30 *Chicago-area parent Richard Shields:* Pickett, Debra. "One Reason Roles Are Changing: Dad's Desire to Be Son's Friend." *Chicago Sun-Times,* April 27, 2003.

31 *The Sun-Times article interviewed:* Pickett, Debra, and Fuller, Janet Rausa. "Teens Shifting Balance of Power." *Chicago Sun-Times,* April 27, 2003.

31 *One family's two daughters convinced:* Pickett, Debra. "Girls Decided When Family Needed a Second Car." *Chicago Sun-Times,* April 27, 2003.

31 *In 1957, 80% of people said:* Mitchell, Susan. 1995. *The Official Guide to the Generations.* Ithaca, NY: New Strategist Publications; p. 92.

32 *doubling since 1982: Statistical Abstract of the United States,* 2004 and earlier years. Available online at www.census.gov/prod/www/abs/statab.html.

32 *the last law antimiscegenation law was not:* en.wikipedia.org/wiki/Miscegenation.

32 *Almost half of Asian women:* Lind, Michael. "The Beige and the Black." *New York Times Magazine,* August 16, 1998.

32 *In a 1997 survey of college freshmen:* Northwestern Mutual Life Insurance survey of college freshmen, cited in Hicks, Rick, and Hicks, Kathy. 1999. *Boomers, Xers, and Other Strangers.* Wheaton, IL: Tyndale; p. 273.

32 *In 2000, 41% of high school seniors:* CBS News. 2001. *The Class of 2000.* Simon & Schuster eBook, available for download; p. 113.

32 *only 10% of white young people:* Arnett, Jeffrey Jensen. 2004. *Emerging Adulthood.* New York: Oxford University Press; p. 84.

32 *In the mid-1960s, Brides magazine:* Wallace, Carol McD. 2004. *All Dressed in White.* New York: Penguin; p. 213.

33 *When former Beverly Hills, 90210 star:* "A Spelling Production," *InStyle,* February 2005.

34 *Wedding gown designer Reem Acra:* Wallace, Carol McD. 2004. *All Dressed in White.* New York: Penguin; p. 265.

34 *Church attendance across:* Putnam, Robert. 2000. *Bowling Alone.* New York: Simon & Schuster; pp. 70–71.

34 *Only 18% of 18-to-29-year-olds:* CBS News. 2001. *The Class of 2000.* Simon & Schuster eBook, available for download; p. 70.

34 *The number of college freshmen who named:* Astin, A. W., et al. 2002. *The American Freshman: Thirty-Five Year Trends.* Los Angeles: Higher Education Research Institute, UCLA. Plus 2003 and 2004 supplements.

34 *In Emerging Adulthood, Jeffrey Arnett:* Arnett, Jeffrey Jensen. 2004. *Emerging Adulthood.* New York: Oxford University Press; p. 172.

34 *Many don't adhere to:* Ibid., p. 172.

34 *In an April 2005 poll:* CNN/USA Today/Gallup poll. See www.cnn.com/2005/US/04/20/us.catholics.poll/index.html.

34 *Interviewed in Emerging Adulthood, Dana:* Arnett, Jeffrey Jensen. 2004. *Emerging Adulthood.* New York: Oxford University Press; pp. 172–174.

35 *Rick Warren, author:* Warren, Rick. "Learn to Love Yourself!" *Ladies' Home Journal,* March 2005.

35 *Groups like the Elks:* Putnam, Robert. 2000. *Bowling Alone.* New York: Simon & Schuster.

35 *In 1976, 46%:* Ibid., Fig. 38, p. 140. From the University of Michigan Monitoring the Future annual survey of high school students.

36 *In 2000, 64% of 18-to-24-year-olds:* Mitchell, Susan. 2003. *American Generations.* 4th ed. Ithaca, NY: New Strategist Publications; pp. 37–38. From the 2000 General Social Survey, National Opinion Research Center, University of Chicago.

37 *In a recent survey of men, 62%:* Orecklin, Michele. "Stress and the Superdad." *Time,* August 23, 2004.

37 *In a 2001 episode of the teen show:* Dawson's Creek. Episode 510: "Appetite for Destruction." Airdate: December 19, 2001.

38 *33% of women in their forties:* Cited in Kamen, Paula. 2000. *Her Way: Young Women Remake the Sexual Revolution.* New York: New York University Press.

39 *"I feel like the X'ers:* Lancaster, Lynne, and Stillman, David. 2002. *When Generations Collide.* New York: HarperBusiness; p. 269.

39 *In one episode of the teen soap: The O.C.* Episode: "The Distance." Airdate: November 4, 2004.

39 *Chris Colin describes Becky:* Colin, Chris. 2004. *What Really Happened to the Class of '93.* New York: Broadway Books; p. 208.

40 *"The older generations are so cautious:* Lancaster, Lynne, and Stillman, David. 2002. *When Generations Collide.* New York: HarperBusiness; p. 259.

40 *Lynne Lancaster, one of the authors:* Ibid.

42 *The scale measures a person's "need:* Crowne, D. P., and Marlowe, D. 1964. *The Approval Motive.* New York: Wiley; p. 39.

42 *follow "conventional, even stereotyped:* Ibid., p. 85.

42 *My student Charles Im and I:* Twenge, J. M., and Im, C. 2005. "Changes in Socially Desirable Responding, 1958–2001." Poster presented at the annual meeting of the Society for Personality and Social Psychology, New Orleans, LA, January 2005; and Twenge, J. M., and Im, C. "Changes in Social Desirability, 1958–2001." Manuscript under review.

43 *Take the line Yippie radical:* Rubin, Jerry. 1976. *Growing (Up) at Thirty-Seven.* New York: Lippincott; p. 117.

2 An Army of One: *Me*

PAGE

45 *Ladies' Home Journal told readers:* Warren, Rick. "Learn to Love Yourself!" *Ladies' Home Journal,* March 2005; p. 36.

45 *while* Parenting *offered:* Lamb, Yanick Rice. "Proud to Be Me!" *Parenting,* April 2005.

45 *The American Academy of Pediatrics guide:* Shelov, Steven, ed. in chief. 1998. *Caring for Your Baby and Young Child: Birth to Age 5.* New York: Bantam.

46 *In a 1976 New York Magazine article:* Wolfe, Tom. "The Me Decade and the Third Great Awakening." *New York Magazine,* August 23, 1976.

47 *When asked what's next in her life:* "Pop Quiz: Kim Basinger." *People,* September 27, 2004.

47 *In answer to the same question:* Laskas, Jeanne Marie. "Sarah's New Day." *Ladies' Home Journal,* June 2004.

47 *Gillon describes Boomers:* Gillon, Steve. 2004. *Boomer Nation.* New York: Free Press; p. 263.

47 *Even food becomes:* Brooks, David. 2000. *Bobos in Paradise.* New York: Simon & Schuster; p. 58.

47 *In 1973, 46% of Boomers:* Smith, J. Walker, and Clurman, Ann. 1997. *Rocking the Ages: The Yankelovich Report on Generational Marketing.* New York: HarperCollins.

47 *Thirty percent of Boomers:* Ibid.

47 *Even stronger evidence:* Astin, A. W., et al. 2002. *The American Freshman: Thirty-Five Year Trends.* Los Angeles: Higher Education Research Institute, UCLA. Plus 2003 and 2004 supplements.

48 *"Instead of seeking:* Rubin, Jerry. 1976. *Growing (Up) at Thirty-Seven.* New York: Lippincott; p. 175.

48 *Aleta St. James, a 57-year-old woman:* Schienberg, Jonathan. "New Age Mystic to Become Mom at 57." cnn.com. November 9, 2004.

49 *In 2004's* Conquering Your Quarterlife Crisis: Robbins, Alexandra. 2004. *Conquering Your Quarterlife Crisis.* New York: Perigee; pp. 51–52.

50   *When a character in the 2004 novel:* Giffin, Emily. 2004. *Something Borrowed.* New York: St. Martin's Press; p. 2.

50   *Dr. Phil, the ultimate in plainspoken: Today.* NBC, December 27, 2004.

50   *Psychologist Martin Seligman says:* Seligman, M. E. P. "Boomer Blues." *Psychology Today,* October 1988: 50–53.

51   *A careful study of news stories:* Patterson, Thomas E. 2000. "Doing Well and Doing Good: How Soft News and Critical Journalism Are Shrinking the News Audience and Weakening Democracy—and What News Outlets Can Do About It." Joan Shorenstein Center on the Press, Politics, and Public Policy; p. 5. PDF available for download at www.ksg.harvard.edu/presspol/Research Publications/Reports/.

51   *In a letter to her fans in 2004:* "The Couples of 2004." *Us Weekly,* January 3, 2005.

51   *In the late 1990s, Prudential:* Hornblower, Margot. "Great Xpectations." *Time,* June 9, 1997.

52   *My colleague Keith Campbell and I looked:* Twenge, J. M., and Campbell, W. K. 2001. Age and Birth Cohort Differences in Self-Esteem: A Cross-Temporal Meta-Analysis. *Personality and Social Psychology Review,* 5: 321–344.

52   *A 1997 survey of teens asked:* "11th Annual Special Teen Report: Teens and Self-Image: Survey Results." *USA Weekend,* May 1–3, 1998.

52   *Another survey found:* Hicks, Rick, and Hicks, Kathy. 1999. *Boomers, Xers, and Other Strangers.* Wheaton, IL: Tyndale; p. 270.

52   *We examined the responses:* Twenge, J. M., and Campbell, W. K. 2001. Age and Birth Cohort Differences in Self-Esteem: A Cross-Temporal Meta-Analysis. *Personality and Social Psychology Review,* 5: 321–344.

53   *Research on programs to boost:* Ibid.

53   *Journal articles on self-esteem:* Hewitt, John. 1998. *The Myth of Self-Esteem.* New York: St. Martin's Press; p. 51.

53   *One children's book:* Loomans, Diane. 1991. *The Lovables in the Kingdom of Self-Esteem.* New York: H. J. Kramer.

55   *One program is called:* Stout, Maureen. 2000. *The Feel-Good Curriculum.* Cambridge, MA: Perseus Books; p. 131.

55   *Another program, called "Pumsy in Pursuit of Excellence":* "Teaching Self-Image Stirs Furor." *New York Times,* October 13, 1993.

55   *The Magic Circle exercise:* www.globalideasbank.org/site/bank/idea.php?ideaId=573; and Summerlin, M. L.; Hammett, V. L.; and Payne, M. L. 1983. The Effect of Magic Circle Participation on a Child's Self-Concept. *School Counselor,* 31: 49–52.

55   *One Austin, Texas, father:* Swann, William. 1996. *Self-Traps: The Elusive Quest for Higher Self-Esteem.* New York: W. H. Freeman; p. 4.

56   *When self-esteem programs:* Hewitt, John. 1998. *The Myth of Self-Esteem,* New York: St. Martin's Press; pp. 84–85.

56   *In one program, teachers:* Payne, Lauren Murphy, and Rolhing, Claudia. 1994. *A Leader's Guide to Just Because I Am: A Child's Book of Affirmation.* Minneapolis: Free Spirit Publishing; and Hewitt, John. 1998. *The Myth of Self-Esteem.* New York: St. Martin's Press.

57   *children are asked to finish:* Hewitt, John. 1998. *The Myth of Self-Esteem.* New York: St. Martin's Press; p. 79.

57   *A sign on the wall:* Kramer, Rita. 1991. *Ed School Follies: The Miseducation of America's Teachers.* New York: Free Press; p. 33.

57   *Perhaps as a result, 60% of teachers:* Scott, C. G. 1996. Student Self-Esteem and the School System: Perceptions and Implications. *Journal of Educational Research,* 89: 292–297.

57   *A veteran second-grade teacher:* Gibbs, Nancy. "Parents Behaving Badly." *Time,* February 21, 2005.

57 *For example, the popular Christian:* Lucado, Max. 1997. *You Are Special.* Wheaton, IL: Crossway Books.

58 *In an article in* Ladies' Home Journal. *Christian author:* Warren, Rick. "Learn to Love Yourself!" *Ladies' Home Journal,* March 2005.

58 *Children in some schools:* Lynn Sherr. "Me, Myself and I—The Growing Self-Esteem Movement." *20/20.* ABC, March 11, 1994.

58 *Other students pen:* Ibid.

58 *An elementary school teacher in Alabama:* Hewitt, John. 1998. *The Myth of Self-Esteem.* New York: St. Martin's Press; p. 81.

58 *The children's museum in Laramie:* Lynn Sherr. "Me, Myself and I—The Growing Self-Esteem Movement." *20/20.* ABC, March 11, 1994.

59 *Don Tapscott, who interviewed:* Tapscott, Don. 1998. *Growing Up Digital.* New York: McGraw-Hill; p. 92.

59 *In a CBS News poll:* CBS News. 2001. *The Class of 2000.* Simon & Schuster eBook, available for download, p. 64.

59 *The 1997 premiere episode:* Daria. Episode: "Esteemsters." MTV, March 3, 1997.

59 *Hewitt, who teaches:* Hewitt, John. 1998. *The Myth of Self-Esteem.* New York: St. Martin's Press; pp. 1–3.

60 *In 2002, the Girl Scout Council:* www.girlscouts.org/program/program_opportunities/leadership/uniquelyme.asp.

60 *In 1999, a carefully researched:* Kling, K. C., et al. 1999. Gender Differences in Self-Esteem: A Meta-Analysis. *Psychological Bulletin,* 125: 470–500.

61 *"We may create:* www.news.wisc.edu/wire/i072899/selfesteem.html.

61 *When my colleague Keith Campbell and I did:* Twenge, J. M., and Campbell, W. K. 2001. Age and Birth Cohort Differences in Self-Esteem: A Cross-Temporal Meta-Analysis. *Personality and Social Psychology Review,* 5: 321–344.

61 *One popular method tells:* Wilde, Sandra. 1989. A Proposal for a New Spelling Curriculum. *Elementary School Journal,* 90: 275–289.

61 *Teacher education courses emphasize:* Kramer, Rita. 1991. *Ed School Follies: The Miseducation of America's Teachers.* New York: Free Press; p. 116.

62 *a British teacher proposed:* "Teachers Say No-One Should 'Fail.'" BBC News, July 20, 2005. See news.bbc.co.uk/1/hi/education/4697461.stm.

62 *office stores have started carrying:* Aoki, Naomi. "Harshness of Red Marks Has Students Seeing Purple." *Boston Globe,* August 23, 2004.

62 *Florida elementary schoolteacher:* Ibid.

62 *In 2004, 48% of American college freshmen:* Astin, A. W., et al. 2002. *The American Freshman: Thirty-Five Year Trends.* Los Angeles: Higher Education Research Institute, UCLA. Plus 2003 and 2004 supplements.

63 *"Each year we think:* Giegerich, Steve. "College Freshmen Have Worst Study Habits in Years But Less Likely to Drink, Study Finds." Associated Press, January 27, 2003. www.detnews.com/2003/schools/0301/27/schools-70002.htm.

63 *Only 33% of American:* Astin, A. W., et al. 2002. *The American Freshman: Thirty-Five Year Trends.* Los Angeles: Higher Education Research Institute, UCLA. Plus 2003 and 2004 supplements.

63 *"Teachers want to raise:* Innerst, Carol. "Wordsmiths on Wane Among U.S. Students." *Washington Times,* August 25, 1994.

63 *As education professor Maureen Stout notes:* Stout, Maureen. 2000. *The Feel-Good Curriculum.* Cambridge, MA: Perseus Books; pp. 3–4.

64 *in 2003, 43% of college freshmen:* Astin, A. W., et al. 2002. *The American Freshman: Thirty-Five Year Trends.* Los Angeles: Higher Education Research Institute, UCLA. Plus 2003 and 2004 supplements.

Notes

64 *educational psychologist Harold Stevenson:* Stevenson, H. W., et al. 1990. Mathematics Achievement of Children in China and the United States. *Child Development*, 61: 1053–1066.

65 *research shows that when people:* Heatherton, T. F., and Vohs, K. D. 2000. Interpersonal Evaluations Following Threats to Self: Role of Self-Esteem. *Journal of Personality and Social Psychology*, 78: 725–736.

65 *Students "look and act like:* Hewitt, John. 1998. *The Myth of Self-Esteem.* New York: St. Martin's Press; p. 84.

65 *There is a small correlation:* Baumeister, R. F., et al. 2003. Does High Self-Esteem Cause Better Performance, Interpersonal Success, Happiness, or Healthier Lifestyles? *Psychological Science in the Public Interest*, 4: 1–44; and Covington, M. V. 1989. "Self-Esteem and Failure in School." In A. M. Mecca, N. J. Smelser, and J. Vasconcellos, eds. *The Social Importance of Self-Esteem.* Berkeley: University of California Press; p. 79.

65 *Several comprehensive reviews:* Ibid.

65 *Even the book sponsored:* Smelser, N. J. 1989. "Self-esteem and Social Problems." In A. M. Mecca, N. J. Smelser, and J. Vasconcellos, eds. *The Social Importance of Self-Esteem.* Berkeley: University of California Press.

66 *Psychologist Martin Seligman has criticized:* Selgiman, Martin. 1996. *The Optimistic Child.* New York: Harper Perennial.

66 *"It is very questionable:* Baumeister, Roy. "The Lowdown on High Self-esteem: Thinking You're Hot Stuff Isn't the Promised Cure-all." *Los Angeles Times,* January 25, 2005.

66 *"What the self-esteem movement:* Stout, Maureen. 2000. *The Feel-Good Curriculum.* Cambridge, MA: Perseus Books; p. 263.

67 *As psychologist Jennifer Crocker documents:* Crocker, J., and Park, L. E. 2004. The Costly Pursuit of Self-esteem. *Psychological Bulletin*, 130: 392–414.

67 *Asians, for example, have lower:* Twenge, J. M., and Crocker, J. 2002. Race and Self-Esteem: Meta-Analyses Comparing Whites, Blacks, Hispanics, Asians, and American Indians. *Psychological Bulletin*, 128: 371–408.

67 *But when Asian students find out:* Heine, S. J., et al. 2001. Divergent Consequences of Success and Failure in Japan and North America: An Investigation of Self-improving Motivations and Malleable Selves. *Journal of Personality and Social Psychology*, 81: 599–615.

68 *"There is no self-esteem movement:* Shaw, Robert. 2003. *The Epidemic.* New York: Regan Books; p. 152.

68 *Narcissists are overly focused:* Campbell, W. Keith. 2005. *When You Love a Man Who Loves Himself.* Chicago: Source Books.

68 *Narcissists are also more likely:* Helgeson, V. S., and Fritz, H. L. 1999. Unmitigated Agency and Unmitigated Communion: Distinctions from Agency and Communion. *Journal of Research in Personality*, 33: 131–158.

69 *In the early 1950s, only 12% of teens:* Newsom, C. R., et al. 2003. Changes in Adolescent Response Patterns on the MMPI/MMPI-A Across Four Decades. *Journal of Personality Assessment*, 81: 74–84.

69 *Psychologist Harrison Gough found:* Gough, H. 1991. "Scales and Combinations of Scales: What Do They Tell Us, What Do They Mean?" Paper presented at the 99th Annual Convention of the American Psychological Association, San Francisco, August 1991. Data obtained from Harrison Gough in 2001.

69 *In a 2002 survey of 3,445 people:* Foster, J. D.; Campbell, W. K.; and Twenge, J. M. 2003. Individual Differences in Narcissism: Inflated Self-Views Across the Lifespan and Around the World. *Journal of Research in Personality*, 37: 469–486.

69 *Lillian Katz, a professor:* Stout, Maureen. 2000. *The Feel-Good Curriculum.* Cambridge, MA: Perseus Books; p. 178.

70 *A scale that measures entitlement:* Campbell, W. K., et al. 2004. Psychological Entitlement: Interpersonal Consequences and Validation of a Self-report Measure. *Journal of Personality Assessment,* 83: 29–45.

70 *A 2005 Associated Press article printed:* Irvine, Martha. "Young Labeled 'Entitlement Generation.'" AP, June 26, 2005. biz.yahoo.com/ap/050626/the_entitlement_ gen eration.html2.v3. Also reprinted in many newspapers.

70 *Stout, the education professor, lists:* Stout, Maureen. 2000. *The Feel-Good Curriculum.* Cambridge, MA: Perseus Books; p. 2.

70 *Several studies have found:* Bushman, B. J., and Baumeister, R. F. 1998. Threatened Egotism, Narcissism, Self-esteem, and Direct and Displaced Aggression: Does Self-love or Self-hate Lead to Violence? *Journal of Personality and Social Psychology,* 75: 219–229; and Twenge, J. M., and Campbell, W. K. 2003. "Isn't it fun to get the respect that we're going to deserve?" Narcissism, Social Rejection, and Aggression. *Personality and Social Psychology Bulletin,* 29: 261–272.

70 *Harris picked up a gun:* Gibbs, Nancy, and Roche, Timothy. "The Columbine Tapes." *Time,* December 20, 1999.

71 *In a set of lab studies, narcissistic:* Bushman, B. J., et al. 2003. Narcissism, Sexual Refusal, and Aggression: Testing a Narcissistic Reactance Model of Sexual Coercion. *Journal of Personality and Social Psychology,* 84: 1027–1040.

3 You Can Be Anything You Want to Be

PAGE

72 *Beginning in May 2005, high school:* Hulbert, Ann. "Unpersuasive." *New York Times Magazine,* May 29, 2005.

74 *The popular school program:* Sykes, Charles J. 1995. *Dumbing Down Our Kids.* New York: St. Martin's Press; p. 42.

74 *The growing primacy:* Twenge, J. M. 1997. Changes in Masculine and Feminine Traits over Time: A Meta-Analysis. *Sex Roles,* 36: 305–325; and Twenge, J. M. 2001. Changes in Women's Assertiveness in Response to Status and Roles: A Cross-temporal Meta-analysis, 1931–1993. *Journal of Personality and Social Psychology,* 81: 133–145.

74 *Yet, as* The Mommy Myth: Douglas, Susan, and Michaels, Meredith. 2004. *The Mommy Myth.* New York: Free Press; pp. 306–307.

74 *Douglas and Michaels refer:* Ibid.

75 Culture Shock! USA, *a guidebook:* Wanning, Esther. 1995. *Culture Shock! USA.* London: Kuperard; p. 70.

75 *One mother says that she treated:* Remley, Anne. "From Obedience to Independence." *Psychology Today,* October 1988: 56–59.

75 *Psychologist Bonnie Zucker, interviewed:* Fields-Meyer, Thomas. "Kids Out of Control." *People,* December 20, 2004.

75 *Another mother didn't make:* Naverrette, Ruben. "Parents Can't Buy Their Children's Respect." *Dallas Morning News,* November 28, 2004.

75 *Other children scream:* Fields-Meyer, Thomas. "Kids Out of Control." *People,* December 20, 2004.

76 *Writer Martin Booe recently:* Booe, Martin. "Generation Me-Me-Me." *Jackson Free Press,* October 21, 2004.

76 *educational psychologist Michele Borba:* Ibid.

76 *Douglas and Michaels argue:* Douglas, Susan, and Michaels, Meredith. 2004. *The Mommy Myth.* New York: Free Press; pp. 307–308.

76 *Paula Peterson's two kids:* Fields-Meyer, Thomas. "Kids Out of Control." *People,* December 20, 2004.

76 *Another parent says of his son:* Ibid.
76 *As* Culture Shock! USA *explains:* Wanning, Esther. 1995. *Culture Shock! USA.* London: Kuperard; p. 68.
76 *After being told to surrender:* Wallis, Claudia. "Does Kindergarten Need Cops?" *Time,* December 15, 2003.
76 *A report from the Tarrant County:* Ibid.
77 *Jerry's parents divorced:* Arnett, Jeffrey Jensen. 2004. *Emerging Adulthood.* New York: Oxford University Press; p. 62.
77 *Chris Colin notes that his classmates:* Colin, Chris. 2004. *What Really Happened to the Class of '93.* New York: Broadway Books; p. 51.
77 *Alexandra Robbins and:* Robbins, Alexandra, and Wilner, Abby. 2001. *Quarterlife Crisis: The Unique Challenges of Life in Your Twenties.* New York: Putnam; p. 109.
77 *Lia Macko, the coauthor:* Macko, Lia, and Rubin, Kerry. 2004. *Mildlife Crisis at 30: How the Stakes Have Changed for a New Generation—and What to Do About It.* New York: Plume Penguin; pp. v, 16.
78 *In a recent survey, a stunning 98%:* Northwestern Mutual Life Insurance survey of college freshmen. www.harrisinteractive.com/harris_poll/index.asp?PID=207; and Hornblower, Margot. "Great Xpectations." *Time,* June 9, 1997.
78 *In 2002, 80% of high school sophomores:* "Numbers," *Time,* February 21, 2005.
78 *In the late 1960s, by comparison:* Schneider, Barbara, and Stevenson, David. 1999. *The Ambitious Generation: America's Teenagers, Motivated But Directionless.* New Haven: Yale University Press.
78 *Seventy percent of late 1990s high school:* Ibid.
79 *In 2003, an incredible:* Astin, A. W., et al. 2002. *The American Freshman: Thirty-Five Year Trends.* Los Angeles: Higher Education Research Institute, UCLA. Plus 2003 and 2004 supplements.
79 *since the number of Ph.D's.:* Statistical Abstract of the United States, 2004 and earlier years. Available online at www.census.gov/prod/www/abs/statab.html.
79 *In 1999, teens predicted:* USA Weekend survey, May 2, 1999, cited in Howe, Neil, and Strauss, William. 2000. *Millennials Rising.* New York: Vintage.
79 *Sixty-five percent of high school seniors:* CBS News. 2001. *The Class of 2000.* Simon & Schuster eBook, available for download, pp. 23–25.
79 *One young employee told:* Raines, Claire, and Hunt, Jim. 2000. *The Xers and the Boomers.* Menlo Park, CA: Crisp Publications; p. 25.
79 Financial Times *writer Thomas Barlow:* Barlow, Thomas. "Tribal Workers." *Financial Times,* July 24, 1999.
80 *Many twentysomethings interviewed:* Robbins, Alexandra, and Wilner, Abby. 2001. *Quarterlife Crisis: The Unique Challenges of Life in Your Twenties.* New York: Putnam; p. 39.
80 *Several interviewees were looking:* Ibid., p. 20.
80 *Rosa, 24, interviewed:* Arnett, Jeffrey Jensen. 2004. *Emerging Adulthood.* New York: Oxford University Press; p. 31.
80 *the story of Charles, 27:* Ibid., p. 37.
80 *Derrick, struggling:* Robbins, Alexandra, and Wilner, Abby. 2001. *Quarterlife Crisis: The Unique Challenges of Life in Your Twenties.* New York: Putnam; p. 84.
80 *Robin, a 23-year-old:* Ibid., p. 83.
80 "*I want to write for sitcoms:*" Ibid., p. 73.
81 *Lara, 29, posted:* weddingchannel.com. Newlywed message boards, "ttc #2," June 4, 2004.
82 *American Idol contestant David Brown:* Gilatto, Tom; Lipton, Mike; and Smolowe, Jill. "The Final 24." *People,* February 28, 2005.
82 *In 2004, a national survey:* Astin, A. W., et al. 2002. *The American Freshman: Thirty-Five Year Trends.* Los Angeles: Higher Education Research Institute, UCLA. Plus 2003

and 2004 supplements and www.earlham.edu/≈ir/surveys/cirp/cirp_national_&_ heds_04.html. See Table 2.

82 *Emily, 22, apparently believes:* Robbins, Alexandra, and Wilner, Abby. 2001. *Quarterlife Crisis: The Unique Challenges of Life in Your Twenties.* New York: Putnam; p. 83.

82 *The book does discuss:* Ibid., p. 76.

83 *Arnett describes Albert:* Arnett, Jeffrey Jensen. 2004. *Emerging Adulthood.* New York: Oxford University Press; p. 158.

83 *Adrianne, 16, dreamed:* Meadows, Bob. "This Teen Wanted to Be Popular. Did That Lead to Her Murder?" *People,* February 14, 2005.

83 *"My big goal is to have:* Hewitt, Bill. "Wearing Out Their Bodies?" *People,* June 13, 2005.

83 *In 1996, 2002, and 2004, the magazine:* Clark, Jane Bennett, et al. Reporter: Elizabeth Kountze. "Dream Jobs (and How to Get One)." *Kiplinger's Personal Finance,* June 2004.

84 *Former Hollywood producer Elisabeth Robinson:* Robinson, Elisabeth. 2004. *The True and Outstanding Adventures of the Hunt Sisters.* New York: Back Bay Books; p. 19.

85 *A website sponsored by the National Clearinghouse:* www.ncfy.com/expseng.htm.

86 *Cowell chided him: American Idol,* FOX, January 27, 2004.

86 *In a later interview with* Star *magazine:* Birn, Jennifer; Hogan, Joyce; and Kim, Maggie. "Introducing William Hung: Untrained, Uncensored, Unstoppable!" *Star,* March 1, 2004, and www.williamhung.net/wst_page16.html.

87 *TV critic James Poniewozik notes:* Poniewozik, James. "Simon Cowell: Picking Our Winners," *Time,* April 26, 2004.

87 *"It's mind-boggling how:* Lopez, Molly. "Chatter: False Idols." *People,* February 14, 2005.

87 *Given the choice between fame:* Smith, J. Walker, and Clurman, Ann. 1997. *Rocking the Ages: The Yankelovich Report on Generational Marketing.* New York: HarperCollins; p. 85.

88 *Al Gore one of the network's founders:* Tumulty, Karen, and Locke, Laura. "Al Gore, Businessman." *Time,* August 8, 2005.

88 *As a New York Times article:* Stanley, Alessandra. "THE TV WATCH: Betting a Network on Youths Who Think." *The New York Times,* August 22, 2005.

88 *Musician Nellie McKay, 19:* " 'I'm Going to Be Famous': Nellie McKay Makes Bid for Stardom." cnn.com, April 13, 2004.

88 *"Ten years after leaving high school:* Colin, Chris. 2004. *What Really Happened to the Class of '93.* New York: Broadway Books; p. 55.

89 *as author Carol Wallace points out:* Wallace, Carol McD. 2004. *All Dressed in White.* New York: Penguin; p. 278.

89 *One bride said, "Finally:* Ibid., p. 280.

89 *Allison Ellis, who moderates:* Tapscott, Don. 1998. *Growing Up Digital.* New York: McGraw-Hill; p. 114.

89 *As part of my dissertation:* Twenge, J. M. 2001. Birth Cohort Changes in Extraversion: A Cross-Temporal Meta-Analysis, 1966–1993. *Personality and Individual Differences,* 30: 735–748.

90 *After 20/20 aired:* Lynn Sherr, "Me, Myself and I—the Growing Self-Esteem Movement." *20/20.* ABC, March 11, 1994.

90 *As Jeffrey Arnett notes:* Arnett, Jeffrey Jensen. 2004. *Emerging Adulthood.* New York: Oxford University Press; p. 73.

91 *One article describes Kathryn, 29:* Barlow, Thomas. "Tribal Workers." *Financial Times,* July 24, 1999.

91 *"Women in relationships tend:* Bartolomeo, Joey. "Jen Moves On," *Us Weekly,* February 21, 2005.

91 *"Commitments imply dependency:* Rubin, Jerry. 1976. *Growing (Up) at Thirty-Seven.* New York: Lippincott; pp. 52, 56.

92 *We gain self-esteem:* Aron, A.; Paris, M.; and Aron, E. N. 1995. Falling in Love: Prospective Studies of Self-Concept Change. *Journal of Personality and Social Psychology,* 69: 1102–1112; and Leary, M. R., et al. 1995. Self-Esteem as an Interpersonal Monitor: The Sociometer Hypothesis. *Journal of Personality and Social Psychology,* 68: 518–530.

92 *Study after study shows:* Myers, David. 1992. *The Pursuit of Happiness.* New York: Morrow.

92 *Research by Sandra Murray:* Murray, S. L., et. al. 1998. Through the Looking Glass Darkly? When Self-doubts Turn into Relationship Insecurities. *Journal of Personality and Social Psychology,* 75: 1459–1480.

92 *narcissists—people who really love themselves:* Campbell, W. Keith. 2005. *When You Love a Man Who Loves Himself.* Chicago: Sourcebooks; and Campbell, W. K. 1999. Narcissism and Romantic Attraction. *Journal of Personality and Social Psychology,* 77: 1254–1270.

92 *They think they are better:* Campbell, W. K.; Rudich, E. A.; and Sedikides, C. 2002. Narcissism, Self-esteem, and the Positivity of Self-views: Two Portraits of Self-love. *Personality and Social Psychology Bulletin,* 28: 358–368.

93 *"If I were to name the top 10:* W. Keith Campbell. Interview, December 28, 2004.

93 *"When the focus of life:* Solomon, Marion. 1992. *Narcissism and Intimacy: Love and Marriage in an Age of Confusion.* New York: Norton; p. 4.

93 *One young woman, interviewed in the book* Flux: Orenstein, Peggy. 2000. *Flux: Women on Sex, Work, Love, Kids, and Life in a Half-Changed World.* New York: Doubleday; p. 73.

93 *In an analysis of data from 47,692 respondents:* Twenge, J. M.; Campbell, W. K.; and Foster, C. A. 2003. Parenthood and Marital Satisfaction: A Meta-analytic Review. *Journal of Marriage and the Family,* 65: 574–583.

94 *Researchers at the National Marriage Project:* Shellenbarger, Sue. "And Baby Makes Stress: Why Kids Are a Growing Obstacle to Marital Bliss." *Wall Street Journal,* December 16, 2004.

94 *in 2004, 8% of twelfth-grade boys:* Hewitt, Bill. "Juiced Up." *People,* May 31, 2004.

96 *In October 2004,* People: "Facing Off Over Plastic Surgery." *People,* October 18, 2004.

96 *In a 1999 survey of 766 college students:* Greif, J.; Hewitt, W.; and Armstrong, M. L. 1999. Tattooing and Body Piercing. *Clinical Nursing Research,* 8: 368–385.

97 *"In the past, people got married:* Grossman, Lev. "Grow Up? Not So Fast." *Time,* January 24, 2005.

98 *GenMe marries later: Statistical Abstract of the United States,* 2004 and earlier years. Available online at www.census.gov/prod/www/abs/statab.html.

98 *the percentage of 26-year-olds living:* Grossman, Lev. "Grow Up? Not So Fast." *Time,* January 24, 2005.

98 *In 2002, 57% of men:* Robbins, Alexandra. 2004. *Conquering Your Quarterlife Crisis.* New York: Perigee; pp. 166–167.

98 *Young people are also taking longer:* Grossman, Lev. "Grow Up? Not So Fast." *Time,* January 24, 2005.

98 *Even at prestigious schools:* money.cnn.com/2004/06/21/pf/college/graduation_rates.

98 *"I want to get married:* Grossman, Lev. "Grow Up? Not So Fast." *Time,* January 24, 2005.

98 *Maroon 5 singer Adam Levine:* Halperin, Shirley. "Maroon 5's Adam Levine." *Us Weekly,* September 13, 2004.

98 *Jeffrey Arnett, author:* Grossman, Lev. "Grow Up? Not So Fast." *Time,* January 24, 2005.

98 *As the Twixters article explains:* Grossman, Lev. "Grow Up? Not So Fast." *Time,* January 24, 2005.

99 *In 1967, when the Boomers:* Astin, A. W., et al. 2002. *The American Freshman: Thirty-Five Year Trends.* Los Angeles: Higher Education Research Institute, UCLA. Plus 2003 and 2004 supplements.

99 *Another survey found that 1990s:* Mitchell, Susan. 1995. *The Official Guide to the Generations.* Ithaca, NY: New Strategist Publications. From the National Center for Education Statistics, "High School Seniors Look to the Future, 1972 and 1992."

99 *Olivia Smith, interviewed for the CBS:* CBS News. 2001. *The Class of 2000.* Simon & Schuster eBook, available for download, p. 14.

100 *College students are fully engrained:* Kiviat, Barbara. "Dressing Up the Dorms." *Time,* October 4, 2004.

100 *"She's a very good girl:* Jeffrey, Nancy. "Proms Gone Wild!" *People,* May 30, 2005.

100 Prom Guide *magazine says:* Ibid.

100 *A Sears ad for girls' clothing:* de Graaf, John; Wann, David; and Naylor, Thomas H. 2002. *Affluenza.* San Francisco: Berrett-Koehler; p. 55.

100 *Marcus Groenig, 28, interviewed:* Colin, Chris. 2004. *What Really Happened to the Class of '93.* New York: Broadway Books; p. 65.

101 *"I want to do things that conform:* "Notebook," *Time.* June 6, 2005.

101 *The coffee choices at Starbucks:* Waldman, S. The Tyranny of Choice: Why the Consumer Revolution Is Ruining Your Life. *New Republic,* January 27, 1992.

101 *"Shopping, like everything else:* Brooks, David. 2000. *Bobos in Paradise.* New York: Simon & Schuster; p. 101.

102 *A show on the cable channel:* "The Latest Entertainment Reviews: Television." *Life & Style,* April 11, 2005.

103 *"Years ago, cell phones:* Ken Belson. "I Want to Be Alone. Please Call Me." *New York Times,* June 27, 2004.

4 The Age of Anxiety (and Depression, and Loneliness):
Generation Stressed

PAGE

105 *Only 1% to 2% of Americans born:* Robins, L. N., et al. 1984. Lifetime Prevalence of Specific Psychiatric Disorders in Three Sites. *Archives of General Psychiatry,* 41: 949–958; Klerman, G. L., and Weissman, M. M. 1989. Increasing Rates of Depression. *Journal of the American Medical Association,* 261(15): 2229–2235; Lewinsohn, P. M., et al. 1993. Age-Cohort Changes in Lifetime Occurrence of Depression and Other Mental Disorders. *Journal of Abnormal Psychology,* 102(1): 110–120; Wickramaratne, P. J., et al. 1989. Age, Period, and Cohort Effects on the Risk of Major Depression: Results from Five United States Communities. *Journal of Clinical Epidemiology,* 42(4): 333–343; and Kessler, R. C., et al. 1994. Lifetime and 12-Month Prevalence of DSM-III-R Psychiatric Disorders in the United States: Results from the National Comorbidity Study. *Archives of General Psychiatry,* 51: 8–19.

105 *In one 1990s study, 21% of teens:* Lewinsohn, P. M., et al. 1993. Age-Cohort Changes in Lifetime Occurrence of Depression and Other Mental Disorders. *Journal of Abnormal Psychology,* 102: 110–120.

106 *In past generations, suicide:* Klerman, G. L., and Weissman, M. M. 1989. Increasing Rates of Depression. *Journal of the American Medical Association,* 261(15): 2229–2235; and Murphy, Jane M. 1994. The Stirling County Study: Then and Now. *International Review of Psychiatry,* 6: 329–348.

106 *The number of people being treated:* Olfson, M., et al. 2002. National Trends in the Outpatient Treatment of Depression. *Journal of the American Medical Association,* 287: 203–209.

106 *8.5% of Americans took:* "Numbers," *Time,* May 30, 2005. Cited source: Agency for Healthcare Research and Quality.

106 *The number of children on mood-altering drugs:* Zito, J. M., et al. 2003. Psychotropic Practice Patterns for Youth: A 10-Year Perspective. *Archives of Pediatrics and Adolescent Medicine,* 157: 17–25. For a nontechnical review, see Linda Marsa, "Are We Hooked on Happy Pills?" *Ladies' Home Journal,* July 2004.

106 *A recent cover of* Time *magazine:* Time, November 3, 2003.

106 *A 2003 government survey asked:* Centers for Disease Control, Youth Risk Behavior Surveillance System. Data available online at http://apps.nccd.cdc.gov/yrbss.

106 *At the Kansas State University:* Benton, Sherry A., et al. 2003. Changes in Counseling Center Client Problems Across 13 Years. *Professional Psychology: Research and Practice,* 34: 66–72. For a nontechnical review, see Shellenbarger, Sue, "Workers Struggle with Kids' Depression," *Wall Street Journal,* April 22, 2003.

107 *As part of my doctoral dissertation:* Twenge, J. M. 2000. The Age of Anxiety? Birth Cohort Change in Anxiety and Neuroticism, 1952–1993. *Journal of Personality and Social Psychology,* 79: 1007–1021.

107 *Twice as many people reported:* Goodwin, Renee D. 2003. The Prevalence of Panic Attacks in the United States: 1980 to 1995. *Journal of Clinical Epidemiology,* 56: 914–916.

107 *40% more people said:* Swindle, R., et al. 2000. Responses to Nervous Breakdowns in America over a 40-Year Period. *American Psychologist,* 55: 740–749.

107 *The number of teens aged 14 to 16:* Newsom, C. R., et al. 2003. Changes in Adolescent Response Patterns on the MMPI/MMPI-A Across Four Decades. *Journal of Personality Assessment,* 81: 74–84.

107 *A 2001 poll found:* Stepp, Laura Sessions. "Perfect Problems: These Teens Are at the Top in Everything. Including Stress." *Washington Post,* May 5, 2002.

107 *One out of three college freshmen:* Astin, A. W. 2002. *The American Freshman: Thirty-Five Year Trends.* Los Angeles: Higher Education Research Institute, UCLA.

108 *Someone commits suicide:* www.suicidememorialwall.com.

108 *While the suicide rate for middle-aged people: Statistical Abstract of the United States,* 2004 and earlier years. Available online at www.census.gov/prod/www/abs/statab.html.

108 *In 2003, 16.9% of high school students:* Centers for Disease Control, Youth Risk Behavior Surveillance System. Data available online at http://apps.nccd.cdc.gov/yrbss.

109 *In 2003, three students committed suicide:* "NYU student jumps to her death," cnn.com, September 6, 2004; and Hoover, Eric. "More Help for Troubled Students." *Chronicle of Higher Education,* December 3, 2003.

109 *Chris Colin describes his classmate Sean Bryant:* Colin, Chris. 2004. *What Really Happened to the Class of '93.* New York: Broadway Books; p. 269.

109 *More students graduate from high school:* Kluger, Jeffrey. "The Kids Are All Right." *Time,* July 26, 2004.

110 *More than four times as many:* Easterbrook, Gregg. 2003. *The Progress Paradox.* New York: Random House; p. 180.

110 *"There is a kind of famine:* Lane, Robert E. 2000. *The Loss of Happiness in Market Democracies.* New Haven, CT: Yale University Press; p. 9.

110 *One 26-year-old participant called it:* "Group Hug." *People,* September 27, 2004.

110 *In Prozac Nation, her memoir:* Wertzel, Elizabeth. 1994. *Prozac Nation: Young and Depressed in America.* New York: Riverhead Books; p. 33.

111 *This has a clear link:* Amato, P. R., and Keith, B. 1991. Parental Divorce and the Well-Being of Children: A Meta-Analysis. *Psychological Bulletin,* 110: 26–46.

113 On Sex and the City, *Carrie compares: Sex and the City*. Episode: "Unoriginal Sin." HBO. Airdate: July 28, 2002.

113 *Laurie, interviewed:* Arnett, Jeffrey Jensen. 2004. *Emerging Adulthood*. New York: Oxford University Press; pp. 110–111.

113 *Another couple described in the book:* Ibid., p. 106.

113 *As Jake puts it, "I could be 35:* Ibid., p. 105.

113 *There are actually thousands more: Statistical Abstract of the United States*, 2004 and earlier years. Available online at http://www.census.gov/prod/www/abs/statab.html.

114 *Twice as many 15-to-24-year-olds:* New Strategist Editors. 2004. *Generation X: Americans Born 1965 to 1976*. 4th ed. Ithaca, NY: New Strategist Publications; p. 172.

114 *A recent in-depth study found that Chicago:* Gorner, Peter. "U. of C. Sex Study Sees Love, Loneliness." *Chicago Tribune*, January 9, 2004.

114 *More than 1 out of 4 people aged 25 to 29:* New Strategist Editors. 2004. *Generation X: Americans Born 1965 to 1976*. 4th ed. Ithaca, NY: New Strategist Publications; p. 84.

114 *Author Chris Colin, 28, sums it up:* Colin, Chris. 2004. *What Really Happened to the Class of '93*. New York: Broadway Books; p. xiv.

115 *"A decade after high school:* Ibid., p. 60.

115 *Seventy-five percent of women aged 25 to 35:* The Next Generation: Today's Professionals, Tomorrow's Leaders. 2001. New York: Catalyst. www.catalystwomen.org.

115 *In The Costs of Living, Barry Schwartz describes:* Schwartz, Barry. 1994. *Costs of Living*. New York: Norton; p. 18.

115 *A mountain of scientific evidence links:* Williams, D. R.; Takeuchi, D. T.; and Adair, R. K. 1992. Martial Status and Psychiatric Disorders Among Blacks and Whites. *Journal of Health and Social Behavior*, 33: 140–157; Robins, Lee, and Reiger, Darrel. 1991. *Psychiatric Disorders in America*. New York: Free Press; Baumeister, R. F., and Leary, M. R. 1995. The Need to Belong: Desire for Interpersonal Attachments as a Fundamental Human Motivation. *Psychological Bulletin*, 117: 497–529; and Myers, David. 2000. *The American Paradox*. New Haven: Yale University Press; chap. 3.

116 *each year, Harvard rejects 50%:* Fallows, James. "New College Chaos." *The Atlantic Monthly*, November 2003.

116 *In 2004, the majority of freshmen:* Davison, James. "Talented Freshman Class Settles in at UW." *Badger Herald*, October 1, 2004. Available at badgerherald.com/news/2004/10/01/talented_freshman_cl.php.

117 *in a 2000 survey, young people were 50%:* Mitchell, Susan. 2003. *American Generations*. 4th ed. Ithaca, NY: New Strategist Publications; p. 47. Data are from the 2000 General Social Survey, National Opinion Research Center, University of Chicago.

117 *A 2002 Washington Post article:* Stepp, Laura Sessions. "These Teens Are at the Top in Everything, Including Stress." *Washington Post*, May 5, 2002.

117 *an amazing 97% of parents said:* Great Expectations Survey, National Center for Public Policy and Higher Education. www.highereducation.org/reports/expectations/expectations_table1.shtml; and Warren, Elizabeth, and Tyagi, Amelia Warren. 2003. *The Two-Income Trap*. New York: Basic Books; p. 41.

117 *The number of high school students:* Wallis, Claudia, and Miranda, Carolina A. "How Smart Is AP?" *Time*, November 8, 2004.

117 *Time magazine interviewed Marielle Woods:* Steptoe, Sonja. "Ready, Set, Relax!" *Time*, October 27, 2003.

118 *In 2004, more than half of medical:* www.aamc.org/data/facts/2004/2004summary.htm.

118 *"When I graduated from college:* Robbins, Alexandra, and Wilner, Abby. 2001. *Quarterlife Crisis*. New York: Tarcher/Putnam; p. 173.

118 A *National Science Foundation study*: Lee, Jennifer. "Postdoc Trail: Long and Filled with Pitfalls." *New York Times*, August 21, 2001.
119 A *recent* New York Times *article described a Harvard*: Ibid.
120 *"You need a college degree*: Grossman, Lev. "Grow Up? Not So Fast." *Time*, January 24, 2005.
120 *Between 1997 and 2002, the amount*: New Strategist Editors. 2004. *Generation X: Americans Born 1965 to 1976*. 4th ed. Ithaca, NY: New Strategist Publications; p. 242.
121 *In June 2005, the median house*: "No cooling the housing market yet." money.cnn.com, July 25, 2005.
121 *In 2004, a record sixty-two*: Max, Sarah. "Hot Housing Markets." cnn.com, February 15, 2005.
121 *Houses in Los Angeles's San Fernando Valley*: Unger, Brian. "Still Renting." *Day to Day*. National Public Radio, February 21, 2005.
121 *In the spring of 2005, the median house*: Christie, Les. "Homes: Hot Markets Get Hotter." cnn.com, May 26, 2005.
121 *In 2004, the average apartment*: Doig, Will. "The Average Apartment Cost a Million Bucks." *New York Magazine*, December 20, 2004.
121 *Where I live in San Diego*: Regnier, Pat. "Are Home Prices Really So Crazy?" cnn.com, May 16, 2005.
122 *The amount of the family budget*: Warren, Elizabeth, and Tyagi, Amelia Warren. 2003. *The Two-Income Trap*. New York: Basic Books.
124 *The number of middle-class families who pay over 35%*: Ibid., p. 133.
124 In Nickel and Dimed, *Barbara Ehrenreich reports*: Ehrenreich, Barbara. 2001. *Nickel and Dimed: On (Not) Getting by in America*. New York: Metropolitan Books; p. 199.
125 *Over the last twenty-five years, the share*: Johnston, David Cay. "Richest Getting Even Richer." *New York Times*, June 5, 2005.
125 *The income of men ages 25 to 34*: Grossman, Lev. "Grow Up? Not So Fast." *Time*, January 24, 2005.
125 *Summarizing data from several large studies*: Putnam, Robert. 2000. *Bowling Alone*. New York: Simon & Schuster; p. 197.
126 *In Oregon, colleges*: Associated Press. "American Colleges Flunk on Affordability." cnn.com, September 15, 2004.
126 *Today's young people*: Statistical Abstract of the United States, 2004 and earlier years. Available online at www.census.gov/prod/www/abs/statab.html.
126 *Average student loan debt*: Grossman, Lev. "Grow Up? Not So Fast." *Time*, January 24, 2005.
127 *"I graduated from college with honors*: *Time*, February 14, 2005.
127 *health care premiums surged 11.2%*: Kiviat, Barbara. "Up, Up, and Away: Health-Insurance Costs Soar." *Time*, September 20, 2004.
127 *almost 1 out of 3 people ages 18 to 24*: New Strategist Editors. 2004. *Generation X: Americans Born 1965 to 1976*. 4th ed. Ithaca, NY: New Strategist Publications; p. 46.
127 *Bankruptcies caused by illness*: "Numbers." *Time*, February 14, 2005.
127 In The Baby Book's *2003 edition*: Sears, William, and Sears, Martha. 2003. *The Baby Book*. New York: Little, Brown; p. 413.
130 *Quarterlife Crisis concludes that twentysomethings*: Robbins, Alexandra, and Wilner, Abby. 2001. *Quarterlife Crisis*. New York: Tarcher/Putnam; p. 109.
130 *Writer Cathi Hanauer sums this up*: Hanauer, Cathi. 2002. Introduction to *The Bitch in the House*. New York: Harper Collins Perennial; p. xv.

130 *In* Quarterlife Crisis, *Joanna says:* Robbins, Alexandra, and Wilner, Abby. 2001. *Quarterlife Crisis.* New York: Tarcher/Putnam; p. 93.

131 *In her book on eating disorders:* Blumberg, Joan Jacobs. 1989. *Fasting Girls.* New York: New American Library; p. 267.

131 As Midlife Crisis at 30 *puts it:* Macko, Lia, and Rubin, Kerry. 2004. *Midlife Crisis at 30: How the Stakes Have Changed for a New Generation—and What to Do About It.* New York: Plume Penguin; p. 59.

131 *Sure enough, research shows:* Shrum, L. J.; Burroughs, J. E.; and Rindfleisch, A. 2005. Television's Cultivation of Material Values. *Journal of Consumer Research;* and Shrum, L. J.; Burroughs, J. E.; and Rindfleisch, A. 2004. A Process Model of Consumer Cultivation: The Role of Television Is a Function of the Type of Judgment. In Shrum, L. J., ed. *The Psychology of Entertainment Media: Blurring the Lines Between Entertainment and Persuasion.* Mahwah, NJ: Lawrence Erlbaum Associates, Publishers; pp. 177–191.

131 *"Whose Ring Is Bigger?" asks Us Weekly:* Us Weekly, March 7, 2005.

132 *because fewer of us ride buses:* Fallows, James. "The Invisible Poor." *New York Times Magazine,* March 19, 2000.

132 *People whose primary motivations:* Kasser, T., and Ryan, R. 1993. A Dark Side of the American Dream. *Journal of Personality and Social Psychology,* 65: 410–422.

132 *And research consistently finds that money:* Myers, David. 2000. *The American Paradox.* New Haven: Yale University Press; chap. 6.

132 *Psychologist Ed Diener got many:* Diener, E.; Horowitz, J.; and Emmons, R. A. 1985. Happiness of the Very Wealthy. *Social Indicators,* 16: 263–274.

132 *People who win the lottery:* Brickman, P.; Coates, D.; and Janoff-Bulman, R. 1978. Lottery Winners and Accident Victims: Is Happiness Relative? *Journal of Personality and Social Psychology,* 36: 917–927.

132 *GenMe writer Chuck Klosterman says:* Klosterman, Chuck. 2004. *Sex, Drugs, and Cocoa Puffs.* New York: Scribner; p. 4.

133 *In a Gallup poll 94%:* Popenoe, David, and Whitehead, Barbara Defoe. 2001. *The State of Our Unions: The Social Health of Marriage in America, 2001.* New Brunswick, NJ: National Marriage Project.

133 *Norval Glenn, an expert:* Bereson, Lisa. "The State of the Union: A Special Report." *Ladies' Home Journal,* March 2003.

133 *The authors of* Midlife Crisis at 30 *call:* Macko, Lia, and Rubin, Kerry. 2004. *Midlife Crisis at 30: How the Stakes Have Changed for a New Generation—and What to Do About It.* New York: Plume Penguin; pp. 89–90.

133 *In the mid-1970s, 69%:* marriage.rutgers.edu/Publications/SOOU/TEXTSOOU 2004.htm. Data are from the General Social Survey.

133 *Compared to those married between 1969 and 1980:* Rogers, S. J., and Amato, P. R. 1997. Is Marital Quality Declining? The Evidence from Two Generations. *Social Forces,* 75: 1089–1100.

133 *"It's as if some idiot:* Seligman, M. E. P. 1988. "Boomer Blues." *Psychology Today,* October 1988, 50–53.

134 *Even with the recent sharp downturn: Statistical Abstract of the United States,* 2004 and earlier years. Available online at http://www.census.gov/prod/www/abs/statab.html. This uses the FBI's Uniform Crime Reports for violent crime.

135 *people who watch many hours:* Romer, D.; Jamieson, K. H.; and Aday, S. 2003. Television News and the Cultivation of Fear of Crime. *Journal of Communication,* 53: 88–104.

135 *"His biggest fear, he told me:* "Utah Scout Feeling 'Good' After Ordeal." cnn.com, June 23, 2005.

5 Yeah, Right: The Belief That There's No Point in Trying

PAGE

138 *"There are plenty of students:* Sacks, Peter. 1996. *Generation X Goes to College.* Chicago: Open Court Press; p. 59.

138 *Or take Ryan, the character: The* O.C. Pilot episode. FOX, August 5, 2003.

139 *Liqing Zhang, Charles Im, and I found 97 studies:* Twenge, J. M.; Zhang, L.; and Im, C. 2004. It's Beyond My Control: A Cross-Temporal Meta-Analysis of Increasing Externality in Locus of Control, 1960–2002. *Personality and Social Psychology Review,* 8: 308–319.

140 *cynical statements such as:* Pharr, S. J.; Putnam, R. D.; and Dalton, R. J. 2000. A Quarter-Century of Declining Confidence. *Journal of Democracy,* 11: 5–25.

140 *High school students increasingly:* Bronfenbrenner, U., et al. 1996. *The State of Americans: This Generation and the Next.* New York: Free Press.

141 *One professor at a "socially progressive" college:* Anonymous review of *Generation X Goes to College.* amazon.com, dated January 31, 2004.

141 *In 2004, only 6%:* Astin, A. W., et al. 2002. *The American Freshman: Thirty-Five Year Trends.* Los Angeles: Higher Education Research Institute, UCLA. Plus 2003 and 2004 supplements.

141 *In 1966, 60% of freshmen:* Ibid.

141 *Fewer freshmen reported:* Ibid.

141 *A recent poll found that 53%:* Long, Kay. "Leave It to Gen-X." *Chicago Daily Herald,* November 7, 2002.

141 *Less than 20% of young people:* Mindich, David T. Z. 2005. *Turned Out: Why Americans Under 40 Don't Follow the News.* New York: Oxford University Press.

142 *Only 32% of people aged 18 to 24:* Ibid.

142 *He found that 60%:* Ibid.

142 *In another poll, high school seniors:* CBS News. 2001. *The Class of 2000.* Simon & Schuster eBook, available for download, p. 126.

143 *"Modern society has become:* Colin, Chris. 2004. *What Really Happened to the Class of '93.* New York: Broadway Books; p. 178.

143 *Young people have heard this so often that Tom: Jack & Bobby.* WB, November 3, 2004.

143 *Voter participation among 18-to-20-year-olds: Statistical Abstract of the United States,* 2004 and earlier years. Available online at www.census.gov/prod/www/abs/statab.html.

144 *Voter participation among those aged 21 to 24:* Ibid.

144 *As a study by People for the American Way:* People for the American Way. 1989. *Democracy's Next Generation.* Washington, DC: Author; p. 27.

146 *As author Neil Postman notes:* Postman, Neil. 1994. *The Disappearance of Childhood.* New York: Vintage; p. 95.

147 *Ryan Beckwith, interviewed:* Colin, Chris. 2004. *What Really Happened to the Class of '93.* New York: Broadway Books; p. 179.

147 *"When there are few winners:* McKeachie, Wilbert. 1994. *Teaching Tips.* Boston: Heath; p. 356.

148 *A sterling example:* Poniewozik, James. "Amber Waves of Self-Esteem." *Time,* April 18, 2001.

148 *"when they encounter teachers:* Stout, Maureen. 2000. *The Feel-Good Curriculum.* Cambridge, MA: Perseus Books; p. 263.

149 *The Yankelovich polling firm found:* Smith, J. Walker, and Clurman, Ann. 1997. *Rocking the Ages: The Yankelovich Report on Generational Marketing.* New York: HarperCollins; p. 82.

149 *An article in* USA Today Magazine *noted:* "Do Workplace Woes Signal the End of the American Dream?" *USA Today Magazine*, August 1995.

150 *"Kids see people like Bill Gates:* Sacks, Peter. 1996. *Generation X Goes to College.* Chicago: Open Court Press; p. 169.

150 *Susan Peterson, who teaches:* amazon.com review of *Generation X Goes to College,* "You Think Gen X Is Bad? Watch Out for Gen Y." Posted April 11, 2003.

150 *"the impulse to flee":* Sykes, Charles. 1992. *A Nation of Victims: The Decay of the American Character.* New York: St. Martin's Press; p. 15.

151 The Myth of Laziness *author Mel Levine:* Levine, Mel. 2003. *The Myth of Laziness.* New York: Simon & Schuster.

151 *As Sykes puts it:* Sykes, Charles. 1992. *A Nation of Victims: The Decay of the American Character.* New York: St. Martin's Press; p. 144.

151 *As Judith Warner points out:* Warner, Judith. 2005. *Perfect Madness.* New York: Riverhead Books; p. 96.

152 *Leroy Wells, 22:* "American Idol: Round #2." *Star*, February 14, 2005.

152 *Clark passed several bad checks:* Tauber, Michelle, and Smolowe, Jill. "*Idol* Under Attack." *People*, May 16, 2005.

152 *In 1940, about 20,000:* Caplow, Theodore; Hicks, Louis; and Wattenberg, Ben J. 2001. *The First Measured Century.* Washington, D.C.: AEI Press; p. 198.

153 *From 1993 to 1996 alone:* Ibid.

153 *One young man sued:* "Former Law Student Stages Hunger Strike." *Chronicle of Higher Education*, January 23, 1998.

153 *Chris Colin was heartened:* Colin, Chris. 2004. *What Really Happened to the Class of '93.* New York: Broadway Books; p. 258.

153 *"Kids today have extremely:* Sacks, Peter. 1996. *Generation X Goes to College.* Chicago: Open Court Press; p. 59.

154 *Another student asked if:* Ibid, p. 16.

154 *Sacks reports with irony:* Ibid., p. 20.

154 *"Students who receive a C, D, or F:* Kazez, Daniel. "A Is for Anybody." *Newsweek*, August 8, 1994; p. 10.

154 *In his 2005 book:* Allitt, Patrick. 2005. *I'm the Teacher, You're the Student.* Philadelphia: University of Pennsylvania Press; p. 211.

154 *After Sacks pointed out:* Sacks, Peter. 1996. *Generation X Goes to College.* Chicago: Open Court Press; p. 122.

154 *In her 2003 book:* Perlstein, Linda. 2003. *Not Much Just Chillin': The Hidden Lives of Middle Schoolers.* New York: Ballantine; p. 183.

154 Time *magazine recently ran:* Gibbs, Nancy. "Parents Behaving Badly." *Time*, February 21, 2005.

155 *Scott McLeod, the headmaster:* Lewis, Michael. "Coach Fitz's Management Theory." *New York Times Magazine*, March 28, 2004.

155 *Between 7% and 15% of children:* Sykes, Charles. 1992. *A Nation of Victims: The Decay of the American Character.* New York: St. Martin's Press.

156 *Some parents also abuse the labels:* Gibbs, Nancy. "Parents Behaving Badly." *Time*, February 21, 2005.

156 *By 1994, almost 5%:* Gibbs, Nancy. "The Age of Ritalin." *Time*, November 30, 1998.

156 *"What if Tom Sawyer:* Ibid.

157 *People who believe that outside forces:* Benassi, V. A.; Sweeney, P. D.; and Dufour, C. L. 1988. Is There a Relation Between Locus of Control Orientation and Depression? *Journal of Abnormal Psychology*, 97: 357–367; Hahn, S. E. 2000. The Effects of Locus of Control on Daily Exposure, Coping and Reactivity to Work Interpersonal Stressors: A Diary Study. *Personality and Individual Differences*, 29: 729–748; Mirowsky, J., and Ross, C. E. 1990. Control or Defense? Depression and

the Sense of Control over Good and Bad Outcomes. *Journal of Health and Social Behavior,* 31: 71–86; and Naditch, M. P.; Gargan, M.; and Michael, L. 1975. Denial, Anxiety, Locus of Control, and the Discrepancy Between Aspirations and Achievements as Components of Depression. *Journal of Abnormal Psychology,* 84: 1–9.

157 *and anxious:* Kilpatrick, D. G.; Dubin, W. R.; Marcotte, D. B. 1974. Personality, Stress of the Medication Education Process, and Changes in Affective Mood State. *Psychological Reports,* 34: 1215–1223; and Morelli, G.; Krotinger, H.; and Moore, S. 1979. Neuroticism and Levenson's Locus of Control Scale. *Psychological Reports,* 44: 153–154.

157 *cope poorly with stress:* Krause, N., and Stryker, S. 1984. Stress and Well-being: The Buffering Role of Locus of Control Beliefs. *Social Science and Medicine,* 18: 783–790; and Sandler, I. N., and Lakey, B. 1982. Locus of Control as a Stress Moderator: The Role of Control Perception and Social Support. *American Journal of Community Psychology,* 10: 65–80.

157 *externals have weakened:* Karabenick, S. A., and Srull, T. K. 1978. Effects of Personality and Situational Variation in Locus of Control on Cheating: Determinants of the "Congruence Effect." *Journal of Personality,* 46: 72–95; and Mischel, W.; Zeiss, R.; and Zeiss, A. 1974. An Internal-External Control Test for Young Children. *Journal of Personality and Social Psychology,* 29: 265–278.

157 *Externality and low self-control:* Baumeister, R. F.; Heatherton, T. F.; and Tice, D. M. 1994. *Losing Control: How and Why People Fail at Self-Regulation.* San Diego: Academic Press; Parrott, C. A., and Strongman, K. T. 1984. Locus of Control and Delinquency. *Adolescence,* 19: 459–471; and Shaw, J. M., and Scott, W. A. 1991. Influence of Parent Discipline Style on Delinquent Behaviour: The Mediating Role of Control Orientation. *Australian Journal of Psychology,* 43: 61–67.

157 *externals consistently achieve less:* Cappella, E., and Weinstein, R. S. 2001. Turning Around Reading Achievement: Predictors of High School Students' Academic Resilience. *Journal of Educational Psychology,* 93: 758–771; Findley, M. J., and Cooper, H. M. 1983. Locus of Control and Academic Achievement: A Literature Review. *Journal of Personality and Social Psychology,* 44: 419–427; and Kalechstein, A. D., and Nowicki, S. 1997. A Meta-analytic Examination of the Relationship Between Control Expectancies and Academic Achievement: An 11-Yr Follow-up to Findley and Cooper. *Genetic, Social, and General Psychology Monographs,* 123: 27–56.

157 *A definitive report concluded:* Coleman, J. S., et al. 1966. *Equality of Educational Opportunity. Report from the Office of Education.* Washington, D.C.: U.S. Government Printing Office.

158 *"Our society has:* Rotter, Julian. "External Control and Internal Control." *Psychology Today,* June 1971, 59.

6 Generation Prude Meets Generation Crude

PAGE

159 *In Valerie Frankel's recent novel:* Frankel, Valerie. 2004. *The Not-So-Perfect Man.* New York: Avon Trade.

159 *It was soon followed by:* Lavinthal, Andrea, and Rozler, Jessica. 2005. *The Hookup Handbook.* New York: Simon Spotlight Entertainment; pp. 2–3.

160 *"I think you can compare friends:* "The 411: Teens & Sex," NBC, January 26, 2005.

160 *62% of people in their twenties:* Mitchell, Susan. 2003. *American Generations,* 4th ed. Ithaca, NY: New Strategist Publications; p. 334.

161 *In a 1999 study, college students' primary motivations:* Regan, P. C., and Dreyer, C. S. 1999. Lust? Love? Status? Young Adults' Motives for Engaging in Casual Sex. *Journal of Psychology and Human Sexuality,* 11: 1–24.

161 *CBS interviewed one young woman:* CBS News. 2001. *The Class of 2000.* Simon & Schuster eBook, available for download, p. 72.

161 *A Glamour magazine article advises:* Kamen, Paula. 2000. *Her Way: Young Women Remake the Sexual Revolution.* New York: New York University Press; p. 93.

161 *In her book Her Way:* Ibid., p. 92.

161 *For her master's thesis with me, Brooke Wells:* Wells, B. E., and Twenge, J. M. 2005. Changes in Young People's Sexual Behavior and Attitudes, 1943–1999: A Cross-Temporal Meta-Analysis. *Review of General Psychology,* 9: 249–61.

162 *in 1970, the average woman:* Statistical Abstract of the United States, 2004 and earlier years. Available online at www.census.gov/prod/www/abs/statab.html.

162 *In 1970, only 36% of women:* Mitchell, Susan. 2003. *American Generations,* 4th ed. Ithaca, NY: New Strategist Publications; p. 333.

162 *An Oregon high school sophomore:* CBS News. 2001. *The Class of 2000.* Simon & Schuster eBook, available for download, pp. 14–15.

163 *84% of single women:* Popenoe, David, and Whitehead, Barbara Defoe. "The State of Our Unions: The Social Health of Marriage in America, 2001." New Brunswick, NJ: National Marriage Project.

164 *In its Summer 2004 issue, Brides magazine:* "The Wedding Report, 2004." *Brides.* Summer 2004: p. 304.

164 *Author Paula Kamen studied:* Kamen, Paula. 2000. *Her Way: Young Women Remake the Sexual Revolution.* New York: New York University Press; p. 225.

164 *A whopping 88%:* Altman, Lawrence K. "Study Finds That Teenage Virginity Pledges Are Rarely Kept." *New York Times,* March 10, 2004.

164 *participants in abstinence programs:* American Psychological Association press release, "Based on the Research, Comprehensive Sex Education Is More Effective at Stopping the Spread of HIV Infection, Says APA Committee," February 23, 2005. At www.apa.org/releases/sexeducation.html; or www.apa.org/releases/sexed_resolution .pdf.

165 *An amazon.com review:* www.amazon.com/exec/obidos/ASIN/0814747337/qid= 1118853685/sr; eq2-2/ref=pd_bbs_b_2_2/002-6957767-3997645.

165 *Numerous newspaper stories:* Stepp, Laura Sessions. "Unsettling New Fad Alarms Parents: Middle School Oral Sex." *Washington Post,* July 8, 1999; Jarrell, Anne. "The Face of Teenage Sex Grows Younger." *New York Times,* April 3, 2000; and Cooke, Barbara. "When Is Sex Not Sex?" *Chicago Tribune,* March 4, 2001.

165 *Many kids say that oral sex:* Denizet-Lewis, Benoit. "Friends, Friends with Benefits, and the Benefits of the Local Mall." *New York Times Magazine,* May 30, 2004.

165 *In the NBC special:* "The 411: Teens & Sex." NBC, January 26, 2005.

166 *Another national survey found:* Kamen, Paula. 2000. *Her Way: Young Women Remake the Sexual Revolution.* New York: New York University Press.

166 *the NBC/People poll found:* Tauber, Michelle; Fields-Meyer, Thomas; and Smith, Kyle. "Young Teens and Sex." *People,* January 31, 2005.

166 *Linda Perlstein, the author:* Perlstein, Linda. 2003. *Not Much Just Chillin': The Hidden Lives of Middle Schoolers.* New York: Ballantine Books; p. 44.

167 *In Alfred Kinsey's studies:* Kamen, Paula. 2000. *Her Way: Young Women Remake the Sexual Revolution.* New York: New York University Press; p. 76.

167 *A recent article in the* New York Times Magazine: Denizet-Lewis, Benoit. "Friends, Friends with Benefits, and the Benefits of the Local Mall." *New York Times Magazine,* May 30, 2004.

168 *In the NBC/People poll:* Tauber, Michelle; Fields-Meyer, Thomas; and Smith, Kyle. "Young Teens and Sex." *People,* January 31, 2005.

168   A 2001 study found that 60%: Denizet-Lewis, Benoit. "Friends, Friends with Benefits, and the Benefits of the Local Mall." *New York Times Magazine*, May 30, 2004.

169   *Young authors Andrea Lavinthal:* Lavinthal, Andrea, and Rozler, Jessica. 2005. *The Hookup Handbook.* New York: Simon Spotlight Entertainment; p. 4.

169   *Features of the hookup:* Ibid., p. 182.

169   *One woman says she knew:* Ibid., p. 221.

169   *As The Hookup Handbook puts it:* Ibid., p. 10.

170   *As The Hookup Handbook notes:* Ibid., p. 232.

170   *Monica, 16, said: Today.* NBC, January 27, 2005.

170   *This is art imitating life:* Ibid.

170   A 2004 study of almost 2,000 teens: "Study Links TV to Teen Sexual Activity." cnn.com, September 7, 2004; and Collins, R. L. 2005. Sex on Television and Its Impact on American Youth: Background and Results from the RAND Television and Adolescent Sexuality Study. *Child and Adolescent Psychiatric Clinics of North America*, 14: 371–385.

171   *young black women who watch:* Wingood, G. M., et al. 2003. A Prospective Study of Exposure to Rap Music Videos and African American Female Adolescents' Health. *American Journal of Public Health*, 93: 437–439.

171   *Thirteen-year-old Maya, interviewed:* Tauber, Michelle; Fields-Meyer, Thomas; and Smith, Kyle. "Young Teens and Sex." *People*, January 31, 2005.

171   *Pediatrician Meg Meeker calls it: Today.* NBC, January 27, 2005.

171   *Linda Perlstein, the author:* Perlstein, Linda. 2003. *Not Much Just Chillin': The Hidden Lives of Middle Schoolers.* New York: Ballantine Books; p. 87.

172   *sexual terms and talk are:* Huner, Marnie. "The Secret Lives of Middle Schoolers." cnn.com, November 19, 2003.

172   *In the New York Times Magazine article on hooking up:* Denizet-Lewis, Benoit. "Friends, Friends with Benefits, and the Benefits of the Local Mall." *New York Times Magazine*, May 30, 2004.

172   *A Kaiser Family Foundation study found:* Jerome, Richard. "The Cyberporn Generation." *People*, April 26, 2004.

173   *Cases of chlamydia in young women:* Centers for Disease Control and Prevention. *Sexually Transmitted Disease Surveillance 2003 Supplement.* Atlanta, GA: U.S. Department of Health and Human Services, Centers for Disease Control and Prevention, October 2004.

173   *Nevertheless, about 25% of people diagnosed:* U.S. Centers for Disease Control and Prevention. *Tracking the Hidden Epidemics: Trends in STDs in the United States 2000.*

173   *between 1 in 3 and 1 in 4 college students:* Civic, D. 2000. College Students' Reasons for Nonuse of Condoms Within Dating Relationships. *Journal of Sex and Marital Therapy*, 26: 95–105.

173   *one young man said he found out:* Arnett, Jeffrey Jensen. 2004. *Emerging Adulthood.* New York: Oxford University Press; p. 92.

173   *A recent study examined the sexual geography:* Wallis, Claudia. "A Snapshot of Teen Sex." *Time*, February 7, 2005. (I calculated the 61% figure myself from the figure in the article.)

173   *A recent Kaiser Family Foundation study found that 75%:* Alexander, Melissa. "Television Programs Lack Safe Sex Message." *Daily Aztec* (San Diego State University student newspaper), March 7, 2005.

174   *When watching TV, says college freshman Joyce Bryn:* Ibid.

175   *It is the fifth leading cause: Statistical Abstract of the United States*, 2004 and earlier years. Available online at www.census.gov/prod/www/abs/statab.html.

175 *Births to teens aged 15 to 17:* Ibid; and "Births: Preliminary Data for 2003." National Vital Statistics Reports, U.S. Department of Health and Human Services, vol. 53, no. 9.

176 *In 1992, when the first wave:* Astin, A. W., et al. 2002. *The American Freshman: Thirty-Five Year Trends.* Los Angeles: Higher Education Research Institute, UCLA. Plus 2003 and 2004 supplements.

176 *In a 2001 poll, 62%:* Popenoe, David, and Whitehead, Barbara Defoe. "The State of Our Unions: The Social Health of Marriage in America, 2001." New Brunswick, NJ: National Marriage Project.

176 *A 1990s study found that 64%:* Michael, R. T., et al. 1995. *Sex in America: A Definitive Survey.* New York: Warner.

177 *Author Linda Perlstein saw a girl's website:* Perlstein, Linda. 2003. *Not Much Just Chillin': The Hidden Lives of Middle Schoolers.* New York: Ballantine; p. 147.

177 *The authors of* Midlife Crisis at 30 *relate:* Macko, Lia, and Rubin, Kerry. 2004. *Midlife Crisis at 30: How the Stakes Have Changed for a New Generation—and What to Do About It.* New York: Plume Penguin; p. 92.

177 *Today in the United States:* Solot, Dorian, and Miller, Marshall. 2002. *Unmarried to Each Other.* New York: Marlowe & Co.; p. 245.

177 *In 2003, 34.6% of babies:* Statistical Abstract of the United States, 2004 and earlier years. Available online at http://www.census.gov/prod/www/abs/statab.html; and "Births: Preliminary Data for 2003." National Vital Statistics Reports, U.S. Department of Health and Human Services, vol. 53, no. 9.

177 *But when Rachel on* Friends: Poniewozik, James. "Reconsidering Friends." *Time,* April 19, 2004.

7 The Equality Revolution: Minorities, Women, and Gays and Lesbians

PAGE

180 *Reflecting on the events:* "From the Front Lines of Freedom." *People,* March 7, 2005.

181 *In 1970, when the first Generation Me babies:* Statistical Abstract of the United States, 2004 and earlier years. Available online at www.census.gov/prod/www/abs/statab.html.

181 " 'Tolerance' and 'acceptance' might: Colin, Chris. 2004. *What Really Happened to the Class of '93.* New York: Broadway Books; p. 102.

182 *In 1970, most blacks did not:* Statistical Abstract of the United States, 2004 and earlier years. Available online at www.census.gov/prod/www/abs/statab.html.

183 *Charles, 27, interviewed:* Arnett, Jeffrey Jensen. 2004. *Emerging Adulthood.* New York: Oxford University Press; p. 129.

183 *Sixty-one percent of black:* Ibid.

184 *In a 2000 poll, 70%:* CBS News. 2001. *The Class of 2000.* Simon & Schuster eBook, available for download, pp. 110, 113.

184 *In 1960, almost 80%:* Myers, David. 1993. *Social Psychology.* 4th ed. New York: McGraw-Hill; p. 378.

184 *among Americans born:* New Strategist Editors. 2004. *Generation X: Americans Born 1965 to 1976.* 4th ed. Ithaca, NY: New Strategist Publications; p. 221.

185 *Back in the 1940s, psychologists:* Myers, David. 1993. *Social Psychology,* 4th ed. New York: McGraw-Hill; p. 378; and Severo, Richard. "Kenneth Clark, Who Fought Segregation, Dies." *New York Times,* May 2, 2005.

185 *Jennifer Crocker and I gathered data:* Twenge, J. M., and Crocker, J. 2002. Race and Self-Esteem: Meta-Analyses Comparing Whites, Blacks, Hispanics, Asians, and American Indians. *Psychological Bulletin,* 128: 371–408.

188 *For example, Asian-American kids:* Ibid.

189 *Women earn 57% of college degrees: Statistical Abstract of the United States,* 2004 and earlier years. Available online at www.census.gov/prod/www/abs/statab.html.

189 *Most women in their twenties:* Mitchell, Susan. 2003. *American Generations.* 4th ed. Ithaca, NY: New Strategist Publications; p. 334.

189 *More than four times as many women:* Riche, Martha Farnsworth. 2003. "Young Women: Where They Stand." In Costello, Cynthia B.; Wight, Vanessa R.; and Stone, Anne J., eds. *The American Woman, 2003–2004.* New York: Palgrave Macmillan.

189 *Couples in which only the husband:* New Strategist Editors. 2004. *Generation X: Americans Born 1965 to 1976.* 4th ed. Ithaca, NY: New Strategist Publications; p. 144.

190 *Attitudes about women's roles continued:* Twenge, J. M. 1997. Attitudes Toward Women, 1970–1995: A Meta-Analysis. *Psychology of Women Quarterly,* 21: 35–51.

191 *Among people under age 29 polled:* Mitchell, Susan. 1995. *The Official Guide to the Generations.* Ithaca, NY: New Strategist Publications. The data are from *Gallup Poll Monthly,* 1993.

191 *While 70% of people 65 and older:* Mitchell, Susan. 2003. *American Generations.* 4th ed. Ithaca, NY: New Strategist Publications; p. 42. Data are from the 2000 General Social Survey, National Opinion Research Center, University of Chicago.

191 *In 1984, for the first time: Statistical Abstract of the United States,* 2004 and earlier years. Available online at www.census.gov/prod/www/abs/statab.html.

192 *In 2004, only 1 out of 1,000:* Astin, A. W., et al. 2002. *The American Freshman: Thirty-Five Year Trends.* Los Angeles: Higher Education Research Institute, UCLA. Plus 2003 and 2004 supplements.

193 *I gathered 103 samples:* Twenge, J. M. 1997. Changes in Masculine and Feminine Traits over Time: A Meta-Analysis. *Sex Roles,* 36: 305–325.

193 *For one thing, more than eight times:* "Women's Sports Foundation, Title IX: What Is It?" womenssportsfoundation.org; and Guttman, A. 1991. *Women's Sports: A History.* New York: Columbia University Press.

193 *It's likely that sports participation:* Butcher, J. E. 1989. Adolescent Girls' Sex Role Development: Relationship with Sports Participation, Self-Esteem, and Age at Menarche. *Sex Roles,* 20: 575–593.

194 *In a 2000 survey, 82%:* Mitchell, Susan. 2003. *American Generations.* 4th ed. Ithaca, NY: New Strategist Publications; p. 43. Data are from the 2000 General Social Survey, National Opinion Research Center, University of Chicago.

194 *Studies have found that girls with working mothers:* Hansson, R. O.; Chemovetz, M. E., and Jones, W. H. 1977. Maternal Employment and Androgyny. *Psychology of Women Quarterly,* 2: 76–78.

195 *I gathered 168 studies:* Twenge, J. M. 2001. Changes in Women's Assertiveness in Response to Status and Roles: A Cross-Temporal Meta-Analysis, 1931–1993. *Journal of Personality and Social Psychology,* 81: 133–145.

195 *My colleague Keith Campbell and I examined 446 studies:* Twenge, J. M., and Campbell, W. K. 2002. Self-Esteem and Socioeconomic Status: A Meta-Analytic Review. *Personality and Social Psychology Review,* 6: 59–71.

196 *In one of the essays, E. S. Maduro:* Maduro, E. S. 2002. "Excuse Me While I Explode: My Mother, Myself, My Anger." In Hanauer, C., ed., *The Bitch in the House.* New York: HarperCollins; p. 8.

196 *Her mother, however, saw:* Hanauer, C. Afterword. In ibid., p. 281–282.

197 *Married fathers spent three times:* Sayer, L. C.; Bianchi, S. M.; and Robinson, J. P. 2004. Are Parents Investing Less in Children? Trends in Mothers' and Fathers' Time with Children. *American Journal of Sociology,* 110: 1–43.

198 *A 2004 poll found that 79%:* Orecklin, Michelle. "Stress and the Superdad." *Time,* August 23, 2004.

198 *Young men are also helping out:* Paul, Pamela. "Whose Job Is This, Anyway?" *Time,* October 4, 2004.

198 *In 1994, the cover of the business magazine:* Holcomb, Betty. 1998. *Not Guilty! The Good News for Working Mothers.* New York: Touchstone; pp. 59–60.

198 *It turned out that if you looked:* Statistical Abstract of the United States, 2004 and earlier years. Available online at www.census.gov/prod/www/abs/statab.html.

198 Time *magazine ran a cover story in 2004:* Wallis, Claudia. "The Case for Staying Home." *Time,* March 22, 2004.

198 *Newspapers breathlessly announced:* Hilton, Lisette. "Census: More Women Are Staying Home to Raise Children." *Silicon Valley/San Jose Business Journal,* August 23, 2002.

198 *This figure was 58% in 1998:* Statistical Abstract of the United States, 2004 and earlier years. Available online at www.census.gov/prod/www/abs/statab.html.

199 *The labor force participation of men:* Ibid.; and New Strategist Editors. 2004. *Generation X: Americans Born 1965 to 1976.* 4th ed. Ithaca, NY: New Strategist Publications; p. 136.

199 *the entering class of medical students in 2004:* www.aamc.org/data/facts/2004/2004summary.htm.

199 *a 1997 article in* Time *magazine proclaimed:* Edwards, Tamala. "The Young and the Nested." *Time,* November 10, 1997.

200 *The median age at first marriage for women in 1990:* Statistical Abstract of the United States, 2004 and earlier years. Available online at www.census.gov/prod/www/abs/statab.html.

200 *older women "who came of age:* Wallis, Claudia. "The Case for Staying Home." *Time,* March 22, 2004.

200 *Yet when these same Boomer women:* Statistical Abstract of the United States, 2004 and earlier years. Available online at www.census.gov/prod/www/abs/statab.html.

201 *As Susan Douglas and Meredith Michaels point out:* Douglas, Susan, and Michael, Meredith. *The Mommy Myth,* New York: Free Press; p. 8.

202 *Writer Peggy Orenstein said:* Macko, Lia, and Rubin, Kerry. 2004. *Midlife Crisis at 30: How the Stakes Have Changed for a New Generation—and What to Do About It.* New York: Plume Penguin; p. 241.

202 *children who attend day care centers:* National Institute of Child Health and Human Development Early Child Care Research Network; and Duncan, G. J. 2003. Modeling the Impacts of Child Care Quality on Children's Preschool Cognitive Development. *Child Development,* 74: 1454–1475; and Schuetze, P.; Lewis, A.; and DiMartino, D. 1999. Relation Between Time Spent in Daycare and Exploratory Behaviors in 9-Month-Old Infants. *Infant Behavior and Development,* 22: 267–276.

203 *Douglas and Michaels label:* Douglas, Susan, and Michaels, Meredith. *The Mommy Myth.* New York: Free Press; p. 5.

203 *In a recent poll, 4 out of 5 parents said:* Hewlett, S. A., and West, C. 1998. *The War Against Parents: What We Can Do for America's Beleaguered Moms and Dads.* New York: Houghton Mifflin.

203 *A sociological study found that despite:* Sayer, L. C.; Bianchi, S. M.; and Robinson, J. P. 2004. Are Parents Investing Less in Children? Trends in Mothers' and Fathers' Time with Children. *American Journal of Sociology,* 110: 1–43.

204 *One* People *magazine cover story:* Douglas, Susan, and Michaels, Meredith. *The Mommy Myth.* New York: Free Press; p. 122.

204 *Peggy Orenstein describes the modern world:* Orenstein, Peggy. 2000. *Flux: Women on Sex, Work, Love, Kids, and Life in a Half-Changed World.* New York: Doubleday; p. 2.

204 *In* Midlife Crisis at 30, *Lia Macko and Kerry Rubin express:* Macko, Lia, and Rubin, Kerry. 2004. *Midlife Crisis at 30: How the Stakes Have Changed for a New Generation—and What to Do About It.* New York: Plume Penguin; p. 3.

204 *As Douglas and Michaels put it, "Both":* Douglas, Susan, and Michaels, Meredith. *The Mommy Myth.* New York: Free Press; p. 12.

205 *As Orenstein puts it, young women have:* Orenstein, Peggy. 2000. *Flux: Women on Sex, Work, Love, Kids, and Life in a Half-Changed World.* New York: Doubleday; p. 18.

206 *When you've always been taught:* Warner, Judith. 2005. *Perfect Madness.* New York: Riverhead Books; p. 9.

206 *Warner argues that many:* Ibid.

206 *Young authors Macko and Rubin found the same thing:* Macko, Lia, and Rubin, Kerry. 2004. *Midlife Crisis at 30: How the Stakes Have Changed for a New Generation—and What to Do About It.* New York: Plume Penguin; p. 25.

206 *Douglas and Michaels sum up:* Douglas, Susan, and Michaels, Meredith. *The Mommy Myth.* New York: Free Press; p. 7.

207 *On a 2005 episode of the teen soap* The O.C.: *The O.C.* FOX. Airdate: February 17, 2005.

207 *Even young Republicans often:* Cloud, John. 2004. "The Right's New Wing." *Time,* August 30, 2004.

207 *While only 30%:* www.cbsnews.com/stories/2004/02/24/national/main601828.shtml.

209 *Sam Hanser, 16, told:* CBS News. 2001. *The Class of 2000.* Simon & Schuster eBook, available for download, p. 120.

209 *In a CBS poll of high school students, 33% said:* Ibid.

210 *"Kids are coming out":* Ibid., p. 117.

210 *In 2002, my graduate school friend:* Cohen, Betsy. "Community of Support: Hundreds Rally Behind Family That Lost Home in Fire Friday Morning." *The Missoulian,* February 10, 2002.

8 Applying Our Knowledge: The Future of Business and the Future of the Young

PAGE

212 *In a recent poll, 53%:* CBS News. 2001. *The Class of 2000.* Simon & Schuster eBook, available for download, p. 36.

213 *Although 17% of teens still said:* Centers for Disease Control, Youth Risk Behavior Surveillance System, data available online at apps.nccd.cdc.gov/yrbss.

213 *births to teens aged 15 to 17: Statistical Abstract of the United States,* 2004 and earlier years. Available online at www.census.gov/prod/www/abs/statab.html.

213 *Fewer teens said they carried:* Centers for Disease Control, Youth Risk Behavior Surveillance System, data available online at apps.nccd.cdc.gov/yrbss.

214 *A recent Associated Press article:* Irvine, Martha. "Young Labeled 'Entitlement Generation.'" AP, June 26, 2005. biz.yahoo.com/ap/050626/the_entitlement_gen eration.html?.v3.

215 *75% of 2003 college freshmen:* Astin, A. W., 2002. *The American Freshman: Thirty-Five Year Trends.* Los Angeles: Higher Education Research Institute, UCLA. Plus 2003 and 2004 supplements.

215 *Given that only 1 in 1,000 incoming college students:* Ibid.
216 *"shockingly high expectations:* Ibid.
216 *Mike Amos, a franchise consultant:* Irvine, Martha. "Young Labeled 'Entitlement Generation.'" AP, June 26, 2005. biz.yahoo.com/ap/050626/the_entitlement_gen eration.html?.v3.
217 *"The manager who says:* Ibid.
218 *The book* Generations at Work *advises:* Zemke, Ron; Raines, Claire; and Filipczak, Bob. 2000. *Generations at Work.* New York: AMACOM; p. 118.
223 *"We are in danger of producing:* Stout, Maureen. 2000. *The Feel-Good Curriculum.* Cambridge, MA: Perseus Books; p. 119.
225 *"We do not need to completely shield:* Rosenfeld, Alvin, and Wise, Nicole. 2000. *The Over-Scheduled Child.* New York: St. Martin's Press; p. 56.
225 *"The risk of over-indulgence:* Tyre, Peg; Scelfo, Julie; and Kantrowitz, Barbara. "Just Say No: Why Parents Must Set Limits for Kids Who Want It All." *Newsweek,* September 13, 2004.
226 *Author Chris Colin quotes his classmate:* Colin, Chris. 2004. *What Really Happened to the Class of '93.* New York: Broadway Books; p. 56.
227 *A whopping 97% of parents:* Great Expectations Survey, National Center for Public Policy and Higher Education. www.highereducation.org/reports/expectations/expec tations_table1.shtml; and Warren, Elizabeth, and Tyagi, Amelia Warren. 2003. *The Two-Income Trap.* New York: Basic Books; p. 41.
229 *As the book* The Two-Income Trap *documents:* Warren, Elizabeth, and Tyagi, Amelia Warren. 2003. *The Two-Income Trap.* New York: Basic Books.
230 *In* Perfect Madness, Judith Warner *writes:* Warner, Judith. 2005. *Perfect Madness.* New York: Riverhead Books; p. 277.
230 *Yet couples in which the husband works:* New Strategist Editors. 2004. *Generation X: Americans Born 1965 to 1976.* 4th ed. Ithaca, NY: New Strategist Publications; p. 144.
230 *in a 2002 poll, 82% of women:* Warner, Judith. 2005. *Perfect Madness.* New York: Riverhead Books; p. 272.
230 *The government pays an average:* Crittenden, Ann. 2001. *The Price of Motherhood.* New York: Holt; p. 217.
231 *Of 168 industrialized nations:* de Graaf, John. 2003. *Take Back Your Time.* San Francisco: Berrett-Koehler.
232 *The authors of* The Two-Income Trap *write:* Warren, Elizabeth, and Tyagi, Amelia Warren. 2003. *The Two-Income Trap.* New York: Basic Books; p. 69.
233 *in 2002, the U.S. birth rate:* Statistical Abstract of the United States, 2004 and earlier years. Available online at www.census.gov/prod/www/abs/statab.html.
234 *A biologically driven shift:* Dement, William C. 1999. *The Promise of Sleep.* New York: Delacorte Press.
234 *When the Edina, Minnesota, school, system:* Ibid.
237 *A huge amount of research:* Anderson, C. A., and Bushman, B. J. 2001. Effects of Violent Video Games on Aggressive Behavior, Aggressive Cognition, Aggressive Affect, Physiological Arousal, and Prosocial Behavior: A Meta-Analytic Review of the Scientific Literature. *Psychological Science,* 12: 353–359.
238 *Raquel Aviva, 32, offers:* Robbins, Alexandra. 2004. *Conquering Your Quarterlife Crisis.* New York: Perigee; p. 130.
239 *Michael Coviello, 25, says:* Ibid., p. 206
239 *You are also less likely to feel:* Ranney, Dave. "KU Study Exploring Treatment for Depression Without Drugs." *Lawrence Journal-World,* June 1, 2005, at www2.ljworld.com/news/2005/jun/01/depression/?ku_news; and Steve Ilardi. Interview, December 16, 2004.
240 *listen to the advice of John Pozniak:* Robbins, Alexandra. 2004. *Conquering Your Quarterlife Crisis.* New York: Perigee; p. 99.

241 *While only 64%:* www.civicyouth.org/PopUps/FactSheets/FS_Volunteering2.pdf.
     Source: Monitoring the Future, University of Michigan.
241 *Among college freshmen, only 66% volunteered:* Astin, A. W., et al. 2002. *The American Freshman: Thirty-Five Year Trends.* Los Angeles: Higher Education Research Institute, UCLA. Plus 2003 and 2004 supplements.
241 *People in their early twenties in 1998:* Putnam, Robert. 2000. *Bowling Alone.* New York: Simon & Schuster; p. 129.

Acknowledgments

As a child, I loved to read so much that I would often stay up past my bedtime to finish a book. My practical midwestern parents, however, had the radical idea that I should get enough sleep. I tried to finish a book in the bathroom once but was promptly busted. After that, I learned to leave on the aquarium light, which was just bright enough to read by but not bright enough to shine under the door and alert the parental units to my stolen reading time. I would lie at the foot of my bed, late into the night, turning the magic pages in the dim light.

Twenty-five years later, I have read the acknowledgments sections of so many books that I can recite the typical one from memory ("It is fiction that it takes only one person to write a book . . . to my agent extraordinaire . . . to my 546 closest friends [Aaron, Adam, Alice, Amanda . . . (insert 540 names here) . . . Zachary, and Zelda] . . . and finally, to my spouse for cooking all the meals for the last year/raising several children by himself while I slaved away at this godforsaken project/reading the whole book/typing the whole book/writing the whole book"). After writing a book myself, I have suddenly realized why acknowledgment sections all sound the same: you're a massive pain in the ass when you're working on a book, and a little ink is small consolation for all of the people who had to put up with it. I was no different, so my acknowledgments will probably sound no different.

I was a pain partially because writing this book was the most fun I've had at work in years, and enthusiasm, although infectious, can get annoying. Everyone, please forgive me. It's just that any project in which I can quote Us Weekly and academic research on the same page is a damn good time.

I owe my first large sums of gratitude to those who made writing this book even more fun than it was already. Brooke Wells wrote her amazingly thorough master's thesis on changes in sexually over time, providing the data for Chapter 6 and enabling me to spend several enjoyable weeks writing about sex. How can I not be grateful for that? W. Keith Campbell, my colleague, coauthor, and friend, has sharpened my thinking on just about everything for six years now, including several parts of this book. I'm not sure I would have made it through the jungle of academia without Keith's hatchet of wry irony to clear the way. Next conference, let's skip the symposia and go talk and eat doughnuts again. I learned more that way anyway.

I am also profoundly grateful to the hundreds of young people who opened their lives to me by contributing stories for the book. A large thanks in particular to those who volunteered their time by submitting material through the www.generationme.org website. Your honesty, insight, and eloquence made this book immeasurably stronger. Your stories and opinions brought your generation to life.

My agent, Jill Kneerim, is the reason I got to write this book in the first place. I am amazed, and truly grateful, at how she was able to guide me so encouragingly toward a book proposal that bore no resemblance to my first pathetic attempts. I can only hope to someday develop even an ounce of Jill's ability to pleasantly guide someone into doing her best. My editor, Leslie Meredith, has been equally delightful. Writing your first book can be terrifying, but all of that melted away once I saw Leslie's enthusiasm for my first few chapters. ;-) Long live the deadline emotion! 8-] The brilliant Brettne Bloom came up with the title and thus deserves a huge high-five.

I have been blessed with truly outstanding academic mentors: Roy Baumeister, Jennifer Crocker, Susan Nolen-Hoeksema, Randy Larsen, Abby Stewart, Dianne Tice, and David Winter all helped guide some aspect of this project. Susan showed me the research on changes in depression and generally gave fantastic advice. David guided me through the uncharted territory of lagged analyses and obscure personality measures, gently shaping my overenthusiastic grad student ideas into a more conventional psychology dissertation. We also had quite a good time just chewing the fat. Roy was the best postdoctoral adviser I could have asked for, and a good friend. His pioneering research on the downsides of self-esteem also strengthened the book considerably. And in the beginning, when I was only 15, Melissa McMillan-Cunningham and Patrick

McCann both told me I would write a book someday. We all thought it would be a book of poetry, but I hope this is just as good.

Charles Im and Liqing Zhang spent hours upon hours in the library collecting some of the data I use here, and they deserve ample praise and gratitude. Your hard work made these projects possible. Mark Reid photocopied numerous articles on changes in depression and provided inspiration through his excellent writing. A true man of many talents, he also designed the www.generationme.org website where I collected stories from young people around the nation.

The library staff at so many locations have been surprisingly tolerant of the mess one of my projects can create: my thanks to the libraries of the University of Iowa, Eastern Michigan University, Case Western Reserve University, Carnegie Mellon University, the University of Wisconsin, San Diego State University, the Library of Congress, and especially the University of Michigan, particularly the Interlibrary Loan Department. You are saints.

Other academic colleagues have provided excellent ideas, inspiration, and friendship. Jeff Bryson, Kate Catanese, Niels Christensen, Natalie Ciarocco, Thierry Devos, Nathan DeWall, Amanda Diekman, Julie Exline, Craig Foster, Linda Gallo, Christine Harris, Benita Jackson, Markus Kemmelmeier, Laura King, Elizabeth Klonoff, Sander Koole, Joseph Lewis, Deborah Megivern, Kathi Miner-Rubino, Claire Murphy, Radmila Prislin, Scott Roesch, Brandon Schmeichel, Tom Scott, Kathleen Vohs, May Yeh, and Alyssa Zucker, thank you for listening to me blather on about this research for years. I am particularly grateful to those of you who told your classes about the www.generationme.org website. I will always remember Mark Leary, whom I got to know later in another line of research, saying kind words about this work—before breakfast, no less—at an APA conference. Alice Eagly was one of the first to cite my work on changes for women and has lent me her expertise as if I were one of her own students. Daniel Cervone, personality psychologist extraordinaire, engineered my first major presentation of this work to the field. I am continually grateful for how Dan saw the promise in this research and was able to articulate its importance even better than I could. Lynne Baker-Ward and James Kalat were also kind enough to encourage me and to believe in the importance of birth cohort work within psychology. The SDSU press office, particularly Jason Foster, Aaron Hoskins, and Jennifer

Zwiebel (now at NYU), have done excellent work to publicize these studies and impress my relatives by getting me on TV.

And to my U of C posse, what can I say except, you rule! Stacey Amodio, Anne Becker Gruettner, Ken Bloom, Lawrence Charap, Rocky Dhir, Sonia Orfield, and Adam Shah, your loyalty and love are unsurpassed. Lawrence and Shasta Charap deserve special mention for their warm hospitality during several Library of Congress sojourns; Ken Bloom also helped with library searches several times. Kim and Brian Chapeau, Shannon and George Ekeren-Moening, Sarah and Dan Kilabarda, Charles and Jane Moening, Brian and Roxanne Moening, Sarah Moening and Rodney Haug, Bud and Pat Moening, and Marilyn, Ray, and Anna Swenson have belied the phrase that you can't choose your relatives—I'd choose you guys every time. And Charles, thanks for your excellent edit of the introduction. Ron Louden and Alice Zellmer, Dave and Amanda Louden, Jillian Berman, and Susie and Jud Wilson have also been the best in-laws I could have ever chosen. Ken and Allene Berman are the coolest "in-in-laws" and the most gracious New York hosts.

I have read enough acknowledgments sections to know that you save the best for last. My brother Dan has grown from my childhood playmate to my steadfast friend and confidant, as well as being the father of the cutest child in the entire world. My parents, Steve and JoAnn Twenge, instilled in me the love of reading and the highest respect for education, and also put their money where their mouth was by subsidizing my time at the University of Chicago. They also provided a window on past decades, always willing to help me understand how things have changed and why. I've lost count of the ideas in these projects that had their genesis in one of our conversations. Finally, to my husband, Craig, for tolerating my hours of (over)work and (over)stress, but mostly for making me the luckiest woman in the world. Here's to many more years of happiness, even if I do write another book.

Index

Page numbers in *italics* refer to illustrations.

Abdul, Paula, 86, 87, 152
abortion, 4, 175, 213
Acra, Reem, 34
Adams, Cecil, 12
advertising, *81*
  job, 188
  prescription drugs, *105*, 106, 142
  sexist, 20, 188
  sexual products, 38–39, 45, 161, *174*
  young people targeted by, 100
African Americans, 244–45
  advances of, 182–83, 184–86
  discrimination against, 21, 25, 180,
    182, 183–84
AIDS, 174–75, *174*
alcohol, 1, 11, 26, 50, 213
"All About Me: Are We Developing Our
  Children's Self-Esteem or Their
  Narcissism?" (Katz), 69–70
Alley, Kirstie, 204
All in the Family, 132
Allitt, Patrick, 154
All My Children, 208
Ally McBeal, 113
"Amber Waves of Self-Esteem," 148
*Ambitious Generation, The: America's
  Teenagers, Motivated But Direction-
  less* (Schneider and Stevenson),
  78–79, 227
American Academy of Pediatrics, 45
American Association of University
  Women (AAUW), 60
American Cancer Society, 241
American Idol, 82, 83, 86–87, 152, 219
American Paradox, The (Myers), 136
American Pie, 170
Amos, Mike, 216–17
Aniston, Jennifer, 96
anxiety disorders, 106–8, 109

Army, U.S., 51
Arnett, Jeffrey, 34, 83, 90–91, 98
Arnett, Kevin, 100
Arthur Murray dance school, 22
Asch, Solomon, 23
Asian Americans, 32, 67–68, 184, 186,
  188
assertiveness, 11, 21, 48, 74, 195
Associated Press (AP), 70, 214, 217
Astin, Andrew, 63
Atkins, Dan, 10
attention deficit/hyperactivity disorder
  (ADHD), 156
Attitudes Toward Women Scale, 190
authority:
  disrespect for, 17–20, 25–36, 39, 43
  questioning of, 25, 28–31
Avenue Q, 130, 172, 183
Aviva, Raquel, 238–39

Baby Book, The (Sears), 127–28
Baby Boomer generation, 7, 8
  abstraction and spirituality of, 34,
    46–48, 49, 50, 51
  as first TV Generation, 6
  GenMe compared to, 19, 24, 28, 34, 46,
    48, 49, 51, 52–53, 74, 89, 98, 99,
    139, 184, 200–201, 215
  group orientation of, 1, 4, 48, 51
  introspection and self-absorption of, 4,
    45–49
  in middle age, 9, 47
  protests and marches of, 1, 4, 48,
    137–38, 141
  rebellion of, 42–43
Baby Einstein, 204
Back to the Future, 21
bankruptcy, 128–29
Barlow, Thomas, 79–80

Barron's, 198
Barrymore, Drew, 145
baseball, 17, 83, 226
Basinger, Kim, 47
Basu, Alo, 88
Batman Begins, 223
Baumeister, Roy, 66, 225
BE A WINNER *Self-Esteem Coloring and Activity Book*, 53–54, *54*, *55*
Beckwith, Ryan, 147
"Believe in Yourself," 78
Bem Sex-Role Inventory, 11
Bend It Like Beckham, 21
Benedict XVI, Pope, 34
Beverly Hills, 90210, 33
Big Chill, The, 143
Billingham, Robert, 30–31
birth control, 4, 161, 176
Bitch in the House, The, 196
blame, 147, 148, 150–57, *151*
Blige, Mary J., 167
Blumberg, Joan Jacobs, 131
Blume, Judy, 38
Bobos in Paradise (Brooks), 47
bodies:
    circadian rhythms of, 234
    obsession with appearance of, 94–97, *95*, 131, 220
    plastic surgery on, 94–96
    tattooing and piercing of, 2, 4, 96–97, 159
    workout-produced muscles on, 94
Booe, Martin, 76
Boomer Nation (Gillon), 47
Borba, Michele, 76
Born to Buy (Schor), 100
Bower, Jocelyn, 100
Bowling Alone (Putnam), 35, 110, 157
Brady Bunch, The, 181
Braff, Zach, 97–98
Brave New World (Huxley), 50
Breakfast Club, 170
Brides, 32, 164
Brooks, David, 47, 101
Brown, David, 82
Brown v. Board of Education, 185
Bryant, Sean, 109
Bryn, Joyce, 174
Burke, Brooke, 95
Burns, George, 238
Bush, George W., 5, 142

business, 82, 149–50
    cheating, crime, and scandal in, 27–28
    competition in, 7, 28
    downsizing and outsourcing in, 27, 120, 150, 199
    pension raiding in, 27
    see also jobs; work

Caccavale, Matt, 241
California, 10, 15, 65, 114
California, University of:
    at Berkeley, 86, 186
    at Los Angeles, 98, 101, 118
California Task Force to Promote Self-Esteem and Personal and Social Responsibility, 65
Campbell, Keith, 52, 61, 69, 92–93, 195
Canada, 7, 231
Cantor, Joanne, 236
Carrey, Jim, 20
Catholic Charities, 241
CBS, 59, 162, 209–10
    Class of 2000 project of, 99, 161, 209
celebrities, 45, 89, 96, 129, 147
    obsession with, 88, 94–95, 131, 145, 149
    as role models, 83, 150
cell phones, 27, 101, 103
Census Bureau, U.S., 200
Channing, Carol, 146–47
Chappelle, David, 183
Chappelle's Show, 184
cheating, 17, 26–27, 91, 92
Chester, Eric, 217
Chiaramonte, Joan, 2
Chicago, Ill., 110, 114
Chicago, University of, 11, 12, 40–41, 108
Chicago Sun-Times, 30–31
children, 1–4, 8, 94, 233–34, 235
    adoption of, 210
    anxiety and depression in, 106–7, 108, 236–37
    behavioral problems of, 154–56
    discipline and punishment of, 1, 76, 140, 236
    impact of divorce on, 3, 77, 111
    independent thinking of, 19, 25, 30–31, 35
    lack of respect and consideration in, 26, 30–31, 75–76
    learning-disabled, 155–56

marketing to, 100

obedience of, 19, 24

parents as friends of, 30–31

praise and boosting self-esteem of, 2, 4, 7, 30–31, 45, 58–59, 74–77, 149, 150

value systems set in, 8

CHiPs, 43

Choose or Lose, 144

church, 26–28

  declining attendance at, 34–35

  fundamentalist Christian, 35, 47, 57–58

  loyalty to, 24

  see also religion; *specific sects*

Civil Rights Act, 188

civil rights movement, 180, 182, 185, 188

Clark, Corey, 152

Clark, Kenneth, 185

Clark, Mamie, 185

Clerks, 20, 40, 166

Clinton, Bill, 88, 145, 166

clothes, 17–19

  comfort and informality of, 17–19, *19*, 32–33, *33*, 218

  cost of, 131

  formal, 17, *18*, 19, *19*, 100

  self-expression and, 17, 25

  sports, 17–18

  styles and fashion in, 43, 95, 100, 171

  wedding, *33*, 34, 89

  work, 17, 19, 218, 221

CNN, 137, 142, 145

Coca-Cola, 7

Cohen, Eric, 103

Cold War, 204

Colin, Chris, 39, 77, 88, 109, 114–15, 147, 153, 181, 226

College Board, 63

colleges, 244–45

  career direction and, 227–28

  cheating in, 27

  classic Dead White Male (DWM) Western literature studies in, 29–30

  competitive admissions to, 2, 116–18, 134, 136, 217, 226

  disrespect for authority in, 28–30

  informality in, 40–41

  Ivy League, 80, 88, 116, 117, 126, 148

  post-graduate study in, 3, 11–15, 79, 118–19, 120

Collins, Rebecca, 171

Columbine High School, 70–71, 134

communication:

  openness in, 36–41, 165, 217, 220

  TMI (Too Much Information) in, 38

  see also Internet

Communists, 20–21

competition, 67

  business, 7, 28

  for college admission, 2, 116–18, 134, 136, 217, 226

computers, 12–14, 109

  generations growing up with, 5–6, 14

  see also Internet

condoms, 39, 174, *174*, 176, 179

conformity:

  honesty vs., 39–40

  peer pressure and, 39

  resistance to, 1, 19–20, 22–25

Congress, U.S., 189

  see also House of Representatives, U.S.

Conquering Your Quarterlife Crisis (Robbins), 49, 238–39, 240

consciousness-raising, 1, 48

constantchatter.com, 38

contentment, 40, 87

Coopersmith Self-Esteem Inventory, 52

Cosby Show, The, 183

Cosell, Howard, 188

Cosmopolitan, 164

Costs of Living, The (Schwartz), 115

Cote, James, 120

Courage to Heal, The, 151

Couric, Katie, 167

Cowell, Simon, 86–87

crack cocaine, 86

Crash, 183–84

Cribs, 238

crime, 134–36, 152, 187

  changing rates of, 52, 53, 109, 152, 213

  corporate, 27–28

  narcissism and, 70–71

  petty, 26–27

  teenage, 234

  violent, 53, 71, 134–35, 136

Crittenden, Ann, 230–31, 232

Crocker, Jennifer, 67

Crosby, David, 48

crystal meth, 36

cuddle parties, 110, 143

culture:
    clash of, 21–22, 40, 41
    popular, 2, 10, 26
Culture of Fear, The (Glassner), 135–36
Culture Shock! USA (Wanning), 75, 76
Current Affair, A, 147
Current TV, 88
cynicism, 137–58
    externality and, 156–58
    feelings of control and, 138–40
    television and, 145–47
    victim mentality and, 150–56
    and waning appeal of politics, 140–45

Daily Show, 147
Dallas, Tex., 32, 35, 63
Damon, William, 225
dancing, 22–23
Daria, 59, 60
dating, 2, 50, 90–91, 111–12, 114, 159,
        167, 168, 169, 198
    Internet, 112
    interracial, 32, 184
    "speed," 221–22
Dawson's Creek, 37, 91, 170, 208
day care, 89, 120, 125–26, 191, 202, 216,
        221, 222, 229, 230–31, 232, 233
Dean, Howard, 142
Degeneres, Ellen, 10, 208
Dement, William, 234
democracy, 29, 30
De Niro, Robert, 22
Denizet-Lewis, Benoit, 167–68
depression, 5, 7, 9, 104–9, 111, 115, 116,
        136, 157, 212–14, 221, 237
    childhood, 106–8, 236–37
    postpartum, 204
    treatment of, 104, *105*, 106, 239
Depression, Great, 105, 129
Diehl, Diane, 26
Diener, Ed, 132
Diller, Lawrence, 156
Disappearance of Childhood, The (Postman),
        171
discos, 1, 48
divorce, 52–53, 112
    effects on children of, 3, 77, 111
    rates of, 90
    social acceptance of, 25
Dolan-Pascoe, Brenda, 61
Donne, John, 227

Douglas, Susan, 74, 201, 203, 204–5, 206
Downs, Hugh, 90, 92
Doyle, John, 153
dreams, 2, 116, 226
    pursuit of, 5, 19, 21, 49, 51, 77–94, 100,
        115, 212, 226
    reality vs., 2, 7, 8, 49, 78–79, 83, 85–87,
        129–34, 212–13, 217, 239–40
driving, 31, 101, 149, 234
    aggressive, 26, 103
drugs:
    addiction to, 50, 86
    illegal, 36, 43, 86, 98
    mood-altering, *105*, 106, 156
    prescription, *105*, 106, 156, 229, 239
Duff, Hilary, 96
duty, 1, 6–7, 19, 45, 217
Dyer, Wayne, 24, 45

Easterbrook, Gregg, 131
eating disorders, 131
economy, 52, 98, 212
    prosperity in, 109
    realities of, 2, 120–29, 149, 219
    recessions in, 105, 109, 114, 199
    rising costs in, 2, 4, 7, 109, 120–29
Ecstasy, 98
education, 1–3, 109
    career path, 227–28
    collaborative approach to, 29–30, 218
    multicultural approach to, 30
    questioning of, 28–30
    rising costs of, 120, 125, 126, 129, 219,
        244
    see also colleges; schools; teachers
Ehrenreich, Barbara, 124
elections, U.S., 142, 144
Elks club, 35, 48
Ellen, 208
Ellis, Allison, 89
Emerging Adulthood (Arnett), 34–35, 77,
        80, 90–91, 98, 113, 173, 183
Emory University, 154
Engelhardt, Tricia, 127
Enron, 27
Entertainment Tonight, 149
"Entitlement Generation, The," 70, 214,
        216–17
Episcopal Church, 35
Erin Brockovich, 84
est, 1, 47, 48

Everson, Howard, 63
"Everyone's a Little Bit Racist," 183
"Express Yourself: A Teenager's Guide to Fitting In, Getting Involved, Finding Yourself," 85

Faludi, Susan, 190
fame, 2, 87–89, 102
families, 5, *18*, *19*, 40
    child-centered, 30–31
    decreasing standards of living in, 215–16
    dysfunctional, 36, 151–52
    middle-class, 4, 215, 232, 244
    relationships in, 110–11
    responsibility for, 2, 4, 8, 48, 86, 120–29, 131
    support for, 229–33
    two-income, 4, 125, 127–29, 189, 198, 230
    see also parents
Father Knows Best, 1
Father of the Bride, 200
Fear Factor, 88
Federal Communications Commission (FCC), 45
Federal Election Committee, 144
Federline, Kevin, 25, 51
feelings, 72, 74, 76, 225
Felicity, 161
feminism, 1, 20, 48, 190
    backlash against, 190
Feminist Fatale (Kamen), 190
Ferguson, Sarah, Duchess of York, 47
Fight Club, 129
Financial Times, 79–80
Finding Nemo, 46
Flux (Orenstein), 93
food, 47, 136
Forbes, 132
Foster, Craig, 93
Foster, Joshua, 69
Fox News, 137, 145
Frankel, Valerie, 159
Franken, Al, 54–55
Freakonomics (Levitt and Dubner), 213
freedom, 5, 20–21, 25, 116
Free Love, 1, 47, 98, 162
Free to Be You and Me, 24, 146–47, 191
Friends, 131, 170, 178, 212
Future Shock (Toffler), 7

Garden State, 97–98
Gates, Bill, 129, 150
gender, 19
    discrimination based on, 188–90
    equality and, 188–92
    stereotypes of, 11–12, 127
Generation Me (GenMe):
    adulthood postponed in, 97–98, 126–27
    Baby Boomer generation compared with, 19, 24, 28, 34, 46, 48, 49, 51, 52–53, 74, 89, 98, 99, 139, 184, 200–201, 215
    challenges of, 4, 5, 7, 116–36, 212–42
    changes for minorities in, 180–88
    combating negative aspects of, 8, 102–3, 223–42
    competition faced in, 2, 5, 7, 116–18, 134, 136, 217
    concentration of business and marketing on, 8, 100–102, 221–23
    consideration for others absent in, 17–43, 51, 90, 102–3
    cynicism of, 137–58
    declining religious and community affiliations of, 34–36, 110
    definition of, 1, 3–4
    depression and anxiety in, 5, 7, 9, 104–9, 129, 136, 157, 212, 213–14
    dissenting views on, 6–7
    feel-good instincts in, 1–2, 7, 10–11, 49, 51, 96, 147
    focus on self needs in, 1–2, 4, 5, 7, 10–11, 43–103, *73*, 147, 221
    freedom and individualism in, 2, 4, 5, 6, 7–8, 17–43, 73–77, 96–97, 98, 101, 119, 129, 192, 212, 229
    internal vs. external control beliefs of, 138–40, 147–58
    labeling of, 1, 3–4, 5–6
    loneliness and isolation of, 110–16
    materialism of, 99–102, 120, 130, 131–32, 219
    obsession with physical appearance in, 94–97, *95*, 131, 220
    open and direct communication in, 36–41, 165, 217, 220
    optimism and high expectations of, 2, 5, 7, 49, 77–94, 99–102, 129–34, 153–54, 212, 219, 241
    predicting future of, 213–16

Generation Me (GenMe): (cont'd)
 realities vs. dreams of, 2, 7, 8, 49,
  78–79, 83, 85–87, 129–34, 212–13,
  217, 239–40
 rejection of authority and tradition by,
  17–20, 25–36, 39, 43
 self-confidence of, 4, 21, 40, 45, 62, 67,
  89, 102, 224–25
 sense of entitlement in, 29, 31, 70,
  100–102, 214
 sexual behavior in, 1, 5, 9, 36, 43, 47,
  98, 159–79
 social rules rejected in, 5, 7, 17–43
 thirty year span of, 3–4, 5–6
 tolerance in, 19–20, 24, 25, 207–9, 214
 victim mentality in, 148, 150–56
 "you can be/do anything" mantra of,
  20, 21, 24, 77–94, 102, 131, 153,
  190, 202, 212
generations:
 age differences vs. differences in,
  246–47
 consistent change in, 9, 12–13
 differing value systems of, 8
 effects of specific events on, 145–46,
  246
 embracing trends of, 2
 labeling of, 1, 3–4, 5–6, 7
 overlapping of, 5–6
 purchasing decisions of, 9
 research on, 3, 9–15, 107, 138–40,
  195–96, 243–47
 resistance to classification in, 2
Generations (Strauss and Howe), 47
Generations at Work (Zemke, Raines, and
  Filipczak), 218
Generation X (GenX), 5, 6, 94, 165, 201
Generation X Goes to College (Sacks), 28,
  64, 138, 150, 154
Generation Y (GenY), 5, 6
George Lopez, 183
Gillon, Steve, 47
Girl Scouts, 25, 60, 61
Gitlin, Todd, 46
Glamour, 161, 164
Glassner, Barry, 135–36
Glenn, Norval, 133
God, 28, 34, 35, 58, 85
Goldblum, Jeff, 143
Good Times, 132
Gore, Al, 88

gossip, 41
Gough, Harrison, 69
government, 25, 28
 family support from, 229–31
Grayson, Carla, 210–11
Great Britain, 7
Greatest Generation, 6, 7
"Greatest Love of All, The," 1, 44
Greenspan, Alan, 212
Gregory, Corinne, 26
Groenig, Marcus, 100
group orientation, 1, 3, 4, 8, 48, 51
Growing (Up) at Thirty-Seven (Rubin), 47,
 49, 91
Growing Up Digital (Tapscott), 10, 24, 29,
 59
guilt, 25, 35, 131, 199

hair styles, 43, 48
Hanauer, Cathi, 130
Hand That Rocks the Cradle, The, 203
Hanser, Sam, 209
happiness, 10–11, 19, 25, 49, 96
 pursuit of, 19, 20, 21, 85, 90, 91–92
 relationships and, 227
Happy Hook-Up, The: A Single Girl's Guide
  to Casual Sex, 159
Hard Copy, 147
Harris, Eric, 70–71
Harry Winston Jewelry, 83
Harvard University, 88, 116
 Medical School of, 118
Hawkins, Brennan, 135
Health and Human Services Department,
 U.S., 85
health care, 109, 210
 rising costs of, 2, 7, 120, 126, 127, 129,
  134, 219, 220, 222
Her Way: Young Women Remake the Sexual
  Revolution (Kamen), 161, 165
Hewitt, John, 56, 59–60
Higher Education Research Institute, 9
Hilton, Paris, 222
hippies, 21–22
Hispanics, 142, 180, 181, 182–83, 184,
 186–87
HIV blood tests, 175
Hollywood, Calif., 83, 85, 152
homosexuality:
 acknowledgement of, 208, 209, 210,
  211

attitudes about, 25, 180, 207–11, 214
    marriage and, 32, 207, 210
    parenting and, 210–11
    suicide and, 210
    see also lesbians
honesty, 10, 50
    consideration and politeness vs., 39–40
    technology and, 27
Hookup Handbook, The, 159–60, 168–70, 178
Houdini, Harry, 14
House of Representatives, U.S., 188
housing, 100–101, 122
    rental, 121, 124
    rising costs of, 2, 4, 7, 99, 109, 120–21, 122–25, *123*, 128, 129, 132, 199, 213, 216, 217, 222, 229
Houston, Whitney, 1, 44, 204
Howe, Neil, 6–7, 47
Hudson, Rock, 174–75
Hughes, John, 112
Hung, William, 86–87
Hurricane Katrina, 146, 183
Huxley, Aldous, 50
Hyde, Janet, 61

I Am Charlotte Simmons (Wolfe), 164
iGeneration (iGen), 6
I Know Black People, 183
Ilardi, Steve, 239
Im, Charles, 139
iMac, 6
iMedia, 6
I'm the Teacher, You're the Student (Allitt), 154
incomes:
    declining buying power of, 4, 7, 120, 124–29, 219
    dual-salary, 4, 125, 127–29, 189, 198, 230
    expectations of, 2, 79, 131, 132
independence, 24, 25, 77, 96, 115–16
individualism, 2, 4, 5, 10, 21, 22, 24, 31, 36, 46, 101, 129, 160, 192, 212, 229
Internet, 27, 48, 122, 146, 169
    availability of information on, 30, 89, 110
    e-mail on, 45, 110, 112, 137, 146, 238
    message boards and chat rooms on, 30, 38, 89, 119, 247
    pornography on, 172–73

Web pages and blogs on, 29, 30, 89, 110, 112, 132, 241
"Invisible Poor, The," 132
iPods, 6, 101
Iran Contra affair, 145
Iran hostage crisis, 4
Iraqi War, 137, 146
It's a Wonderful Life, 84–85
It's Never Too Soon to Discipline (Peters), 236
I Want a Famous Face, 94–95
I Want That, 102

Jack & Bobby, 143, 145
Jackson, Janet, 167
Jackson, Michael, 216
Jackson, Shar, 25
James, LeBron, 83
Jeffersons, The, 183
Jesus Christ, 35
Jiang, Jennie, 98
jobs, 24, 149–50
    blue-collar, 120
    dead-end, 97–98
    downsizing and out-sourcing of, 27, 120, 150, 199
    dream, 80, 83–84
    education for, 227–28
    flexible schedules in, 218
    fringe benefits of, 219–20
    lack of fulfillment in, 4, 79–80, 102, 104, 130, 221
    paid parental leave from, 231–32
    part-time, 220
    searching for, 2, 97, 98, 109, 118–19, 120, 127, 217, 228
    service, 89, 124
    white-collar, 82, 120
    see also business; work
Jonathan Livingston Seagull (Bach), 45–46
Jones, Marcus, 98
Joplin, Janis, 116
Jordan, Michael, 83, 129
Judaism, 31, 32, 34–35
Jump Cats, 80

Kaiser Family Foundation, 172, 173–74
Kamen, Paula, 161, 164, 190
Kansas, University of, 78, 239
Kansas State University, 106
Kaplan New SAT 2005, 72

Kato, Lesley, 226
Katz, Lillian, 69–70
Kazez, Daniel, 154
Keaton, Diane, 200
Kennedy, John F., 216
Khalil, Matthew, 101
Kids, 175
"Kids Out of Control" (Zucker), 75, 140
Kilibarda, Sarah, 241
King, Billie Jean, 188
Kinsey, Alfred, 167
Kiplinger's Personal Finance, 83–84
Klebold, Dylan, 70–71
Klosterman, Chuck, 132–33

Ladies' Home Journal, 45, 58
Lamb, Corvin, 83
Lancaster, Lynne, 40
Lane, Robert, 110
Las Vegas, Nev., 102, 121
Latham, Eric, 241
Lavinthal, Andrea, 169
Law & Order: SVU, 168
leadership, 141, 189–90
Legoland Park, 83
lesbians, 178, 180, 182, 207–11
Letterman, David, 41
Levine, Adam, 98
Levine, Mel, 151
Lewinsky, Monica, 145, 165, 166
Lewis, John, 180
Lewis, Karen Gail, 91
Liberace, 181
Library of Congress, 14
Lichtenberger, Drew, 119–20, 240–41
Life & Style Weekly, 102
light exposure, 239
Loggins, Kenny, 87
loneliness, 110–16
Lopez, Jennifer, 129, 131
Lovables in the Kingdom of Self-Esteem, The
    (Loomans), 53
love, 25, 53, 55, 59, 84
    Free, 1, 47, 98, 162
    romantic, 84, 111–14, 132–33
    of self, 2, 44, 45, 50, 90–94
loyalty, 10, 24
Lutheran Church, 31

McCain, John, 142
McCarthyism, 20–21

McDonald's, 7, 152
McGraw, Phil, 50
McKay, Nellie, 88
Macko, Lia, 77, 204, 206
McLeod, Scott, 155
Madonna, 204
Maduro, E. S., 196
Majestic, The, 20–21
makeovers, 84
manic-depression, 107
manners, 26, 40, 41
marijuana, 43
Marlowe-Crowne Social Desirability
    Scale, 42
marriage, 31–34, 90–91, 97, 176–78
    age at, 1, 19, 20, 48, 98, 99, 112,
        113–14, 116, 189, 192, 195,
        199–200, 221
    arranged, 21, 111–12, 116
    childless, 93, 129, 215, 229
    mixed race, 19, 32, 184
    mixed religion, 19, 21, 32
    same-sex, 32, 207, 210
    satisfaction in, 93–94, 132–34
    stable, 91–92
    unhappy, 115
    wedding traditions of, 23, 24, 31,
        32–34, *33*, 89
    see also divorce
Martin, Ricky, 86
Martin, Steve, 200
Maryland University Law School, 118
Maslow, Abraham, 47, 92
Massachusetts, University of, 59
Massachusetts Institute of Technology
    (MIT), 88
Massey, Morris, 8, 246
materialism, 99–102, 120, 130, 131–32, 219
Mayer, John, 119
Me Decade, 1
medical insurance, 126, 127, 134
meditation, 47
Meeker, Meg, 171
Meet the Fockers, 21–22
Meet the Parents, 21
Me Generation, 1, 46
men, 196–98, 215
    gay, 207–10
    parenting of, 197, 215, 220–21
    self-esteem of, 52, 61, 195–96
    stereotypical traits of, 12, 197

Merritt, Virginia, 210
metrosexuals, 94
Michaels, Meredith, 74, 201, 203, 204–5,
    206
Michigan, University of, 3, 12–14
Michigan Daily, 175
Middletown study, 24
Midlife Crisis at 30 (Macko and Rubin), 77,
    131, 133, 177, 204
military draft, 109, 149
Millennials, 6
*Millennials Rising: The Next Great Genera-
    tion* (Howe and Strauss), 6–7
Millionaires' Hawaii, 131
Mindich, David, 142
miscegenation laws, 32
Missoula First United Methodist Church,
    210–11
Mommy Myth, The (Douglas and
    Michaels), 74, 201
Mona Lisa Smile, 20
Moral Majority, 190
movies, 4, 10, 129
    children's, 24–25, 146–47, 191
    culture clash in, 21–22, 40, 41
    inspirational, 5, 84–85
    political content in, 20–21
    R-rated, 41
    time travel in, 20–22
MTV, 91, 94–95, 144, 186, 238
Murray, Sandra, 92
music, 10, 26, 82, 83, 167, 184
Myers, David, 136
My Guidewire, 221
My Life, 186
My Super Sweet 16, 101–2
Myth of Laziness, The (Levine), 151
Myth of Self-Esteem, The (Hewitt), 56

Nanny 911, 76
narcissism, 55, 68–71, 74, 77, 223, 225
    measuring of, 244
    relationships and, 92–93
*Narcissism and Intimacy: Love and Marriage
    in an Age of Confusion* (Solomon),
    93
Narcissistic Personality Inventory, 69
National Clearinghouse on Families and
    Youth, 85
National Institute of Child Health and
    Human Development, 202

National Institutes of Health, 202
National Job Training, 173
National Marriage Project, 94
National Science Foundation, 118–19
Nation of Victims, A (Sykes), 150–51,
    155–56
Native Americans, 186
NBC, 160, 165, 166, 167, 168
Neff, Adrianne, 210–11
Negroponte, Nicolas, 142
Net Generation, 5–6
New Age, 47, 92
New Atlantis, 103
*New Rules: Searching for Self-Fulfillment in a
    World Turned Upside Down*
    (Yankelovich), 46
Newsweek, 154
New Yorker, 30
New York Magazine, 46–47
New York Times, 88, 119, 188
New York Times Magazine, 132, 155, 159,
    167, 168
New York University, 109
Nichols, Kristy, 25
Nickel and Dimed (Ehrenreich), 124
Nixon, Richard M., 144
noise, 26, 103
Nolen-Hoeksema, Susan, 238
Northwestern University, 12, 17–18
*Not Much Just Chillin': The Hidden Lives of
    Middle Schoolers* (Perlstein), 154,
    166–67
Notre Dame University, 116
Not-So-Perfect Man, The (Frankel), 159
'N Sync, 78

obedience, 19, 24
obsessive-compulsive disorder, 106
O.C., The, 39, 138, 170, 207
O'Connor, Sandra Day, 188
Offspring, 44–45
Onion, 147
Orenstein, Peggy, 202, 204, 205
Over-Scheduled Child, The (Rosenfeld and
    Wise), 225

Pak, SuChin, 186
Paltrow, Gwyneth, 83, 89
panic attacks, 105, 106, 107
Parenting, 45

parents, 9, 24, 28, 41
    blaming of, 151–52
    choices offered to children by, 75–76,
        100
    disrespect of children for, 26, 30–31,
        75–76
    financial help for, 230–33
    as friends, 30–31
    hopes and expectations of, 5, 24
    indulgence and self-esteem promoted
        by, 2, 4, 7, 30–31, 45, 58–59, 74–77,
        149, 150
    living with, 34, 97, 127
    parenthood as choice of, 4, 19, 94
    suggestions for, 235–37
    teachers and, 154–56, 236
    worry and concern of, 5, 26, 117
    see also families
Paul, Pamela, 112
pensions, 27
People, 25, 75, 76, 83, 96, 127, 140, 143,
    148, 166, 171, 204
People for the American Way, 144
Perfect Madness: Motherhood in the Age of
    Anxiety (Warner), 151–52, 203,
    205–6, 230
Perlstein, Linda, 154, 166–67, 171–72, 177
personality, 10
    changes in, 192–96
    gender and shaping of, 11–12
    measuring traits of, 3, 11–13, 42, 74,
        89, 243–44
Peters, Ruth, 236
Peterson, Abby, 76
Peterson, Joey, 76
Peterson, Paula, 76
Peterson, Susan, 150
philosophy, 10–11, 25, 48, 51
plastic surgery, 94–96
Pleasantville, 21
PoliteChild, 26
politeness, 26, 41, 42
politics:
    conservative, 5, 153, 191, 197
    participation in, 1, 48, 137–38, 139
    waning appeal of, 137, 138–45, 229–30
Poniewozik, James, 87, 148, 178
pop culture, 2, 10, 26
pornography, 172–73
Postman, Neil, 146, 171
Pozniak, John, 240

pregnancy, 38, 199
    biological clock and, 113
    teenage, 67, 109, 175–76, 213, 234
Princeton University, 80, 117, 136
profanity, 26, 40–41
Prom Guide, 100
Promise of Sleep, The (Dement), 234
Prozac Nation (Wertzel), 110–11
Prudential Life, 51
Psychological Bulletin, 60–61
psychology, 62, 67, 68, 74, 80, 157, 185
    clinical, 118
    educational, 76, 148
    group, 4
    personality, 3, 9
    pop, 90
    social, 23–25
Psychology Today, 158
psychotherapy, 23–24, 36, 47, 91, 106,
    107, 111, 152
Purpose-Driven Life, The (Warren), 35
Putnam, Robert, 35, 110, 125, 157

Quarterlife Crisis (Robbins and Wilner),
    11, 77, 80, 82–83, 118, 130
Queer Eye for the Straight Guy, 208–9

race:
    behavior and fate dictated by, 19
    discrimination and, 21, 25, 180, 182,
        183–84
    marriage outside of, 19, 32, 184
    segregation and, 180, 182
    tolerance and, 32, 214
radio, 45, 101
Rainbow Party, 167
Reagan, Ronald, 190, 216
Real World: Philadelphia, 91
Rebel Billionaire, 88
rebellion, 21, 39–40, 42–43
Reddy, Helen, 200
relationships, 136, 227
    break-up of, 3, 25, 52–53, 77, 90, 91,
        93, 111
    cheating in, 91, 92
    dysfunctional, 107
    narcissism and, 92–93
    quarrels in, 93
    romantic, 68, 84, 90–91, 111–14,
        132–34, 167–68

social, 89, 110, 115, 136, 238–39
see also families; marriage
religion, 24, 25
    abandonment of, 34–35, 209
    restrictive rules of, 34–35
    see also church; *specific religions*
Republican Party, 142, 207
responsibility, 6, 19, 28, 75
    declining belief in, 5, 140, 147, 148,
        150–56
Reviving Ophelia (Pipher), 60
*Revolution from Within: A Book of Self-
    Esteem* (Steinem), 60
Rice, Condoleezza, 183
Riggs, Bobby, 188
Ritalin, 156
Robbins, Alexandra, 77, 83
Roberts, Julia, 20, 96
Robinson, Elisabeth, 84
Roe v. Wade, 142
rolfing, 47
Roman Catholic Church, 26–27, 31, 34,
    35, 113, 160, 207
Roper Youth Report, 2
Rosenberg Self-Esteem Scale, 52
Rotter, Julian, 157–58
Rozler, Jessica, 169
Rubin, Jerry, 43, 47, 48, 49, 91
Rubin, Kerry, 204, 206
Rudy, 84
Running on Ritalin (Diller), 156
Ryan, Joan, 2

Sacks, Peter, 28, 29, 64, 154
sacrifice, 140, 191
safety measures, 149
San Diego State University, 10, 116, 126,
    142, 228
Sanford and Son, 132
San Francisco Chronicle, 2
San Francisco Giants, 83
Sarbanes-Oxley law, 27
Saturday Night Live, 54–55
Scalzo, Richard, 143
Schneider, Barbara, 78–79
Scholar, The, 72
schools:
    Advanced Placement (AP) classes in,
        117
    advertising in, 100
    cheating in, 27

grade inflation in, 62–64, 62
public preschool, 231–32
SAT exams in, 63, 72, 116–17
segregation of, 182
shifting start times at, 233–35
teaching self-esteem in, 1–2, 53–57,
    61–65, 68, 72, 188, 217
victim mentality in, 153–56
see also colleges; education; teachers
Schor, Juliet, 100
Schwartz, Barry, 115
Sears, Martha, 127–28
Sears, William, 127–28
Seinfeld, 170, 208
self, 10, 49
    being true to, 39–40, 45, 47
    belief in, 21, 45, 50, 77–89
    core, 39
    duty and, 1, 6–7, 19
    focus on needs of, 1–2, 4, 5, 7, 10–11,
        43–103, 73, 147, 221
    knowledge of, 1, 91, 101
    language of, 2, 48–49, 50–51
    traditional, 50–51
Self, 50
self-absorption, 4, 225
self-confidence, 4, 21, 40, 45, 62, 67, 89,
    102, 224–25
self-control, 67, 225, 235–36
self-destruction, 26
self-esteem, 44–45, 52–71, 90, 102, 212
    academic performance and, 61–65, 62,
        66, 70, 187–88, 223–24
    changes in, 52–53, 60
    of minorities, 185–88
    promotion and teaching of, 1–2, 7, 45,
        53–65, 54, 55, 62, 71, 72, 188, 217,
        218, 223, 224
    protection of, 147–48, 152, 218
    reality vs., 147–49, 187–88, 225–26
    rebelling against, 87, 223–27, 235–36
    rejection of criticism and, 64–65, 68,
        87, 223–24
    self-control vs., 225
    socioeconomic status and, 195–96
    see also narcissism
"Self-Esteem," 44–45
self-expression, 2, 17–19, 34, 50, 74, 85,
    96–97, 98, 101, 148
self-fulfillment, 45–49, 50, 51
self-help books, 23–24, 45, 50, 92, 151

self-importance, 4, 31, 49, 69, 75–77, 103
self-improvement, 46–47, 50
selfishness, 4, 5
self-love, 2, 44, 45, 50, 90–94
Self Matters (McGraw), 50
self-protection, 147–48, 152, 218
self-reliance, 4, 24, 36, 77
self-respect, 45, 50
self-sufficiency, 77
Seligman, Martin, 50–51, 66, 133
Selma, Ala., 180, 182
September 11, 2001 terrorist attacks, 146, 246
Sesame Street, 78, 181
7th Heaven, 58–59, 85, 90
sex:
　　ages at initiation of, 5, 9, 36, 160, 162–63, 173
　　hookup, 159–60, 168–70, 178
　　openness about, 36, 38–39, 43, 165
　　oral, 165–67
　　products associated with, 38–39, 45, 146, 161, *174*
　　radical behavioral changes in, 5, 9, 36, 43, 159–79
　　see also homosexuality
Sex in the City, 40, 111, 113, 170
sex therapy, 21, 22, 47
sexually-transmitted disease (STD), 173–75
Sexual Revolution, 161–62
"Sexy New Moms, The," 204
Shanian, Charlie, 33
"She Bangs," 86
shoplifting, 27
Simpsons, The, 22
Sinatra, Frank, 88
sleep loss, 234
Slipakoff, Robin, 62
Smith, Howard, 188–89
Smith, Kevin, 20
Smith, Olivia, 99
Smith College, 142
social class, 78
Social Security, 215, 220, 229, 232, 233
society:
　　accelerated pace of change in, 8
　　American cultural influence on, 7–8
　　civic disengagement in, 34–36
　　cultural and technological advance-
　　　ment in, 8

disregard for norms and rules in, 5, 7, 17–43
family-first, group-oriented, 3, 6
me-centered, 26–28
molding of generations by, 2, 8
need for approval in, 42–43
new informality in, 17–19, *19,* 28, 29, 36–41
trends of, 2, 5, 7–8, 42–43
Solomon, Marion, 93
Something Borrowed (Griffin), 50
Song of Solomon, 90
Sopranos, The, 106
Spano, John, 217
Spears, Britney, 25, 51
Special Olympics, 67
speech:
　　disrespectful, 26, 39–40
　　freedom of, 20–21
　　profane, 26, 40–41
Spelling, Tori, 33
sports, 17, 82, 83
　　female participation in, 5, 17–18, 21, 188, 193–94, *194*
Stanford Law School, 188
Star, 86
Starter Marriage, The (Paul), 112
Statistical Abstract of the United States, 9
Steinem, Gloria, 60
steroids, 94
Stevenson, David, 78–79
Stevenson, Harold, 64
Stewart, Jon, 147
Still Killing Us Softly, 20
St. James, Aleta, 48
Stout, Maureen, 28, 64, 66, 67, 68, 70, 148, 224
"Straight Dope, The" (Adams), 12
Strauss, William, 6–7, 47
suicide, 104–5, 106, 108–9, 210, 213
Supernanny, 76
Supreme Court, U.S., 32, 142, 176, 185, 188
Survivor, 88
Swan, The, 94
Swarthmore College, 116
Swingers, 114
Sykes, Charles, 150–51, 155–56

Talking Heads, 212
Tapscott, Don, 29, 30, 59

Taylor, Niki, 204
teachers, 26, 28
    blaming of, 153–55, 236
    as "facilitators," 29–30
    gay, 207–8
    lack of respect for, 28–30, 76
    parents and, 154–56, 236
    seeking approval from, 24
    self-esteem taught by, 1–2, 53–57,
        61–65, 68, 72, 188, 217
    see also colleges; education; schools
teamwork, 6, 29
technology, 8, 136, 247
    dishonesty facilitated by, 27
    see also computers; Internet; television
telekinesis, 14
television, 4, 6, 10, 45, 101, 136
    cable, 41, 102, 106, 110, 131, 137, 142,
        145
    commercials on, 38–39, 106, 146–47,
        172
    dramas and soap operas on, 33, 37, 39,
        40, 50, 90, 91, 106, 111, 113, 131,
        132, 133, 138, 208
    growing up with, 6, 129, 130
    impact of, 171, 236–37
    limiting exposure to, 236–37, 238
    news broadcasts on, 137, 142, 145–46,
        236–37
    reality, 72, 76, 88, 94–95, 101–2
    sitcoms on, 131, 170, 178, 183, 208,
        212
    tabloid shows on, 147, 149
    violence on, 236–37
Teresa, Mother, 162
terrorism, 134, 136, 137, 146, 149
Texas, 10, 15, 32, 210
Texas, University of, 165
Texas A&M University, 27
Texas Tech University, 11
thirtysomething, 50
Timberlake, Justin, 4
Time, 117–18, 127, 148, 178, 199–200,
        207
    "The Case for Staying Home," 198
    covers of, 88–89, 106, 154, 198
    "Does Kindergarten Need Cops?," 76
    "Twilight of the Boomers," 8
    "What Teachers Hate About Parents,"
        154–55
Titanic, 70

TiVo, 6, 101
Today show, 50, 170
tolerance, 19–20, 24, 25, 32, 214
Toxic Parents, 151
tradition, challenging of, 17–20, 26,
        28–36
Trinkaus, John, 26–27
Trudeau, G. B., 62
trust, decline of, 28, 35–36
truth, 24
tsunami of 2005, 145–46
Tuned Out: Why Americans Under 40 Don't
        Follow the News (Mindich), 142
TV Generation, 6
20/20, 90
Two-Income Trap, The (Warren and Tyagi),
        128–29, 229, 232–33

UFOs, 145
Unexpected Legacy of Divorce, The (Waller-
        stein, Lewis, and Blakeslee), 111
Unger, Brian, 121–22
USA Today Magazine, 149
Us Weekly, 88, 91, 98, 131

Viagra, 45, 146
Victory gardens, 136
Vietnam War, 4, 48, 141
Virginia Technical University, 240
volunteerism, 4–5, 102, 241
voting, 137, 138, 143–45, 144, 180, 229

Wake Forest University Law School, 153
Wallace, Carol, 89
Wal-Mart, 27
Walters, Barbara, 90, 165
war, 7, 19, 59, 149
Warhol, Andy, 22
Warner, Judith, 151–52, 203, 205–6, 230
Warren, Rick, 35, 58
Washington, D.C., 14, 15, 207–8
Watergate, 4, 145
Weakest Link, The, 148
We Are All Special, 1, 54
Wellesley College, 20
Wells, Brooke, 161–62
Wells, Leroy, 152
Wertzel, Elizabeth, 111
What Really Happened to the Class of '93
        (Colin), 39, 77, 88, 100, 109, 143,
        147, 181

What You Think of Me Is None of My Business (Cole-Whittaker), 24
When Generations Collide (Lancaster), 40
When You Love a Man Who Loves Himself (Campbell), 92
White House, 17–18, 162
"Why Georgia," 119
Wilde Lake Middle School, 154
Will and Grace, 208
"William Has a Doll," 191
Wilner, Abby, 77, 83
Windows Millennium Edition (ME), 6
Wisconsin, University of, 61, 116, 118
Wolfe, Tom, 1, 46–47, 49, 164
women:
    attitudes toward, 190–92
    changing roles of, 188–96, 198–207
    college degrees of, 182, 189, *189*, 199, 214, 221
    goals of, 130–31, 133, 214–15
    health concerns and diseases of, 37–39
    housework of, 190, 192, 196, 197
    leadership of, 189–90
    "masculine" traits of, 5, 12, 193–95, 197
    motherhood and child care, 20, 38, 113, 182, 189, 191–92, 198, 199, 201–7, 210–11, 215–16, 220, 230
    professions of, 188–90, 214–15
    self-esteem of, 52, 60–61, 95
    sports participation of, 5, 17–18, 21, 188, 193–94, *194*

Women Who Think Too Much (Nolen-Hoeksema), 238
Woods, Marielle, 117–18
Woodstock concert, 4
Woodward, Louise, 203
work, 140, 149–50, 153, 216–21
    dressing for, 17, 19
    longer hours at, 221
    love of, 84
    new democracy and informality at, 17, 19, 29, 39
    open communication at, 39
    personal lives impacted by, 115, 218
    see also business; jobs
WorldCom, 27
World War II, 6, 7, 9, 116, 129, 184, 194

Yale Law School, 118
Yankelovich, Daniel, 46, 149
yoga, 1, 47
You Are Special, 57–58
"You Are the Sunshine of My Life," 45
You Can Be Anything!, 78
Your Erroneous Zones (Dyer), 24, 45
"You're the Inspiration," 23
YO-YO (You're On Your Own), 4

Zapata, Christine, 31
Zhang, Liqing, 139
Zoloft, *105*, 106
Zucker, Bonnie, 75

About the Author

JEAN M. TWENGE, PH.D., is associate professor of Psychology at San Diego State University and the author of more than forty scientific journal articles and book chapters. Accounts of her research have appeared in *USA Today*, *The Wall Street Journal*, *Time*, and *Newsweek* and have been featured on the *Today* show and *Dateline NBC*. In addition to her work on generations, she has published numerous studies on the effects of social rejection. She received a B.A. and an M.A. from the University of Chicago in 1993 and a Ph.D. in personality psychology from the University of Michigan, Ann Arbor, in 1998. After living in Texas, Chicago, Michigan, Minnesota (twice), and Cleveland, she is happy to be settled with her husband in beautiful San Diego, California. When not slaving over a hot computer writing something, she can usually be found swimming, reading, sitting in the sun, or reading and sitting in the sun—though usually not swimming while reading and sitting in the sun.